LLEWELLYN'S 2020

HERBAL

ALMANAC

© 2019 Llewellyn Publications
Llewellyn Publications is a registered trademark of
Llewellyn Worldwide Ltd.

Cover Designer: Kevin R. Brown
Editor: Lauryn Heineman

Interior Art: © Fiona King
Garden plan illustrations on pages 286–87
by Llewellyn Art Department

You can order annuals and books from *New Worlds,*
Llewellyn's catalog. To request a free copy, call 1-877-
NEW WRLD toll-free or visit www.llewellyn.com.

ISBN: 978-0-7387-4944-0
Llewellyn Worldwide Ltd.
2143 Wooddale Drive
Woodbury, MN 55125-2989

Printed in the United States of America

Contents

DIY and Crafts

Plant Profiles

Gardening Resources

Introduction to
Llewellyn's Herbal Almanac

Holistic care for the mind, body, and soul starts in the garden. Gardeners of all skill levels and climates can find common ground in early morning weeding, combating pests, marveling at this year's abundant harvest, and impatiently waiting to plan next year's plot. The work is hard, but the rewards are bountiful. Growing herbs is good for the spirit, and using them in home-cooked meals, remedies, and crafts is clean, healthy, and just plain delicious.

The 2020 edition of the *Herbal Almanac* is a love letter and guidebook to the hands-on application of herbs in our daily lives. With sage advice appealing to novice gardeners and experienced herbalists alike, our experts tap into the practical and historical aspects of herbal knowledge—using herbs to help you connect with the earth, enhance your culinary creations, and heal your body and mind.

In addition to the twenty-four articles written by Master Gardeners, professors, and homesteaders, this book offers reference materials tailored specifically for successful growing and gathering. Use this book to log important dates, draw your garden plan, practice companion planting, find a helpful herbal remedy, and keep track of goals and chores in the personal logbook pages.

Reclaiming our connection to Mother Earth in our own backyards can bring us harmony and balance—and a delicious, healthy harvest. May your garden grow tall and your dishes taste divine!

Note: The old-fashioned remedies in this book are historical references used for teaching purposes only. The recipes are not for commercial use or profit. The contents are not meant to diagnose, treat, prescribe, or substitute consultation with a licensed health-care professional. Herbs, whether used internally or externally, should be introduced in small amounts to allow the body to adjust and to detect possible allergies. Please consult a standard reference source or an expert herbalist to learn more about the possible effects of certain herbs. You must take care not to replace regular medical treatment with the use of herbs. Herbal treatment is intended primarily to complement modern health care. Always seek professional help if you suffer from illness. Also, take care to read all warning labels before taking any herbs or starting on an extended herbal regimen. Always consult medical and herbal professionals before beginning any sort of medical treatment—this is particularly true for pregnant women. Herbs are powerful things; be sure you are using that power to achieve balance.

Llewellyn Worldwide does not participate in, endorse, or have any authority or responsibility concerning private business transactions between its authors and the public.

Growing
and
Gathering

Incredible Neem

by Jill Henderson

Among the billions of plant allies that have ever been used by the human race, there are few that are as revered and honored as the neem tree. This hardy, drought-loving tree is known to have been used for so many different things that a list of all the ways it can and has been used to aid humankind could easily fill dozens of pages. Suffice it to say that every part of the neem tree is used as food, fodder, medicine, and shelter. It has also been used for building and making many useful things, not least of which are deep-seated spiritual and cultural traditions.

Ancient History of Neem

It is often said that neem is native to the Indian subcontinent, which

encompasses the countries of India, Pakistan, Bangladesh, Sri Lanka, and Nepal, but its earliest origins actually begin with the legend of the sunken Dravidian island civilization known as Kumari Kandam or Lemuria some 50,000 years before Christ. Known as *nimba* in ancient Sanskrit, the neem tree has always been a vitally important plant to East Indian cultures. The Hindu Vedas suggest the neem tree was the creation of a sublime deity whose love and compassion for human life was manifested in a single drop of heavenly elixir from which the "miracle tree" grew. This wondrous tree not only grew where other trees and plants would not, but every single part of it was enormously useful to humans, animals, and the earth itself.

Siddha medicine, often referred to as Tamil medicine, eventually developed into what we know as Ayurveda—which is among the oldest known medical systems in the world. Nimba is so ancient that it can be said that the very roots of every branch of natural and allopathic medicine known to man are deeply and ritually entwined with those of the sacred neem tree. It has even been suggested that many bodhisattvas, including the Buddha, utilized the divine shade of the neem tree to achieve enlightenment.

After hearing such a glowing description of neem, you might almost expect it to simply materialize out of thin air and shimmer like the spectral visage of Devi, mother of Shiva. However, unless you sit under a neem tree and meditate until you reach enlightenment, you're more likely to see a simple but attractive tree that in some regions of the world is so prolific that it is considered a weed. Because of neem's versatility, astounding medicinal properties, and ability to grow in the most desolate of places, the tree was spread far and wide. As people moved, so did the neem tree. It traveled by way of land and sea through ancient trade routes for thousands and thousands of years. Today, the ancient neem tree can be found growing in more than thirty countries.

Botanists refer to neem by its Latin name, *Azadirachta indica*, which was derived from the Persian words *azad*, which means "free," and *dirakht*, which means "tree," to describe what the local people thought of as the "free tree of India." Once you've seen a mature neem tree, it's easy to recognize that this freely giving tree belongs to the Meliaceae, or mahogany, family, which contains roughly fifty-three genera and upward of six hundred species of flowering trees, shrubs, and a few herbaceous plants. Many resources suggest that there are other species of neem that have different botanical names, but my in-depth research into this suggests that all other Latin names used for neem come from an earlier era of botanical nomenclature.

Whatever you call them, neem trees are stately evergreens with fairly straight trunks that can reach upward of a hundred feet in height. Young neem trees have mostly smooth gray-brown bark that becomes rough, furrowed, and reddish-brown in color as the tree ages. Neem trees bear pinnately compound leaves that may or may not have a terminal leaflet. Each individual leaflet has beautifully serrated edges and a very pointy tip, giving neem trees a full "leafy" appearance. If grown in the tropical and subtropical climates they prefer, neem trees will produce a profusion of simple, five-petaled white flowers that emit a luscious perfume that smells a lot like honey. Panicles of flowers are followed by a multitude of small, thin-skinned, olive-shaped fruits, each of which contains a single hard seed. When given the right conditions and room to grow, mature neem trees will develop a wide, spreading canopy that can reach some seventy feet in diameter to provide ample shade and loads of curb appeal.

Grow Your Own Natural Insecticide

In its native habitat, neem often prefers to grow in dry, shallow soils in areas of full sun. The monsoonal nature of the Indian subcontinent is marked by heavy flooding rains and long periods of extensive heat and drought, which is typical of the environment that neem prefers. And although they may drop their leaves temporarily in very extended periods of severe drought, they will die if exposed to standing water or temperatures that drop below 39 degrees Fahrenheit. This intolerance to cold and excessively wet soil is the primary reason that many Americans don't grow neem. However, if you are able to control these factors by cultivating neem in pots and providing winter shelter, you can grow neem just about anywhere you want to.

The cool things about neem trees are the ease with which they can be propagated and their undemanding soil requirements. Neem trees are very easy to grow from seed and are cultivated much like garden peppers, with plenty of warmth and sunshine. Neem seeds are readily available online, but if you live in an area where neem trees are growing outdoors, simply gather the fruits after they ripen and turn yellow. Each olive-shaped fruit contains one oblong seed. If fruits are fresh, they can be planted whole. Otherwise, simply squeeze the large seed out of the fruit and plant one per pot. Most commercial neem seeds have been extracted from the fruit and carefully dried before being shipped. Sow the seed one inch deep in a four-inch pot filled with a light seed-starting mix and keep it at or above 70 degrees Fahrenheit. At these temperatures, seeds often germinate within a week. If the soil dries out often or is too wet or if the temperature stays below 70 degrees, the seeds may take up to three weeks to germinate.

Another way to propagate neem trees is through stem cuttings taken in mid to late spring before twigs get brown and woody. Select a stem that is green all the way to the tip and cut it so that it comes away with at least four leaves. Do not confuse the pinnate leaves with the actual stem of the tree. A single **pinnate leaf** consists of several leaflets. Each stem cutting should have at least four **compound leaves** attached to it. Once you've cut the stem, remove all but the topmost leaf stem. Dip the cut end in rooting hormone and then plant it in the soil deep enough to cover two of the leaf nodes, leaving the third leaf node and the single pinnate leaf above the soil line. Place the cutting in a warm, shady location for several weeks, keeping the soil moist but not soggy. You will know when the cutting has taken root when you see the first signs of green emerging from the exposed leaf node. Allow the cutting to grow in this pot for at least four more weeks before repotting it to a larger container.

After a month or two, the seedling will begin to outgrow the original starting pot and will need to be transplanted. Although it seems normal to move the seedling incrementally to a slightly larger and larger pot each time, the fact is that neem trees spend the first year of their life sending their roots deep into the soil. If you wait too long to plant your seedling in the ground, it may become root-bound in the pot and be stunted for life. For the best root development, either plant your seedling in the ground where it will grow for the rest of its life or transplant it into a sturdy five-to-seven-gallon pot, which should be plenty of room for the first year or two of its life. If you need to keep your neem tree in a pot, you will eventually want to transplant it into a very sturdy ten-to-fifteen-gallon pot, where it can remain for many more years with proper pruning.

For those who do not live in frost-free regions, your neem tree will grow best if allowed to live outside in full sun during the warm months and brought indoors or kept in a heated greenhouse during times when frost or freezing is likely. As summer wanes, prepare your tree for life indoors by reverse hardening it off to indoor conditions. Start the process in early fall by moving your neem tree to shadier and shadier locations, with the final move being into the house or greenhouse where you must provide it with plenty of sunshine from south-facing windows. Of course, in order to move a very large, heavy pot like the one your tree will need to live in for the remainder of its life, having wheels under the pot can be a huge help.

When it comes to growing neem trees in pots, you may want to fertilize your tree at least once during the growing season. I'm not big on chemical fertilizers, so I suggest using a balanced organic fruit or ornamental tree fertilizer very sparingly. Be sure to water your tree lightly but regularly during the summer months, and always allow the soil to dry completely in between—this goes for indoor trees as well as outdoor ones. For indoor trees that have reached a semidormant state in winter, very light watering coupled with leaf misting is the way to go. Waterlogged soil leads to root rot and can very easily kill your tree. Because neem trees are natural insect repellents in their own right, they are not bothered by insect pests and may even help deter or eliminate plant pests bothering your other indoor plants.

Neem trees respond well when major pruning cuts are done in early spring. Light pruning or thinning and shaping can be done in late summer without harm. Pruning mature neem trees hard results in many new leafy shoots. Like fruit trees, neem trees respond best to early spring pruning, but you can also do a little light pruning of branches in late summer without any ill effects. Once your neem tree is mature, either in the pot or in the ground, it can be **pollarded** by cutting back the branches almost to the trunk of the tree. Pollarding is traditionally used to manage the size of trees in urban landscapes and to produce fodder for livestock. For medicinal purposes, potted neem trees are sometimes pollarded in spring to obtain an abundance of leaves and twigs for making medicine. It takes a lot of energy to regrow stems and leaves, so anytime you prune or pollard your neem tree, be sure to give it a bit of extra fertilizer afterward.

Using Neem in the Garden

Although neem has been grown and used for hundreds of thousands of years, most Westerners are just beginning to learn about what this amazing tree can do. The most well-known use of neem these days is as a safe and natural insecticide and fungicide. Many of the common neem insecticidal products on the market today are made with neem oil that has been extracted from the dried and ground seeds and mixed with surfactants and other agents to help the oil stick to and persist on plant leaves. Neem oil contains many naturally occurring compounds, but the one that gets the credit for repelling insects is called **azadirachtin**, which can also be found in the roots, twigs, bark, and leaves of neem trees. Once an insect ingests treated plant material, it quickly loses its appetite and stops eating. Some insects die of starvation, while others perish because they can no longer molt their old skins. Azadirachtin also stops some insects from laying eggs, and the oils laid over existing eggs can prevent them from hatching.

Neem oil and neem leaf spray are effective against a wide array of chewing or sucking insects, including caterpillars, aphids, mealy bugs, slugs, snails, whiteflies, bean beetles, and many more. That being said, it doesn't work on all garden pests, and according to the National Pesticide Information Center, "Neem oil is practically non-toxic to birds, mammals, bees, and plants" and is "slightly toxic to fish and other aquatic organisms." In addition to its effectiveness against garden pests, the (NPIC) authors suggest there is little concern for the long-term or negative side-effects of neem on the environment: "Azadirachtin, a component of neem oil, is rapidly broken down. Microbes and light break down the pesticide in soil, water and on plants. The half-life of azadirachtin in soil ranges from 3–44 days. In water, the half-life ranges from 48 minutes to 4 days. It also rapidly breaks down on plant leaves; the half-life is 1–2.5 days. The remaining components of neem oil are broken down by microbes in most soil and water environments."

Neem Insecticidal Sprays
Neem oil is difficult to make at home because it takes an awful lot of seeds and specialized extraction equipment to produce it. However, people in India and elsewhere have made insecticidal sprays from both the seeds and the leaves for hundreds of thousands of years—and so can you. If you have access to

neem fruits, simply lay them out in the sun for several days until they are dry. Next, wrap the dried fruits up in a tarp and stomp or pound on them until the outer shells break away from the seeds. Discard all the white seeds, which have no azadirachtin in them. Separate the seed from the chaff by using a tarp, a box fan, and two five-gallon buckets. Pour the threshed shells and seeds from one bucket into the next set on top of the tarp to catch stray seeds from being lost. Use the fan to blow away the lighter chaff while the heavier seeds land in the second bucket. The seeds can then be pounded down with the blunt end of a two-by-four or other sturdy pestle-like instrument. Once the seeds are powdered, they can be soaked in cold water for twenty-four hours. The liquid is then strained through a cloth and sprayed on crops.

The leaves of neem can also be used to make an effective insecticide for home and garden. To make one gallon of neem leaf spray, place three-quarters of a pound of fresh macerated neem leaves in a five-gallon bucket and cover with a gallon and a half of water. Allow the tea to steep anywhere from twenty-four hours to a week. The longer the leaves steep, the stronger (and fouler-smelling) the brew. When ready, simply strain the tea through a fine cloth and spray plants until dripping.

If you've never used them before, be aware that neem oil and neem leaf spray don't smell particularly nice. Even in its purest form, the smell actually stops people from using neem on their bodies for medicinal purposes. In fact, the first year I used neem in my garden I quickly realized that the smell of the premade "organic" concentrate that I bought deterred persistent pests like deer, squirrels, and even my own cats from coming anywhere near my garden after spraying. Yet not all neem products have the same effect. The following year, I decided to blend my own neem spray using organic cold-pressed neem oil and liquefied castile soap. I realized too late that the neem oil I bought was meant for use on the body and not in the garden. Apparently, it contained little if any azadirachtin and the deer actually loved it, grazing every single plant I sprayed it on! In the end, a simple neem leaf spray made from your own trees will not only be cheaper and more natural but also superior to almost anything you can buy. Besides, by using your own neem leaves, stems, or seeds, you can customize both the level of azadirachtin and the stinky smell that you want for the best all-around natural insect and pest deterrent available anywhere.

For more great ways to incorporate neem into your life,
check out Birgit Bradtke's fantastic noncommercial website,
Discover Neem, at discoverneem.com

The Medicinal Miracle of Neem

In order to convey just some of neem's miraculous medicinal properties and current and cultural uses in this monograph, I must necessarily be brief. Let me begin by saying that all parts of the neem tree and the various preparations made from them are exceedingly valuable to man, mammal, plant, and soil. At this time, neem is known to contain some one hundred fifty known natural compounds, the actions of which are still being studied. Second, the physical method in which neem is employed or "administered," be it oil, powder, or extract, is the only limiting factor in its application. Third, studies show that neem is considered nontoxic and safe for human use. However, caution has it that neem should not be given to or used on babies or toddlers, pregnant women or women who are trying to become pregnant, or those with severe liver or kidney disease (neem has a strong action on these organs) without consulting a licensed medical practitioner before using medicinally. Always talk to your primary care provider before beginning an herbal regimen.

Neem is adaptogenic and alterative, which means it has an overall positive effect on the body and its systems by helping it adapt to stress and illness by gradually removing toxins and waste materials from the blood through the stimulation of liver function. It is also antimicrobial and antiseptic, meaning that it helps the body resist, inhibit, or destroy all forms of microorganisms, such as bacteria, fungi, viruses, and their resultant infections. Neem is analgesic, anti-inflammatory, astringent, and antiseptic all in one, aiding the body's natural resistance to infection, relieving pain and inflammation, and also reducing swelling, bleeding, and diarrhea. In this regard it is a perfect candidate for wound treatments, rashes, and periodontal disease.

In terms of healing wounds and diseases, neem excels. Its strong antioxidant and antitumor properties help prevent or inhibit oxidation of body cells by free radicals, helping prevent benign lumps, certain cancers, and skin diseases as well as signs of aging seen in the skin, hair, and nails. Neem is also a beneficial cardioactive and circulatory tonic that strengthens the heart muscle and heartbeat, and it tones and improves the function of the circulatory system. It does this by widening and tonifying the overall condition of vessels, arteries, and capillaries to increase blood flow. And speaking of blood flow, neem has been used since ancient times as both a form of nonabortive birth control and an aphrodisiac that is said to stimulate sexual desire and sensitivity. This makes sense because neem also addresses issues with the heart and blood. As a hypotensive, neem has been shown to reduce blood pressure while also acting as a hypoglycemic that has helped many people reduce their need for insulin over time.

In general, extracts and teas of neem taken over a long period of time act as an invigorating and nourishing tonic that improves the function of one or more body systems by imparting vitamins, minerals, and trace minerals to the body. It also acts as an immunostimulant that strengthens autoimmune functions, generally by forming antibodies in the blood and lymphatic systems. By this very nature, neem can also be regarded as a lymphatic herb that strengthens or improves the functions of the lymph system, which is responsible for cleansing cellular tissues and for producing antibodies and white blood cells.

As a digestive, carminative, stomachic, and bitter tonic (cholagogue), neem stimulates the appetite and digestive functions in the mouth, stomach, and liver while simultaneously easing multiple forms of digestive distress. And speaking of distress, neem is considered a gentle nervine, which not only aids in the proper function of the nervous system but also acts as a mild sedative that has a calming action on the entire body. Additionally, neem oil can be used internally as a demulcent that soothes and protects irritated tissues like the gums and mucous membranes or as an emollient to soothe, soften, and encourage the growth of healthy skin, hair, and nails. It's also an effective vulnerary that helps speed the healing of all manner of external wounds.

In addition to neem's well-known use as a safe and effective garden insecticide, it is also an excellent insect repellent that is often used to keep bed bugs, biting flies, ticks, chiggers, and mosquitoes away. Therefore, it shouldn't come a surprise to learn that neem is also a very powerful vermifuge that kills and expels parasitic worms, fungi, bacteria, and viruses that are commonly found in the digestive tract of both man and animal.

Among the dozens of common names assigned to the neem by various cultures around the world, that of *miracle tree* is likely the most descriptive. Just an hour's worth of research on neem will surely have you convinced that this deceivingly modest tree is about as close to a natural panacea as any the world has ever known. From its fine-grained wood come homes, cabinetry, musical instruments, tools, and many other sturdy and beautiful items. From its roots and shoots, people are fed. With its leaves, flowers, twigs, and bark, pests and diseases in all living things are deterred and health and balance restored. From its very life, desertified wasteland and soil vitality are miraculously renewed. What other plant could do all these things and more without being utterly and truly divine?

Resources

Bond, C., K. Buhl, and D. Stone. "Neem Oil: General Fact Sheet." National Pesticide Information Center. 2012. http://npic.orst.edu/factsheets/neemgen.html.

Kumar, Venugopalan Santhosh, and Visweswaran Navaratnam. "Neem (*Azadirachta indica*): Prehistory to Contemporary Medicinal

Uses to Humankind." *Asian Pacific Journal of Tropical Biomedicine* 3, no. 7 (July 2013): 505–514. doi:10.1016/S2221-1691(13)60105-7.

"Neem in the history/Neem and India." Nature Neem. Accessed August 29, 2018. http://www.natureneem.com/index_fichiers /Neem_history_Neem_and_India.htm.

Staughton, John. "13 Impressive Benefits of Neem." Organic Facts. Last modified September 28, 2018. https://www.organicfacts .net/health-benefits/herbs-and-spices/neem.html.

Ferns: Ancient Herbs
for Modern Gardens

❧ by James Kambos ❧

It's an afternoon in late May. I've been working in my herb and perennial gardens most of the day, readying them for summer. A storm is building, the sky darkens, and thunder rumbles. I begin to hurry as I gather my tools and head back to the shed. On the way I pause a moment to admire my old red peony. Its stems bend down beneath the weight of its large ruffled flowers. Worried that the approaching rain will ruin the flowers, I quickly cut a bouquet to enjoy indoors.

The rain begins. But I suddenly remember—no peony bouquet is complete without some elegant fern foliage to lend its old-fashioned charm. Ignoring the rain, I rush around the herb garden cutting several fern fronds.

Once inside, I arrange the peonies and fern stems in a vintage vase and place it on an entry hall table. Admiring the simple beauty of the ferns and the elegance they add to such an ordinary floral arrangement makes me pause. I begin to think about the ferns. My mind wanders as I think about the charm, mystery, and lore of this ancient herb, as well as its place in the modern herb garden.

Fern History and Lore

Ferns are one of the most ancient herbs on earth. Before the dinosaurs walked the earth, and before humans arrived on the scene, the ferns were here. And they were already ancient. Most experts agree that even before many mountain chains were formed, the ferns were growing. Ferns seem to have appeared 300 to 365 million years ago. Fossilized ferns also show us that the shape and appearance of most ferns have remained virtually unchanged for eons. Ferns pre-date all flower and seed-producing plants.

As an herb, ferns were once used to treat tapeworms. However, finding the correct dosage was difficult. Too little was ineffective, and too much could cause serious side effects. For these reasons, I don't encourage ingesting ferns. Instead, enjoy ferns for the landscape value they'll add to your herb and perennial gardens.

In magical lore, ferns were used to draw good luck, health, and wealth, which is why they were planted near an entrance or kept as a houseplant. Used in a bouquet, ferns symbolize wealth and safe shelter. Ancient magicians were drawn to ferns. They didn't yet understand that ferns reproduced by a system of spores. Since ferns didn't produce flowers or seeds but still multiplied, early magicians thought that ferns held great magic. They believed that whoever discovered the fern's secret of reproduction would possess enormous magical power.

To this day these ancient plants go about their life cycle in a quiet manner. They may not dazzle the eye with bright flowers, they don't need to. These elders of the plant kingdom are remarkable in other ways. They seem to be almost sentient. Although frequently found growing along streams and in the sheltered, shady margins of the forest, ferns are tough and resilient. They've practically witnessed the creation of our planet. They were here when the earth convulsed and the mountains rose. They witnessed the rise and extinction of great species such as dinosaurs. They've seen empires rise and fall.

Like shamans, in their quiet, subtle way, ferns seem to possess the wisdom and secrets of the ages.

Growing and Planting Ferns

For the purpose of this article, I am writing about hardy ferns only. **Hardy** ferns are ferns that have root systems that can tolerate deep cold. These are ferns that, once planted outside, will come back year after year. During the winter, only their foliage will die back. Then in the early spring, new small fronds (leafy stems) will appear. These small curled leaves and stems are called **fiddleheads**. Since ferns return each year, they are classified as a **perennial**.

The ferns you find in hanging baskets at garden centers each spring are not hardy. They are meant for outdoor use during the warm months only. They'll begin to die completely beginning with the first hard frost. They're lovely to use on a porch during the summer, but don't confuse them with hardy ferns, which are meant for garden use.

Since ferns have been around for millions of years, you can be sure that ferns are one of the easiest plants to grow. I have ferns in my herb garden that are over twenty years old. They return each year more beautiful than ever. Once planted, ferns will give you years of carefree beauty.

When planting ferns, the main considerations should be light, moisture, and soil type. Let's start with light.

Ferns are one of the few herbs that grow in shade. Most ferns require sheltered, shady areas to do their best. However, many ferns also do well in sun-dappled areas, in partial shade, and in areas with some morning sun. When in doubt, remember the warmer your climate, the more shade your ferns will require. In my Ohio garden I have ferns growing in locations that face east, west, and north. The south-facing section of my garden is too hot and dry for ferns.

As far as moisture needs, ferns usually require a moisture-retentive soil. This doesn't mean soggy. It means that the soil feels slightly cool and damp to the touch, even in warm weather. Once established, ferns usually don't need to be watered. The only time I've watered my ferns is during long hot, dry spells.

The soil requirements for ferns can be summed up in one word: organic. Ferns need a well-drained soil rich in organic matter. Since ferns grow wild in forested areas, I try to duplicate the woodland soil. To do this, I work compost, pine bark, peat moss, and bags of rich top-soil into the garden soil. Don't plant ferns in heavy clay soil unless you amend it first with organic matter. Here's another tip: I never use chemical fertilizers on ferns. Enriching the soil with organic matter should be enough.

Once the soil is prepared, you'll be ready to purchase and plant your ferns. Ferns usually come in pots. The pot sizes can be four inches, one quart, or one gallon in size. Potted ferns can range in price from six to fifteen dollars, depending on size and variety. Some retailers sell bare-root ferns. These will probably come packed in a plastic bag with peat moss. Bare-root ferns can average six to eight dollars each.

To plant a potted fern, dig a hole two to three inches deeper and wider than the pot. Add water to the hole. Gently remove the fern, with the soil intact, from the pot. Place into the hole and water again. After the water is absorbed, begin to firm the garden soil around the base of the fern. Once in place, mulch around the fern with organic material. Water again.

To protect ferns during the winter, don't cut back the dead foliage. Remove the dead growth in the spring when the fiddleheads appear.

When planting a bare-root fern, dig a hole slightly deeper and wider than the roots. Mound some soil in the bottom of the hole. Spread the roots over the mounded soil. Water well. When the water is absorbed, fill the hole with soil. Press the soil firmly around the plant **crown** (the part where the stems meet the roots) until the fern is in place. The top of the crown should be visible. Mulch with organic matter and water well.

Water newly planted ferns two to three times a week the first month.

Some Ferns to Try

There is a large variety of ferns available for you to grow in your herb garden. Here are several of my favorites that I've enjoyed for years. If possible, plant in groups of two or three for a lush effect.

Autumn Fern (**Dryopteris erythrosora**): This beautiful, slow-growing fern gets its name due to the bronze / coppery color of its fronds when they emerge in the spring. Later the foliage turns green. The foliage has a slightly glossy sheen. Reaches 18 to 24 inches high and wide.

Christmas Fern (**Polystichum acrostichoides**): Unlike most ferns, this fern is evergreen. It's fun to see the green fronds surrounded by snow. It grows about 2 feet high and wide. I cut back the old growth in early spring.

Japanese Painted Fern (**Athyrium niponicum**): These beautiful ferns will light up a shady nook of your herb garden with their silvery foliage. The fronds are streaked with blue-green and burgundy. The stems, which are an attractive burgundy, add more interest. They grow 1 to 2 feet tall and wide. These are a nice change from the usual green ferns.

Lady Ferns (**Athyrium filix-femina**): These grow in shade, or with morning sun. They grow 2 to 3 feet high and wide. Stunning when planted around garden statuary.

Maidenhair Fern (**Adiantum**): Plant this airy, delicate fern at the edge of the garden. With striking black stems, it grows to 1 foot.

Combined with other shade-loving plants, ferns will give you years of carefree beauty. This noble, ancient herb deserves a place in today's gardens.

An Indoor Mini Garden for Your Cat

⤜ by Thea Fiore-Bloom ⤛

My cat Tsunade and I share an exotic obsession—white tulips. I like to look at them. Tsunade, being the down-to-earth type, prefers to eat them.

Do you have a cat that likes to nibble on your flowers or houseplants? Sacrificing an occasional bouquet to your cat wouldn't be the end of the world except for three things:

You don't want your fluffy pal to get in the habit of regularly eating houseplants or cut flowers because certain ones are toxic if swallowed in large enough amounts. For example, lilies pose a serious poison hazard for felines. Tulips too can be dangerous for cats as well as dogs.

Store-bought flowers are often grown with pesticides and other chemicals that probably aren't good for your kitty.

Eating floral bouquet leaves that contain dried flowers (or rough outdoor grasses) can damage the lining of your cat's throat, especially on the way back up, if you know what I mean.

Why Do Cats Want to Eat Your Flowers?

Theory is cats go bananas for leaves and grasses because the right ones may aid digestion, supply trace minerals, or reduce intestinal parasites. Some vets say cats eat plants to help them throw up material they can't digest, such as hair balls. Other authorities claim there are no definitive studies done on the subject that prove any of the above and that cats may eat plants, even plants that are bad for them, just because they're there.

Whatever the reason, I am happy to report the War of the Roses (or in my case, the War of the Tulips) seems over. Tsunade hasn't tried to bouquet binge in ages. Why?

I found a few things Tsunade likes to eat more than tulips, plants that not only are nontoxic but also seem to be good for her digestion and make her happy. I've road tested a bunch of cat-friendly plants in my house and will share the greatest hits here.

Since I started growing good greens for my two cats, neither seems interested in going after the orchids I used to have to hide on crazy high shelves or eating mysterious bits of straw or chair stuffing they find at night. It also has decreased the amount of plant-based "regifting" that typically happens on my favorite carpet.

How can you be sure the plants and flowers you bring into your home aren't toxic to the hairy love of your life? Check out these two great webpages for safety tips to protect your dog or cat:
https://bit.ly/2glxetC
https://bit.ly/13cunsF

And it's not just me. Many cat owners I talk to report that giving their cat healthy greens, such as the ones we'll cover here, has drastically reduced their feline's desire to eat weird stuff.

Indoor cat gardens are also good for mostly outdoor cats. If you have a cat that forages out in the neighborhood every day, providing healthy plant alternatives to treated lawn grass is a smart idea. You too may find less half-digested plant or hair ball surprise packages on your floors.

Before we learn how to assemble our garden, let's meet the green stars of the show.

Three Green Go-Tos for Your Feline

A Standing "O" for Oat Grass (*Avena sativa*)

Cats go insane for fresh oat grass. And the good news is it's easy to grow and even easier to buy in pet supply store chains.

Confusingly, oat grass, like its sister wheatgrass, is often referred to as "cat grass." The cat grass sold in pet supply stores is often a combo of oat grass, wheatgrass, and ryegrass. Your cat will probably like the cat grass combo, but if the store sells straight-up oat grass, snag it. Cats adore it even more.

You usually can buy little four-inch square plastic containers of cat grass or oat grass there for under six bucks. You could just the take container out of bag and put it on the floor. After your cats figure out it's legal to eat, they will devour it. Easy, right? But the grass will wilt or yellow pretty quickly.

Why not pop the grass out of the plastic and plant it in your mini garden? Or you could buy an inexpensive pet grass self-grow kit. The Cat Ladies brand is one of several options you can find on Chewy.com or Amazon.

I grow my own oat grass from scratch for two reasons: it's fun (I enjoy feeling like a cross between Martha Stewart and a mad scientist), and the oat grass at my local pet chain looks a little worse for wear sometimes.

I just buy a cup or two of organic oat groats at my local health food store from the bulk bins for less than ninety-nine cents. I place one cup organic soil in a glass container and a handful of seeds on top of soil. I then cover the seeds with the second cup of soil, and pour in about a cup of water. Done!

The water will sink down eventually. I then place the container on a super sunny, south-facing windowsill in my house for seven days. Sprouts usually peak up between day two and day three. Check out the YouTube video in the resources list for a short, easy-to-follow video on how to grow oat grass for your cat.

Growing oat grass is another kid-friendly project. Cats love this project even more, though, so you might want to protect your oat grass seedlings with a barrier until they are hardy enough to survive your cat's attentions.

When the seedlings transform into a lovely bowl-o'-grass, I just place the container on the floor or plant it in my cat garden. I try to remember to start a new batch of seedlings (groatlings, actually) the same day I put out the grown grass. This way Totoro and Tsunade have a continually refurbished cat lawn to mow down.

The Wonder of Wheatgrass (*Triticum*)

Wheatgrass is the freshly sprouted beginnings of the common wheat plant. Seen it before? The next time you are in a health food store or real juice bar, you'll notice trays of the emerald green stuff still in soil up on a shelf or over the fridge, waiting to be made into "power shots" by your vegan barista.

Wheatgrass is sometimes sold at pet supply chain stores and is also available to buy in trays at health food stores. You might like to get a kit online to help you grow it yourself.

Give your cat a wheatgrass taste test before you go to the trouble of growing it at home. Wheatgrass is packed with nutrients, but it takes more tending to than oat grass. Sarah Moore's article, listed in the resources section, highlights the health benefits of wheatgrass for cats and how to grow it at home for them.

Cuckoo for Catnip (*Nepeta cataria*)

You could stop at a one-or-two-grass mini garden and I'd still respect you. But if you're feeling frisky, try growing catnip. Often referred to as catmint, catnip (*Nepeta cataria*) is a hardy perennial that resembles its cousins in the mint family. While mint leaves are forest green and usually fairly soft, catnip leaves are gray-green, appear dappled with light lavender whorls, and are kind of hairy. You can buy a little container of catnip at your local nursery and plunk it right into your cat garden.

Why does your cat go cuckoo for catnip? She's responding to the seemingly magical power of the catnip's star chemical,

nepetalactone. However, kittens, picky adults, and older cats are often immune to nepetalactone's charms in fresh catnip. They want it dead and dried.

Tsunade and Totoro couldn't care less about the fresh, green catnip I grow in pots on my patio. However, normal adult cats (i.e., not mine) are often fond of the fresh plant, and you might have to place a net over it while you grow it in your house or garden so it won't be inhaled before it has a chance to propagate.

If you are growing catnip from seed indoors, try for a south-facing window. The key to catnip success is tons of sun, daily watering, and good drainage.

To make your own catnip, wait until the leaves are big—say, the size of a quarter—and cut a few green sprigs. Tie the base of the sprigs together with cotton cooking string or kite string and hang upside down to dry for two weeks in a cool, dry place. Then crush the leaves and store in a Ball or mason jar to keep potent, or save the dried leaves whole in a baggie and crush as needed.

That's it. You've made organic catnip! You're a wonder.

DIY Mini Garden

Now let's put it all together. Here's all you'll need for a DIY indoor mini cat garden:

Fairly Shallow Pot: A pot size of a big salad bowl is good, but it doesn't need to as deep as a salad bowl. It can be half the height, no problem. The pot's width can depend on your cat's width. Get a pot big enough for three small plants in one half and your cat in the other. The shape or size of the pot is less important than the presence of a drainage hole. Want to know the difference between black-thumbed and green-thumbed patio gardeners? It comes down to drainage holes.

One Small Bag Organic Potting Soil: An eight-quart or six-pound bag should be more than enough soil. I would avoid soil with chemical fertilizers and the like because your cat will be in it, on it, and eating the stuff that grows from it.

Smooth River Rocks, Beach Glass, or Shells: Because your cat will love these plants so much they will sit in the pot as opposed to grazing politely from the side of it. If you don't want them lying on top of the plants like a lounging odalisque, do this: plant half the pot. Leave the other as just soil. Then lightly press smooth river-type rocks; large, polished glass floral beads; seashells; or other smooth, nontoxic, unswallowable stuff into the just-dirt half of the pot. These rocks or shells will serve two other purposes: they make your mini garden lovely to look at, and they will prevent your cat from digging in the dirt or leaving soil samples on your newly mopped floor.

Optional Decorations: It's also fun to add some height or motion to your mini cat garden. Consider pinwheels, plastic hummingbirds with spinning wings, or little hanging chimes that catch your eye at the garden center.

Fill your pot, with a drainage hole, halfway up with soil. Loosen the root balls of the oat grass, wheatgrass, or catnip you've purchased or grown. Place plants in the little holes you've created on one side of the pot. Now press the river rocks flat into the just-soil half of your pot. Water the side with the plants. Presto! You are done.

Water a bit every day, every other day, or when soil seems dry to you. Taller plants tend to look good at the back of your arrangement with shorter guys in front. But your cat won't care much if you sweat over things like harmonious placement, right?

If you don't have a cat, you can still have fun making a mini garden for friends who do. Mini gardens make great housewarming presents, new-cat gifts, or sweet holiday offerings. Just make sure the recipient is equipped to take care of it.

Happy Cat, Happy Home

Try this version of the cat garden or invent your own version. Your cats will love you for it.

No, I take that back. If you have a cat, you know the best you'll get is momentary excitement followed by mild indifference. But it will be health-saturated mild indifference. And that's still good.

Even though our cats don't show their gratitude to us for specific actions we take on their behalf like dogs do, they do manage to communicate their love for us in their own healing way. St. Francis is said to have claimed, "A cat purring on your lap is more healing than any drug in the world, as the vibrations you are receiving are pure love and contentment." He knew what he was talking about!

Resources

Moore, Sarah. "How Do I Grow Wheatgrass for Cats?" SFGate. Accessed March 14, 2019. https://homeguides.sfgate.com/grow-wheatgrass-cats-90908.html.

Poolsidedreamer. "Growing Oat Grass for Cats." November 13, 2014. YouTube video, 3:31. https://www.youtube.com/watch?v=zZv CpqWt5B4&feature=youtu.be.

Building Quality Soil

by Corina Sahlin

In my twenty-five years of organic gardening and growing tons of food (literally), I have learned several effective strategies to build quality soil. Even if you're not a gardener, you still should be concerned about soil.

Officials at the UN warn that the world's topsoil could be depleted in just over half a century—a major concern given that it takes a thousand years to produce three centimeters of it. *Scientific American* reports that about a third of the world's soil has already been degraded. Furthermore, intensive farming is costing us thirty soccer fields of soil every minute. When soil has richer organic matter, it can withstand a longer dry spell and rely less on irrigation and fertilizer.

Since our earth will have to feed nine billion people in the future, the health of our soil is a matter of life and death.

In organic farms, where soil is rarely plowed, you can find up to 450 worms per square meter. Compare that to farmed soil, where there are fewer than thirty earthworms per square meter, according to the World Wide Fund for Nature (WWF). But why should you care about these slimy invertebrates? Earthworms burrow through the earth and fertilize it with their nutrient-rich waste. They also aerate the soil so oxygen and plant roots can reach further down. Thus, earthworms help form and regenerate new soil, improving its ability to absorb water. In these times of changing climate and increasing droughts, this is hugely important. Soil that contains too few earthworms is dense, poorly aerated, and unabsorbant. The WWF calls this a "dangerous chain reaction for humanity" and encourages farming practices that are healthy for soil. Therefore, it is important to protect earthworms for the sake of soil fertility and feeding the growing population of the world.

For healthier, more fertile soil, you need to increase organic matter and mineral content, and whenever possible, you should avoid tilling the soil and leave its structure undisturbed. Kathy LaLiberte of Garden Supply writes that the small amount of necessary organic matter binds together soil particles into porous crumbs, which allow air and water to move through the soil. She explains, "Organic matter also retains moisture (humus holds up to 90 percent of its weight in water), and is able to absorb and store nutrients. Most importantly, organic matter is food for microorganisms and other forms of soil life."

Let me show you my favorite ways to improve soil—the same strategies I have used for two decades to build incredibly productive gardens on my homestead.

Compost

One of the best-known ways to increase soil health, organic matter, and fertility is by using compost. Eliot Coleman, author of *The New Organic Grower*, *Four Season Harvest*, and *The Winter Harvest Handbook*, has written extensively on the subject of organic agriculture and has more than fifty years of experience in all aspects of organic farming. He says that fertile soil is filled with life, and compost is a life preserver.

John Jeavons, cofounder of the group Ecology Action and father of the modern biointensive gardening movement, explains that compost has a dual function. It improves soil structure and speeds up the formation of soil humus, which makes it easier to work with, gives it good aeration and water retention, and makes it resistant to erosion. Compost also provides nutrients for plant growth and helps make nutrients in the soil more available to plants. Fewer nutrients leach out in a soil with adequate organic matter. In his book *How to Grow More Vegetables*, Jeavons writes, "Improved soil structure and nourishment produce a healthy soil. A healthy soil produces healthy plants better able to resist insect and disease attacks. Most insects look for sick plants to eat. The best way to control insects and diseases in plants is with a living, healthy soil rather than with poisons that kill beneficial soil life."

I make lots of compost on our homestead. When I dig into a chunk of my homemade compost, hundreds of earthworms wriggle in it. Earthworms are especially good composters.

Jeavons writes that "their castings are 5 times richer in nitrogen, 2 times richer in exchangeable calcium, 7 times richer in available phosphorus, and 11 times richer in available potassium than the soil they inhabit." We're lucky because we raise dairy goats who produce lovely manure and bedding, which transforms into great compost. We also raise chickens for eggs and meat, and their droppings get incorporated into our compost scene as well.

Over the course of forty to sixty years, farmed soil will lose between forty and sixty percent of its original organic matter, notes Michigan State University.

But even if you don't have animals, you can make wonderful compost. Compost is made with the help of prolific micro-organisms, organic matter, air, moisture, and time. The recipe for compost is like lasagna: you build layers with green and brown matter. The green is young, moist, nitrogen-rich, fresh plant matter, like kitchen and garden waste (vegetable scraps, fresh grass clippings, or discarded plants from the garden). Coleman plants alfalfa and keeps harvesting it for the green layer. Alfalfa grows fast, has deep roots, and is a strong feeder on nutrients from the lower levels of the soil and therefore is high in minerals. If you have animal manure like we do on our homestead, this is a great source of nitrogen (the green layer). Never put manure directly on the garden, since it can burn plants. The other "lasagna" layer for building compost is brown matter, consisting of older, drier materials that take longer to decompose, such as straw, sawdust, and dried leaves.

You can put your layers inside a purchased compost bin or hold together the pile with wooden crates or even bales of straw.

How to Build a Compost Pile

Start by putting down a layer (about 3 inches) of dried matter, then add a layer (about 6 inches) of green matter, then sprinkle a little bit of soil (¼ to 1 inch) on top of that layer. Moisten each layer lightly so it has the texture of a wrung-out sponge. For your initial pile, build six or more layers like this, then add to the pile for the next two months. When it reaches 4 feet high, it's big enough. Add a cover such as a tarp, metal sheet, or plywood.

The pile will heat up (140 to 160°F) as the microorganisms inside the heap break down the organic materials. These organisms need air, which is why straw is an ideal component since it is hollow. You will know when things go wrong if the compost heap smells. This can happen if the pile is too wet or compacted and the process becomes **anaerobic** (without air), which encourages bad bacteria that make the heap stink. Another problem arises if there is too much green material, which produces too much heat and kills all the good stuff in the pile. Or it won't heat up at all because there is too much dry material, in which case you have to moisten it or add some liquid fish fertilizer or blood meal.

The heat of decomposition reaches its peak a few weeks after the heap is completed and then dies down. By that point, you can turn the pile to aerate it to get the process going again. I do this by moving the materials on the pile with a pitchfork into a new heap next to it.

When the compost pile is cooled down, you can use the compost even if it's not completely broken down and you can still distinguish some of the original materials. Put this in the garden in the fall, and it will finish decomposing by spring. You can let it go longer in the compost pile for one or two years to make it crumbly, dark, and sweet smelling. It will have the texture of a delicious chocolate cake by then.

Sprinkle the finished compost on top of a garden bed (½ inch to 1 inch yearly) and mix it into the top 2 inches of soil. Earthworms and other soil creatures will mix it in all the way.

A fun alternative to composting is **vermicomposting**, using earthworms to convert nutrient-dense materials, such as manures, food wastes, and green crop residues, into food for plants. Earthworm castings feed plant roots and also carry a huge load of beneficial microbes that boost the soil organism community. You can easily start vermicomposting with a small container under the sink as worm bin, and you can find a lot of free information on how to start the bin online.

Use a Broadfork—Don't Till

When I studied organic, sustainable agriculture in college, I came across a tool called a **broadfork**, which is exactly what its name describes: it's a very large fork that's broad. It looks like a big pitchfork but with a handle on each side and a crossbar you step on, and when you thrust it into the soil and pull back on the handles, the tines break up and loosen the soil. It's used to aerate the soil manually instead of with a rototiller. I have successfully used a broadfork in my fruitful career as a homesteader and organic gardener for over a decade and even made a demonstration video on how to use it, found on my YouTube channel here: https://youtu.be/V_crd4xGUio.

Why would you want to use a broad fork instead of a rototiller? Although rototillers make the job of tilling and plowing large patches of dirt easy and fast, they tear up lots of earthworms. Tilling also disrupts the **rhizosphere**, the band of soil containing plant roots, their secretions, and associated soil microorganisms. A broadfork, however, doesn't mix and chop soil but gently loosens it, which keeps the useful little critters that are so good for the soil intact and happy.

Rototillers usually only reach and aerate four to six inches of soil, which can leave the layers underneath compacted and hardpan, messing with drainage and root growth. Broadforks, on the other hand, reach down further, loosening the soil deeper down and creating tunnels, making room for plants to reach deeper. It's easier for deeply rooted plants to reach water during dry spells and also to reach soil nutrients in the deeper layers of the soil.

You cannot rototill soil that's too wet because you will completely destroy soil structure by creating small bricks that tender roots can't penetrate. This can be very frustrating because gardeners are so dependent on a dry weather spell in the spring for tilling the soil to get it ready for planting. Good luck waiting for a solid dry spell here in the Pacific Northwest! With a broadfork, you can work the soil earlier, since it doesn't have to be so dry. This allows the gardener to plant earlier in the season.

Weed seeds can patiently wait to germinate for many years, staying dormant until a rototiller brings them to the surface by mixing and chopping the soil. With light and water, they will sprout, even if they're very old. This doesn't happen as much when using a broadfork, since it doesn't mix the soil, and the old weed seeds stay deep down where it's dark and they can't germinate.

Broadforks work great for raised beds with wooden or stone edges, since you don't need to lift a heavy rototiller over them. If you have an area in a garden bed that needs loosening up but would be impossible to reach with a rototiller, just whip out your broadfork and easily work around the plants.

Rototillers are noisy and stinky. When you use a broadfork, you can smell the roses and can hear the birds sing. Working in the garden with a broadfork counts as exercise! It's a great workout!

Another key strategy for protecting soil structure is to grow in wide permanent beds prepared by a broadfork and to never step on the beds. I only step on designated pathways and never on the garden beds, because this would compact the growing areas. Raised, wide beds are perfect for planting as closely as possible in the beds. Close planting shades the soil surface, which benefits both soil life and plants by conserving moisture and moderating temperature extremes.

Grow Green Manure

Growing **green manures**, also called cover crops, is a wonderful way to improve and protect soil. In the north, gardeners plant cold-hardy crops such as vetch and winter rye. In my neck of the woods, it rains 100 inches per year, so I like to tuck my garden under a blanket of green to protect it from all the heavy rain in the winter. The cover crops lie dormant in the winter and begin growing again in early spring. I then use a shovel or garden fork to dig them under, a shallow procedure that kills the cover crop and feeds the soil. The channels opened up by the decaying roots of cover crops permit oxygen and water to penetrate the soil. Green manures have to decompose for at least three weeks before you can sow seeds or transplant seedlings.

You can also plant these green manures in a new garden area the year before you plant it with vegetables. The cover crop will choke out weeds and add organic matter. Harvey Ussery of *Mother Earth News* recommends growing legumes (field peas, soybeans, alfalfa), which contribute nitrogen and organic matter. Fast-growing grains and buckwheat generate the most organic matter and smother weeds. Mixes of grasses and clovers are great because "the grasses add a large amount of biomass and improve soil structure because of the size and complexity of their root systems, and the legumes add nitrogen to help break down the relatively carbon-rich grass roots quickly."

The green manure can be then buried under mulch to decompose, or it can be pulled up and left on the soil to act as a mulch. Ussery warns that some cover crops are difficult to kill without tilling them, "but cutting them immediately above the crowns after seed stalks or flowers form will kill them. Use the upper ends of the plants as a mulch to help break down the roots more rapidly." Additionally, if you keep chickens, they can till in your cover crops for you. Not only does their enthusiastic scratching kill the cover crop, but in our garden they also eat slugs or damaging insects, while at the same time fertilizing the soil with their droppings.

Some people sow cover crops under a vegetable crop. It's fun to experiment with this: Ussery recommends sowing Dutch white clover in a bed where you also grow tall crops, like tomatoes or pole beans, because the clover grows quickly, deters weeds, and helps retain moisture. It also looks pretty and attracts beneficial insects!

Talking of mulch, even if you don't grow green manure on your garden beds, always cover them in winter to protect the soil against cold temperatures and drying out. You can use straw or fall leaves in a pinch.

Nutrient-Rich Soil

We are what we eat, but we should also keep in mind that the food we eat is as good as the soil it grows in. Over the years, and because of industrialized farming, soil all over the world is becoming depleted of minerals. This is reflected in the nutritional content of the plants it grows. We're missing a percentage of the minerals and trace elements that used to be there. *Scientific American* reports that the University of Texas studied USDA nutritional data from 1950 and 1999 for many different fruits and vegetables and found "reliable declines" in several main nutrients and vitamins in that time period. A Kushi Institute report noted that "average calcium levels in 12 fresh vegetables dropped 27 percent; iron levels 37 percent; vitamin A levels 21 percent, and vitamin C levels 30 percent." This means that to consume the same amount of nutrition that earlier generations enjoyed, we need to eat several times the produce today.

Before you begin a fertilizer regimen, test your soil to see what you're working with. You can generally send a sample to your local cooperative extension or university for a small fee. Many synthetic fertilizers offer a combination of three key elements: nitrogen, phosphorus, and potassium. Your plants will also need small amounts of calcium, magnesium, and sulfur. Some farmers choose to add **rock dust** for a natural way to reintroduce a wider variety of minerals and micronutrients.

Adding **fish emulsions** and **bone meal** is another natural way to add nutrients to your soil.

Consider also that your plants can't make use of these nutrients if they can't absorb them. LaLiberte writes, "Most essential plant nutrients are soluble at pH levels of 6.5 to 6.8, which is why most plants grow best in this range. If the pH of your soil is much higher or lower, soil nutrients start to become chemically bound to the soil particles, which makes them unavailable to your plants." To improve the fertility of your soil, you need to get the pH of your soil within this range, though it is a slow and careful process. Limestone and ash are sometimes used to raise the pH, and ground sulfur and pine needles are sometimes used to lower it.

I hope you are now inspired to build gorgeous, healthy soil in your garden! And the next time you encounter an earthworm, don't recoil, but marvel at all the hard work it is doing.

Resources

Arsenault, Chris. "Only 60 Years of Farming Left If Soil Degradation Continues." *Scientific American*. Accessed January 31, 2019. https://www.scientificamerican.com/article/only-60-years-of-farming-left-if-soil-degradation-continues/.

Coleman, Eliot. *The New Organic Grower*. White River Junction, VT: Chelsea Green Publishing Company, 1993.

———. *The New Organic Grower's Four-Season Harvest*. White River Junction, VT: Chelsea Green Publishing Company, 1992.

Jäger, Karin. "Earthworm Numbers Dwindle, Threatening Soil Health." DW.com. January 30, 2017. https://www.dw.com/en/earthworm-numbers-dwindle-threatening-soil-ealth/a-37325923.

Jeavons, John. *How to Grow More Vegetables*. Berkeley, CA: Ten Speed Press, 1995.

LaLiberte, Kathy. "Building Healthy Soil." Gardener's Supply. Last modified February 21, 2017. https://www.gardeners.com/how-to/building-healthy-soil/5060.html.

Melakeberhan, Haddish, Sieglinde Snapp, and Kim Cassida. "No Matter How You Slice It, Healthy Soil Is Important." Michigan State University AgBioResearch. July 26, 2015. https://www.canr.msu.edu/news/no_matter_how_you_slice_it_healthy_soil_is_important.

Scheer, Roddy, and Doug Moss. "Dirt Poor: Have Fruits and Vegetables Become Less Nutritious?" EarthTalk, *Scientific American*. Accessed February 6, 2019. https://www.scientificamerican.com/article/soil-depletion-and-nutrition-loss/.

Ussery, Harvey. "8 Steps for Making Better Garden Soil." *Mother Earth News*. June/July 2007. https://www.motherearthnews.com/organic-gardening/8-steps-to-make-better-garden-soil-zmaz07jjzsel.

Blending Herbs into Any Garden

꒰ by Kathy Vilim ꒱

No matter what kind of garden you grow, herbs can be blended into your garden design. Herbs can easily be tucked into vegetable gardens, perennial gardens, English cottage gardens, or wild native plant gardens.

When my neighbor Judith had hip replacement surgery, she asked me to help her design a garden that would be easier for her to manage. So she could avoid getting down on hands and knees to reach her plants, I suggested she would benefit from a raised bed built close to the house. This would put her favorite flowers and herbs at eye level and within reach while she was sitting in a chair.

Trailing rosemary could be planted along the edge of the bed and allowed to hang gracefully.

Judith got me thinking about mixing herbs into the garden. When we think of gardening with herbs, most of us envision an herb box placed in a sunny spot by a kitchen door or a planter box hung underneath a kitchen window. Perhaps we recall seeing pots of herbs grown indoors on a kitchen counter.

The other day while I was at the nursery, I stopped to look at the herbs. Observing the lacy leaves of cilantro and the delicate gray color of sage leaves, I thought to myself, *Can't I grow these herbs right next to my flowers? Aren't they just as beautiful?* Of course, some gardeners prefer to keep their herbs separate from the rest of the garden. For one thing, it can be helpful to keep them close at hand for cooking. But can't herbs be ornamental as well? How can I make them part of the landscape?

Does sage grow in a rose garden? Can lavender survive alongside my flowers? I have a native plant garden in the coastal mountains of Southern California. Can I plant herbs alongside succulents and drought-tolerant perennials? Why not give it a try? And why not try to blend herbs into Judith's garden?

Therapeutic Raised Garden Beds

Raised beds are an excellent way to bring herbs into your garden, especially for seniors. For the most part, seniors have more time to garden than busy working adults, but they can be put off by the physical strain of keeping a garden. My research has shown that gardens can contribute to overall wellness, including relief from depression. Aromatic herbs create calmness. Romantic scents can bring back memories of special times. The herb rosemary can help you remember future tasks to be done, referred to as *prospective memory*.

There are many different types of raised beds. The possibilities are limitless, but here are some considerations: height, depth, amount of sun, location of trees, distance from the kitchen, access to water, and material to use. Judith's bed was built to table height and was no deeper than arm's length so that plants were in easy reach. We used reclaimed wood that was sealed to avoid rot, though be sure your wood has not been treated with chemicals unsafe for ingestion should you plan to eat plants grown in this bed. We picked a flat spot and first took out a patch of lawn using the lasagna gardening method to make it easy. This method of lawn removal uses layers of cardboard, newspapers, compost, peat moss, and grass clippings. It is less labor-intensive than digging or tilling, and you can do it yourself without hiring a contractor or using any chemicals.

I took advantage of Judith's well-tended pink roses by transplanting them into the raised bed. Around the edges of the bed I planted trailing rosemary (*Rosmarinus officinalis* 'Prostratus') with tiny blue blossoms. In between the rosemary, I tucked silver-leafed santolina (*Santolina chamaecyparissus*) and gray lamb's ears (*Stachys byzantina*). The pastel color combination created a wonderfully calming effect.

For everything you ever wanted to know about raised-bed gardening, check out the *joe gardener* podcast series by Joe Lampl noted in the resources section.

Companion Planting in the Vegetable Garden

What is a companion plant? Two plants that have a harmonious relationship are called **companions**. Often companion plants are plants that can provide pest control for others. This is notable in the vegetable garden, where smart vegetable gardeners take advantage of this natural arrangement and place their vegetables close to friends, where the strong smell of one plant can deter insects from another. This keeps the garden organic with little to no need for chemicals. (See page 272 for a companion planting guide.)

Since Judith loves salads, she asked that I also create a small, raised vegetable garden for her. Because leeks do well when planted with carrots, I made sure to include both. Leeks put off a smell that will repel the carrot fly, and carrots put off a smell that will repel the leek moth, for a mutually beneficial relationship.

Another big insect enemy of plants in the vegetable garden is the white cabbage butterfly. For example, if you plant vegetables that are in the cabbage family (such as kale, broccoli, and cauliflower), my research indicates that they benefit from being planted near celery, dill, chamomile, sage, peppermint, rosemary, onions, and potatoes, which help keep the caterpillars away. In the 1800s, gardeners in Holland planted hemp (*Cannabis*) as a hedge around the cabbage patch to keep the white cabbage butterflies away. Companion plants can also be beneficial when a taller plant creates shade for its neighbor, or when a plant with deep roots brings nitrogen up to the surface.

Basil is an especially good companion plant for tomatoes and asparagus, and there are quite a number of varieties. Plus, it just looks pretty. And who says you can't have a pretty vegetable garden? Sweet Thai basil (*Ocimum basilicum* var. *thyrsiflora*), with its long, purple flower spikes speckled with white, is a graceful addition to any vegetable garden. Thai basil was one of the herbs I used in the edging along Judith's long gravel walkway.

Edible flowers can also be helpful companions in the vegetable garden. Marigolds, dahlias, zinnias, and nasturtiums can be useful to keep pests away. Plant marigolds with your tomatoes to deter snails. I made sure to plant nasturtiums to attract aphids and draw them away from Judith's vegetables. Nasturtiums (*Tropaeolum majus*) are not herbs but are edible flowering plants that can be added to salads for a colorful effect. Dahlias provide protection from nematodes.

Some herbs just naturally go together, like the herbs that get thrown into an Italian spaghetti sauce or pizza sauce: oregano, rosemary, basil, and garlic. One fun way to blend herbs into your garden design and get the attention of your kids is to create a pizza garden!

A Child's Pizza Garden

Define a circular area of dirt in which to grow your pizza "pie plate." Divide it into triangular "slices" of six or eight pieces. In each slice will be planted an ingredient for your child's pizza. Tomatoes are a must-have; perhaps make them the centerpiece surrounded by onion, green or red bell pepper, garlic, and Italian herbs such as oregano, rosemary, and basil. Since the herbs are set in a circle, they are always within easy reach. For a vegetarian pizza, spinach is one of my favorites to add to the pizza garden.

Let your children help you plant from seedlings. Kids who grow their own vegetables eat their vegetables. They become participants, engaged in the process of knowing where their food comes from.

The Wild Native Plant Garden

Perhaps you want to have a native plant garden. You absolutely can include herbs that are native to your region. Sage

(*Salvia*) is a great example. No matter where you live in North America, there is a native variety of sage in your climate.

Since these plants are hummingbird magnets, you'll want to place them near a bench where you can spend endless time watching the hummers' antics. Plant in full sun, and even on hot summer days they will continue to bloom. Native sages can live as much as thirty years, and the plants can get bushy. When planning a native sage garden, it is necessary to allow room for their growth. Resist the urge to place your plants close together.

Native sages should be grown with pollinators in mind, rather than for culinary use. For the kitchen garden, grow garden sage (*Salvia officinalis*). One exceptional variety of native sage for pollinators is the Texas sage (*Salvia texana*), possibly the best hummingbird magnet of them all.

For more info on which varieties of sage are native to your region and nurseries that carry them, visit your local branch of the North American Native Plant Society (NANPS.org).

In the California garden, native herbs are staples in the native plant garden design, sometimes taking center stage as the garden's focal point all year long. In California alone, there are seventeen different native varieties of sage that can withstand our sandy soil and lack of rain. Even in drought years, native varieties will survive and continue to bloom, much to the delight of the hummingbirds. Some varieties prefer living along the coast, while others are happy inland, and still others prefer higher altitude mountain locations.

Another benefit to planting native varieties of sage is attracting pollinators such as bees, wasps, and especially hummingbirds. One pairing that I love is Cleveland sage (*Salvia clevelandii*) and milkweed (*Asclepias tuberosa*). Not only do they look good together, but while the sage brings in the hummingbirds, the milkweed will bring in the monarch butterflies!

The Xeric Succulent Garden

If you live in part of the country where water use is restricted due to drought, such as the Southwest, you may be using **xeric plants**, including a lot of succulents. What is xeriscaping? Denver Water coined the term *xeriscape* in 1981 by combining *landscape* with the Greek prefix *xero-*, from *xeros*, meaning "dry." Xeric plants refer to the plants used in a xeriscaped garden.

Can you use herbs here? Of course. Many native sage varieties are drought tolerant and look wonderful planted amid the succulents. They add a vibrant splash of color to the gray and green xeriscaped garden, and you don't have to worry about watering. In fact, too much water will kill *Salvia*. Just be careful to leave room for succulent growth.

In the xeric garden, small fleshy succulents like *Sedum* 'Autumn Joy' add interest. Cliff stonecrop (*Hylotelephium cauticola*) offers up a bluish tint for a nice change from green. Blue fescue grass (*Festuca glauca*) can grow alongside sedums in the xeriscaped garden. All of those mix well with thyme (*Thymus*).

Another plant for the xeric garden, and one of my favorites, is hens and chicks. The hens and chicks that are commonly sold in California are *Echeveria* ×*imbricata*. These are native to Mexico. If you live in cold winter areas, you would want to look for *Sempervivum*, also commonly called hens and chicks. The main difference is that *Sempervivum* is frost-resistant while *Echeveria* is not. It can be confusing when buying them: both plants have a tight ring of fleshy rosettes. One tip is that *Echeveria* leaves are thick and rounded, sometimes with sharp points; while *Sempervivum* leaves come to sharp points also, they are not thick. Both offer fascinating possibilities mixed with herbs in the xeric garden.

You will want to use herbs that are drought tolerant in your xeric garden. Some recommendations include yarrow (*Achillea*), anise hyssop (*Agastache*), scented geraniums (*Pelargonium*), hyssop (*Hyssopus officinalis*), lavender (*Lavandula*), lamb's ears (*Stachys byzantina*), and garden sage for culinary use. In general, plants with gray leaves will be more drought tolerant than those with green leaves.

The Perennial Garden

In my California garden, there is always lavender. Most of the country can enjoy fragrant lavender blossoms. A member of the mint family, lavender blends well with other perennials in borders all over the country.

Spanish lavender (*Lavandula stoechas*), French lavender (*L. dentata*), and English lavender (*L. angustifolia*) are sun-loving plants that grow well in Southern California's Mediterranean climate, where it is hot and arid. Lavender plants grow taller and wider in areas with mild winters and hot summers. All the lavenders have abundant blue or purple blooms, are drought tolerant, and are highly fragrant. Both the flowers and leaves can be used, either as lavender oil or as an herbal tea. Lavender is also beloved by gardeners for attracting beneficial insects.

Spanish lavender has dark purple flower spikes with purple bracts (wings). This variety is the best choice for hot humid places in the southeast. Spanish lavender is lovely and fragrant, attracting butterflies and bees. Growing twelve to fourteen inches tall and fifteen to eighteen inches wide, Spanish lavender can be tucked in between other perennials in areas where there is slightly alkaline soil and full sun. Spanish lavender is even drought tolerant. It can be planted in the cutting garden or grown in rows for a sweeping display of purple color in the perennial garden. This versatile plant can also be used in rock gardens.

Provence French lavender (*L. ×intermedia* 'Provence') is intensely fragrant and produces lavender-blue blooms. French lavender is a drought-resistant perennial and thrives in hot, sunny sites with fast-draining soils. This lavender absolutely needs well-drained soil. You can plant it on mounds to improve drainage. Since it grows twenty-four to thirty inches tall by eighteen to twenty-four inches wide, choose this lavender to fill large spaces in the garden. Lavender makes wonderful cut flowers, so I like to grow French lavender with roses and native Pacifica iris for a contrast of blooms and colors: pink roses, baby blue lavenders, and either yellow, deep purple, or delicate shades of blue Pacifica iris.

English lavender is the most cold hardy of the three lavenders, especially a variety called *L. angustifolia* 'Vera' (zones 5 through 10). Despite its name, English lavender did not originate in England; rather, it is native to the Mediterranean. This variety was the original lavender, known to the Greeks and Romans. Choose dwarf varieties of English lavender for small spaces. Sweetly fragrant, English lavender is suitable for flower cutting, sachets, and oil production. A summer bloomer,

English lavender grows into large compact mounds eighteen inches tall and twenty-four to thirty inches wide with thin stems that hold small purple blossoms at the very ends. Use this lavender for a sweeping effect. They grow bigger in areas with mild winters, so leave lots of room. English lavender is drought tolerant and looks stunning when planted with milkweed (*Asclepias*) for the monarchs. Other pairings include oriental poppies (*Papaver orientale*), yarrow (*Achillea*), and montbretia (*Crocosmia*). Another benefit: English Lavender is rabbit and deer resistant.

In warmer zones, rosemary (*Rosmarinus officinalis*) brings a unique minty-pine fragrance and delicate pale blue flowers to the perennial garden. Rosemary can be used as a border plant. A woody perennial with needle-like deep green leaves, rosemary can be trimmed into tight hedges. Walking down a garden path edged with rosemary, you can run your hand along the green leaves, pick up the rustic fragrance, and take it with you throughout the day. Upright rosemary can also be shaped into topiaries or grown in pots. A drought-tolerant perennial, it can be grown alongside xeric plants.

Besides the upright rosemary, there is also a trailing or creeping variety of rosemary, *R. officinalis* 'Prostratus'. This type of rosemary is useful in raised garden beds like Judith's, where cascading branches of rosemary's glossy deep green needle-like leaves and prolific baby blue flowers can soften walls of wood or stucco. Creeping rosemary can also be used to make attractive hanging plants for patios. One of my favorite pairings to use in garden designs is the blue blooms of trailing rosemary with the happy yellow faces of daffodils (*Narcissus*).

Groundcovers

The other day I spied an interesting pairing of spearmint, cabbage, and marigolds. The spearmint (*Mentha spicata*) spread out as a groundcover between cabbage plants, while the marigolds dotted the scene with happy yellow blooms that deterred whiteflies and killed bad nematodes.

What about chamomile (*Chamaemelum nobile*)? There is something special about stepping on a groundcover and having it release a delicate aroma. I have done garden designs using chamomile between flat stones in areas where there was a garden bench for viewing the garden. Thyme (*Thymus vulgaris*) is also another aromatic herb that can be used as an aromatic groundcover.

Rock Gardens

I have a soft spot for compact, ground-hugging herbs that can spill over rocks or fill in between flat stones. Chamomile, wooly thyme, and mints all do this. If you have a rock garden, an interesting pairing is a low-growing herb like thyme placed to spread softly over bulbs. You can enjoy the herbs when the bulbs are dormant and when they are blooming. I especially like to plant daffodils (*Narcissus*) that naturalize here in Southern California and do not require freezing winter temperatures.

Edgings

Border edgings are necessary to tie together all the elements of a garden bed. In a formal setting, you will want the herbs used to be perennials, so they will not disappear for part of the year.

A row of soft herbal foliage, such as the delicate lacy leaves of cilantro (*Coriandrum sativum*), makes an attractive garden border. Low-growing mounds of cilantro can work in front of peppers, tomatoes, or green beans.

The curry plant (*Helichrysum italicum*) is a lovely addition to the herb border. This is a compact Mediterranean shrub with golden flower heads that pop out of narrow silver-gray leaves and smell strongly of curry when rubbed. Curry plants (zone 7 to 11) are easy to grow and are drought tolerant.

In the book *Herb Garden Design* by Faith H. Swanson and Virginia B. Rady, the authors take a perennial garden, an herb garden, a cutting garden, and a vegetable garden and put them all together in the landscape. However, the plants are all still separated by borders: herbs stay in their beds, perennials stay in theirs, and vegetables have their own bed. The one thing that is interesting about having so many beds is that it offers the opportunity for lots of borders, all edged with herbs. Suggested herbs for borders are Greek oregano (*Origanum heracleoticum*), bush basil (*Ocimum minimum*), common thyme, lemon thyme (*Thymus citriodorus*), chives (*Allium schoenoprasum*), rosemary, winter savory (*Satureja montana*), and germander (*Teucrium chamaedrys*).

The Cutting Garden

I have had success adding herbs to wildflowers such as California poppies (*Eschscholzia californica*) and lupines (*Lupinus albifrons*). What I did was hand-scatter seeds in a bed that was planted with herbs and let them grow in together. I used a seed mix of flowers that were medium to low growing, to keep herbs visible. In this way, herbs can be easily added to bouquets.

Some of my favorite foliage herbs to add to bouquets are white or silver-leafed plants, such as lamb's ears (*Stachys byzan-*

tina) and silver mound artemisia (*Artemisia schmidtiana*). The herbs in the genus *Artemisia* are also popular for their aromatic foliage. While these foliage herbs do bloom, their flowers are generally of only secondary interest to their foliage.

You might like to try planting tansy. Tansy (*Tanacetum vulgare*) is an herb enjoyed for its clusters of tightly packed yellow flowers, which pop out nicely in a bouquet of cut flowers and herb foliage. Silver feather tansy (*T. ptarmiciflorum*) is a good choice for silvery-white plants with twice-cut feathery leaves and is a good alternative to dusty miller (*Jacobaea maritima*).

Rosemary adds interest both with its aromatic, deep green, glossy, needle-like leaves and its soft blue flowers that add a nice contrast to almost any flower colors. In California, rosemary can grow easily in a patch of wildflowers and can be easily cut along with them. For bouquets, use upright rosemary rather than the trailing form.

For a bouquet that uses more herbal blooms, try chives and woolly yarrow. Common chives add a soft pink, while woolly yarrow (*Achillea tomentosa*) delights with unique yellow flower clusters. Add old-fashioned pink roses to a bouquet of: lavender, tansy flowers, chives, purple basil seed heads (*Ocimum basilicum* var. *purpurascens*) and anise hyssop (*Agastache foeniculum*). They all work together nicely. Indeed, ideas for herbal bouquets are limited only by our imagination.

A Scented Herb Garden

To create a scented herb garden, I would start with scented geraniums (*Pelargonium crispum*). Scented geraniums can bring in the scent of lemon, lime, oranges, rose, or mint. Besides delightful fragrance, they also offer a variety of colorful flowers. Lemon verbena (*Aloysia citrodora*), lemon balm (*Melissa officinalis*), green lemon-scented thyme (*Thymus citriodorus*), and lemon basil (*Ocimum ×africanum*) can also be used to bring the scent of citrus to your garden.

For a licorice scent, plant fennel or anise hyssop. Wild fennel grows tall and bears lots of yellow flowers with ferny foliage. Anise hyssop, native to the Great Plains, has dark gray-green licorice-scented foliage and mauve flowers in late summer. Try growing bee balm (*Monarda didyma*) for a bouquet of mint, thyme, oregano, orange peel, and black tea when you rub its leaves; grow it also for the bees and hummingbirds it attracts.

Whatever fragrant herbs you plant, be sure to place them where you can enjoy the fragrance. Warm breezes will bring smells to walkways and garden benches where you can touch their leaves or brush against them.

Smells, of course, carry memories with them. I'll never forget walking through a park of tall, minty eucalyptus trees in a grassy meadow where sweet fennel had naturalized. The smell of eucalyptus and licorice filled the air. The park (Ellwood Beach, Goleta, CA) turned out to be an overwintering grove for the monarch butterflies, who roost up high in the trees. Wild fennel seeds also attract ladybugs in great number, always welcome in any garden.

Herbs in Every Garden

Gardening with herbs is so rewarding. They give us so much more than just beautiful flowers. They add leaves of different shades, textures, shapes, and aromas that either delight or heal. They add flavoring to our meals and oils for our bodies. They bring pollinators to our gardens.

In today's modern garden, we can enjoy all that herbs offer just as generations of gardeners have done since ancient times. So go a little wild, let your hair down, and put herbs just about anywhere in the landscape without restriction. Just be careful to note any herb's requirements on temperature, soil, and moisture.

Be bold! Try different pairings in your garden and see what happens. For my part, I can't wait to dig up more of Judith's garden and try out some new combinations.

Resources

Lampl, Joe. "Raised Bed Gardening, Pt. 1: Getting Started." *joe gardener* (blog), episode 42. March 8, 2018. https://joegardener.com/podcast/raised-bed-gardening-pt-1/.

Riotte, Louise. *Carrots Love Tomatoes: Secrets of Companion Planting for Successful Gardening.* Pownal, VT: Storey Books, 1988.

———. *Roses Love Garlic: Companion Planting and Other Secrets of Flowers.* Pownal, VT: Storey Books, 1983.

Swanson, Faith H., and Virginia B. Rady. *Herb Garden Design.* Hanover, NH: University Press of New England, 1984. Page 30.

"Salvia." BONAP's North American Plant Atlas. The Biota of North America Program. Last modifed December 15, 2014. http://bonap.net/Napa/TaxonMaps/Genus/State/Salvia.

Wilson, C., and J. R. Feuch. "Xeriscaping: Creative Landscaping." Colorado State University Extension. October 2007. https://extension.colostate.edu/topic-areas/yard-garden/xeriscaping-creative-landscaping-7-228/.

Wilson, Jim. *Landscaping with Herbs.* New York: Houghton Mifflin, 1994.

Cooking

Kombucha Craze: Making, Flavoring, and Cooking with Fermented Tea

➳ by Monica Crosson ➳

If you ask any of my friends or family members, they will say receiving a gift from me is always . . . interesting. You never know what might be peeking from beneath the tissue paper and ribbon—it might be homemade soap made with oil that had been steeped for months with bark or buds of locally foraged medicinal plants; it might be a hand-sculpted kitchen witch whose crocheted shawl matches the trim on one's good china; or it might be a collection of herbal teas from plants that I had cultivated in my very own garden. I have been known to plop a giant home-smoked ham or a brick of homemade cheese in someone's lap, and there was one time, when I had forgotten a friend's

birthday, that I quickly gathered eggs and placed them in a basket with a vintage piece of fabric I had been hoarding for just such an occasion.

The bonus to receiving a "Monica gift" is that it comes with a tale of how I screwed up on the first batch or how I had to start over three times or why I will never try this project again. Most explanations begin before the recipient has a chance to tear the paper, leaving them dumbfounded, to say the least. If you're very lucky, I will tear the gift from your hands and point out the tiniest of flaws. "See, right here? I swear I did not sculpt those tiny fingers to look like sausages, but they do!"

So, one April afternoon when the sun streamed through thick gray clouds that dared to rain on a gathering celebrating my sister's fifty years on this earth, I arrived with a sloshing gallon jar of amber liquid with a thick pancake-like substance floating on top.

"Happy birthday!" I said and plopped it on a table laden with brightly colored gift bags and cards.

My sister smiled nervously. "What is that?"

"You said you wanted to learn to make kombucha." I pointed to the jar. "Well, that's the starter and a healthy SCOBY for your kombucha. I ordered you some bottles with stoppers too. They'll be here in a couple of days." I was feeling pretty satisfied with my gift.

"Oh."

"What?! You don't like it?"

"No, I love it! I buy it all the time. I just didn't know that it would include a giant fungus-looking thing." She pointed to the leathery SCOBY with gelatinous fringe floating above the tea and sugar mixture. "I love it, really."

"You're welcome." I gave her a punch on the arm.

If you're a fan of the fizzy, fruity fermented tea called kombucha, you know how expensive it is to purchase: typically, a twelve-ounce bottle sells for between three and five dollars. So, here is an easy-to-follow guide with everything you need to know about making kombucha at home. It's easier than you think, and it will save you money.

In Case You Didn't Know

Rich in probiotics, fermented teas were thought to have originated in China over two thousand years ago. The first recorded use of fermented tea comes from the Tsin Dynasty in 221 BCE, when it was called the "Tea of Immortality." And though there are many types of fermented teas that can be divided into categories by their fermentation processes, by far the most popular is kombucha.

Kombucha was popular in Eastern Europe, Russia, and Japan for centuries and has been known by many names. Why we call the popularly consumed fermented tea *kombucha* is actually unclear, but the name may have originated in Japan. The term actually refers to kelp tea in Japan, which is a completely different beverage made from sea kelp, but it was from this Japanese name that the name for our fermented brew may have been adopted. Though the etymology may be uncertain, there is no uncertainty about the recent craze for this fermented beverage. Made from tea and sugar, it is slightly effervescent, lightly fruity, and praised for the alleged benefits of promoting weight loss, aiding joint repair, lowering cholesterol, protecting your liver, and boosting heart health (among other benefits). But have you ever wondered how this magical concoction is formed?

The Secret's in the SCOBY

If you've peeked inside the pantry of a friend or family member who makes kombucha, you may be familiar with the gelatinous pancake that is seen floating on top of a jar of the fermenting beverage. That is the mother culture, mushroom, or **SCOBY**, which stands for **symbiotic culture of bacteria and yeast**, a virtual housing unit for specific bacteria and yeast strains that live together in a mutually supportive community. Though not all kombucha cultures will contain the exact same strains, generally, you may expect: *Acetobacter, Saccharomyces, Brettanomyces, Lactobacillus, Pediococcus, Gluconacetobacter kombuchae, Zygosaccharomyces*, or a combination of these. While each SCOBY's exact makeup may vary, what is common to all kombuchas is gluconic acid, acetic acid, and fructose.

There are three ways you can obtain a SCOBY if you want to make your own kombucha:

1. Layers from a Friend or Family Member

If you know someone who makes their own kombucha, odds are they will have an extra SCOBY, as each batch creates a new one, adding layers to the original that can be peeled and passed on. Be sure to put your new SCOBY in a glass jar with approximately one cup of kombucha tea. Avoid using a metal lid to seal your jar in transport. If the metal comes in contact with your SCOBY, it can kill it, so use a plastic lid or a piece of plastic and a rubber band.

2. Purchased from a Reputable Company

You can buy a SCOBY online or from your local health food store or co-op. Look for a source that uses organic products.

3. Growing Your Own

You can grow your own through a relatively simple process that utilizes raw kombucha (that can be sourced through your local health food store), tea, and sugar. The process can take up to one month, so if you're in a hurry to start making bottles of kombucha, you might go ahead and skip this.

Making Kombucha

Before you get started, you will need a few supplies: primarily, a brewing vessel and a cover for the container. The container you use to brew your kombucha in is the most crucial component, and though you have several options, I find a glass jar works the best. I use one-gallon glass jars that can be purchased inexpensively at any big-box store. Avoid metal (though stainless steel is okay) and crystal containers, which contain lead.

During the fermentation process, you will need to employ a non-airtight cover system that allows the brew to breathe as well as keeps harmful insects or debris from entering your container. The easiest method is a coffee filter and a large rubber band; you can also use a paper towel, tea towel, or layered cheesecloth in the same manner.

The following are other tools that are useful but not necessary:

- Tea ball, if brewing loose tea
- Strainer
- Funnel
- Glass jar with a lid and a plastic spigot for storing and enjoying your finished brew

- Old-fashioned (flip-top) air-tight twelve-ounce bottles, a fun way to store individual servings

Tea for Kombucha Making

Black Tea: Traditionally used for brewing kombucha and provides the most nutrition for the SCOBY. Provides a bold apple-like flavor and a dark amber color.

Green Tea: Commonly mixed with black tea but can be used alone. Green tea lends a softer color and taste to your kombucha.

White Tea: Creates a flowery and delicate kombucha. Best used in combination with black or green tea.

Red Rooibos: Lends an earthy flavor but is recommended in combination with black tea.

Oolong Tea: Provides an amber-colored tea with a somewhat fruity flavor.

Herbal Teas: Because herbal teas do not contain the nutrients necessary to feed the SCOBY, they should be used in combination with black tea.

Teas Containing Essential Oils (Earl Grey, Flavored Ceylon, or Chai): Volatile oils often added to tea are generally harmful to the SCOBY and may become rancid during the brewing process.

For the healthiest SCOBY, brew black, green, or white tea (or a combination). Herbal teas, such as rosehip, licorice root, and hibiscus, can be used in combination with black tea for added flavor and healthful benefits.

Basic Kombucha Recipe (Makes 1 Gallon)

> 1 gallon filtered water
>
> 12 tea bags
>
> 1 cup organic sugar or pasteurized honey (Don't skimp on the sugar; this is what the yeast feeds on.)
>
> 1 cup kombucha (Use the kombucha that came with your SCOBY or purchase a bottle of unflavored kombucha.)
>
> SCOBY
>
> Gallon-size jar, wide mouthed
>
> Coffee filter, tea towel, paper towel, or cheesecloth
>
> Large rubber band

Heat the water and add tea bags and let steep for approximately 10 minutes. Remove from heat.

Add the sugar and allow to cool to below 90°F to avoid damaging the SCOBY. Pour your tea in the jar and add the kombucha and the SCOBY. Place the coffee filter over the mouth of the jar and secure with a rubber band. Let sit in a warm, dark place (in a cupboard or on a shelf of your pantry) for 7–10 days. You will know it's done when the tea is slightly effervescent with a sweet, tangy flavor.

Once it has finished fermenting, set aside the SCOBY and 1 cup of the kombucha to use with your next batch. Bottle and refrigerate the remaining brew.

Giving Your Kombucha Flair

One of the great benefits of making your own kombucha is that you have the ability to influence the flavor of your brew. You can do this by combining different teas or experimenting with fermentation time. But if you really want to amp up the flavor of your brew, you can incorporate fresh or dried fruit, juices, extracts, or herbs and spices just prior to drinking or in a second fermentation.

While kombucha is great on its own after the initial fermentation time, a second fermentation can be done after the SCOBY is removed. For a second fermentation, you will need to bottle your kombucha in combination with flavorings in air-tight bottles and allow them to sit at room temperature between two and four days. To prevent your bottles from building up with too much CO_2, monitor and burp them (open them to release carbonation) during the second fermentation. When the second fermentation is complete, strain the fruit (if desired) and rebottle and store in the refrigerator or cupboard. This second fermentation allows the flavors to meld and lends a more complex flavor profile.

Don't be afraid to experiment with flavor combinations, because this allows you to come up with a brew that suits your taste preference. Here are a few guidelines to get you started:

- If flavoring with fruit juice, measure 10 to 20 percent juice to 80 to 90 percent kombucha.

- If using extracts, herbs, or spices, start small (½ to 1 teaspoon) and adjust to taste.

- If using fresh fruit, measure 25 percent fruit to 75 percent kombucha.

Great Flavor Combinations
Strawberries and basil
Strawberries, almond extract, and honey
Blueberries, ginger, and lemon
Raspberries, lime, and chili pepper
Cherries and almond extract

Peaches and vanilla bean

Pears and cinnamon

Pineapple, coconut water, and mango

Cranberries, ginger, and cinnamon

Maple syrup, ginger, and cinnamon

Orange zest, chamomile, and honey

Blackberries and thyme

Plums, candied ginger, and cinnamon

Watermelon, basil, and coconut water

Lemon zest, rum extract, and ginger

Lavender, rose water, and honey

Kombucha in the Kitchen

Kombucha is more than just a flavorful drink containing gut-loving probiotics—it can also be used as a marinade, salad dressing, or replacement for apple cider vinegar in many of your favorite recipes. Here are a few of my favorite ways to use kombucha in the kitchen:

Kombucha Tahini Dressing

½ cup tahini

⅓ cup kombucha (well fermented)

¼ cup water

¼ cup tamari

3 tablespoons nutritional yeast

2 cloves garlic

½ teaspoon sea salt

¼ cup olive oil

In a food processor, add all ingredients except the olive oil and blend until smooth. Slowly drizzle in olive oil and serve.

Kombucha Fennel Slaw

    5 tablespoons kombucha (well fermented)

    3 tablespoons extra-virgin olive oil

    1 teaspoon lemon juice

    Pinch of sugar

    2 fennel bulbs (plus 2 tablespoons chopped fennel fronds)

    1 firm apple (Granny Smith or Gala)

    3 stalks celery (plus ⅓ cup loosely packed leaves)

    Salt and pepper to taste

Whisk together the first four ingredients. Set aside. Thinly slice fennel, apple, and celery. Add all ingredients to a bowl and toss with dressing. Add salt and pepper to taste. Serves 2.

Kombucha Marinade

    2½ cups kombucha (well fermented)

    3 tablespoons tamari or soy sauce

    1 tablespoon Worcestershire sauce

    2 teaspoons Tabasco sauce

    ½ teaspoon garlic powder

    1 teaspoon red pepper flakes (optional)

    Salt and pepper to taste

    ⅓ cup olive oil

Combine all ingredients in a food processor except olive oil. While processing, slowly add olive oil. Makes approximately 3½ cups.

Kombucha Fruit Pops

    2 cups of your favorite fruits or fruit combination

    12 ounces flavored or plain kombucha

Blend ingredients in high-speed blender until smooth. Use a popsicle mold to fill and freeze until frozen (approximately 6 hours). Makes 6 frozen fruit pops.

What to Do with That Extra SCOBY

Because a new SCOBY is created with each batch of kombucha you make, you can easily become overrun with it. If you have friends or family who are interested in making kombucha, make sure to share the love. Here are a few other ideas for how to use your extra SCOBY around the home:

Face Mask: A SCOBY face mask is alleged to improve skin tone and combat the appearance of wrinkles.

Pet/Livestock Food: With probiotics and high percentages of protein, fiber, calcium, and phosphorus, SCOBYs are a nice addition to your animal's diet or make a healthy treat.

SCOBY Jerky: Try marinating and drying your extra SCOBY in a food dehydrator to make healthful vegan jerky for your family.

Compost: SCOBYs are a good source of nitrogen for your compost.

Sushi: Because the SCOBY has a consistency that is similar to squid, it makes a great ingredient in vegan sushi recipes.

Recommended Resource

Crum, Hannah, and Alex LaGory. *The Big Book of Kombucha: Brewing, Flavoring and Enjoying the Health Benefits of Fermented Teas.* North Adams, MA: Storey Publishing, 2016.

Herbs in Baked Goods

⋙ by Suzanne Ress ⋘

I love baking homemade desserts and experimenting with ingredients to create original and delicious new recipes, and because my family produces much of our own food, I always try to use what is on hand rather than buy ingredients at the store. I decided to try using more aromatic herbs in desserts after my first successful experiment, lemon bars with lavender.

Many aromatic herbs contain some of the same chemical compounds found in spices that are commonly used in baked goods and other desserts and blend very well in combination with those spices or in place of them. For example, cloves, which are a usual ingredient in pumpkin pie,

peach desserts, and cherry desserts, contain **eugenol**. This is what gives cloves their aroma and flavor. Eugenol is also found in basil leaves, bay leaves, and lemon balm. Basil leaves also contain **estragole**, which is similar to **anethole**, found in fennel and anise. Bay leaves also contain **cineole**, which is a component of cardamom. It seemed to me that adding basil to a peach pie rather than cloves would give it a familiar yet different flavor that would not be so different as to be unpleasant.

Many aromatic herbs have a lemony scent and flavor that blends naturally well with fruity and sweet flavors. Some of these are lemon thyme (which contains **geranial**, a compound used to create artificial fruit flavors in the laboratory), lemon verbena, lemon grass, lemon balm, and lemon basil. All of these can be used successfully to enhance the flavors of desserts.

More unusual perhaps are rosemary, marjoram, dill, thyme, and oregano, which are usually associated with savory dishes. But, on closer inspection, marjoram contains one of the same natural chemicals found in nutmeg, so why not try using it in apple pie, for example? Rosemary, which traditionally pairs so well with potatoes, also tastes surprisingly right with apricots; and thyme, when paired with orange, creates a flavor redolent of mandarin orange.

Oregano's distinctive taste, which often makes people think immediately of Italian tomato sauces and pizza, comes from **carvacrol**, found in savory and in Egyptian lavender. I have heard of oregano ice cream and chocolate with oregano, but I have not yet tried using it in home baked goods.

Dill, which goes so classically well with beets or with lemon, contains **carvone**, also found in spearmint and in caraway seed, and would blend nicely into orangey desserts, carrot cakes, and possibly even chocolate brownies!

When experimenting with aromatic herbs in sweet dishes, use your sensory imagination to find new flavor combinations that work in surprising ways.

Among all food categories, herbs, in general, have the highest antioxidant level. Although there is large variation between different herbs, common peppermint and oregano both are very high in antioxidants.

In most of my recipes, I use honey rather than sugar, partly because as a beekeeper, I always have a lot of honey on hand and partly because I try to avoid eating refined white sugar at all. Feel free to substitute sugar for honey, if desired, in the same amount. By "light honey," I mean a delicately flavored honey, such as clover or spring wildflower. A medium honey would be summer wildflower or most monofloral fruit tree honeys, such as apple, cherry, or plum. In all cases, if you use honey, use it in its liquid form.

Beet Cake with Bay Leaf and Cardamom

    2 fresh raw beets
    1 cup medium honey
    ½ cup vegetable oil
    2 eggs
    1½ cups flour
    2 finely chopped bay leaves
    1 teaspoon ground cardamom
    1½ teaspoon baking powder

Pinch salt

¾ cup chopped black walnuts or English walnuts

Wash, peel, and finely grate the beets. Squeeze out excess liquid.

Whisk honey and oil together in a bowl, then beat in eggs, one at a time.

Mix together all dry ingredients in a separate bowl and then stir them into the oil mixture.

Stir in beets and nuts.

Pour into a greased and floured loaf pan (I use a pan that's 4 × 12 × 3 inches), and bake at 350°F for 25–30 minutes.

This is a rich, dense cake that does not require frosting.

Tomato Cake with Basil Frosting

After one failed attempt that tasted more like pizza than cake, I came up with this very tasty recipe.

For the cake:

½ cup butter, softened

1 cup light honey, such as clover

2 eggs

1 teaspoon vanilla

2¼ cups flour

1 teaspoon baking powder

½ teaspoon salt

1 teaspoon cinnamon

½ teaspoon cardamom

2 whole fresh medium tomatoes, pureed

Cream together the butter and honey in a medium bowl using an electric mixer. Mix in the eggs one at a time, and then add vanilla and mix well.

In a separate bowl, blend together all the dry ingredients.

Alternating with the flour mixture, add the pureed tomatoes to the butter mixture and blend well.

Pour into a greased and floured loaf pan and bake at 350°F for 40–50 minutes.

Let cool completely before frosting.

For the basil frosting:
- ½ cup basil, packed
- 2 cups powdered sugar, separated
- ¼ cup softened butter
- 1 teaspoon vanilla
- Green food coloring

Into an electric herb chopper or food processor, put ½ cup of the powdered sugar and all the basil leaves and process until it forms a paste.

Mix in the softened butter, vanilla, and the rest of the powdered sugar. This can all be done in the food processor. Blend in a few drops green food coloring.

Frost the cake when it is cool, and store it in the refrigerator.

Six Yellow Cupcakes with Marjoram and Lavender
These are very pretty and festive, decorated with rose petals and lavender flowers.

For the cupcakes:
- ⅓ cup butter, softened
- ¾ cup light honey
- 1 egg
- 1 teaspoon vanilla or rose water
- 1¼ cup flour
- 1 teaspoon baking powder

¼ teaspoon salt

½ cup milk

Zest of 1 lemon

1 tablespoon fresh lavender flowers

1 tablespoon marjoram buds

Cream the honey with the butter, using an electric mixer. Mix in the egg and the vanilla or rose water.

In a separate bowl, mix together the flour, baking powder, and salt. Alternating with the milk, add this to the butter mixture. Stir in the lavender, marjoram, and lemon zest. Pour into cupcake tins lined with cupcake papers, and bake at 350°F for 25–30 minutes.

For the buttercream frosting:

¼ cup butter, softened

2¼ cups powdered sugar

Lemon juice

Zest of ½ lemon

A few rose petals

A few lavender buds

Cream the butter and powdered sugar together using an electric mixer. Add enough lemon juice to make it a spreadable consistency. Stir in the lemon zest.

Frost the yellow cupcakes when they are cool. Decorate them with rose petals and lavender buds.

Apricot Pie with Rosemary

For the almond crust:

1 cup almond flour (finely ground almonds)

1¼ cups regular flour

1 teaspoon nutmeg

½ teaspoon salt

⅔ cup cold butter

⅓ cup cold water

Mix together the two flours, the nutmeg, and the salt. Cut in the cold butter till it looks like crumbs. Make a well in the center and pour in the cold water, then quickly mix with a fork until the dough comes together. Form into two balls and refrigerate. Meanwhile, make the filling.

For the filling:

2 pounds fresh apricots, stoned and sliced

1 tablespoon lemon juice

1 cup light honey

½ cup cornstarch

½ teaspoon nutmeg

1 tablespoon crumbled dried rosemary

Mix together all the ingredients in a large bowl. Roll out one ball of dough to a circular shape that will fit into your pie pan. Carefully fold it into quarters, put it into the pie pan, and unfold. There should be a little overlap around the edges of the pie pan. Spoon all the filling into the crust, and then roll out the other ball of dough for the top crust. Crimp the edges of the two crusts together and use a sharp knife to cut an X in the center of the top crust to let steam escape. Bake at 375°F for 50 minutes.

Lemon Bars with Lavender

1 cup flour, plus 2 tablespoons

½ cup butter, softened

2 eggs

1 cup light honey

½ teaspoon baking powder

2 tablespoons lemon juice

1 teaspoon lemon zest

2 tablespoon fresh lavender buds, crumbled

Combine 1 cup flour and the butter and pat the mixture into an 8-inch square pan. Bake at 350°F for 20 minutes.

Beat the eggs and add the honey. Mix in the dry ingredients and the lemon juice. Stir in the zest and the lavender. Pour over the crust.

Bake at 350°F for 25 more minutes.

Gingerbread with Lemongrass

I am a huge fan of gingerbread and have tried many different recipes over the years, discovering that the more gingery it is the more I like it. The lemongrass in this recipe exalts the ginger flavor, making for a smooth and perfectly gingery taste experience.

2¼ cups flour

2 teaspoons baking powder

½ teaspoon salt

½ cup vegetable oil

½ teaspoon ground cloves

1 teaspoon powdered mustard

1 teaspoon cinnamon

1 teaspoon powdered ginger

1 cup dark molasses

1 egg

1 cup hot water

1 tablespoon finely chopped fresh or dried lemongrass

1½ inch piece fresh ginger root, peeled and finely
chopped

Sift together the flour, baking powder, and salt in a small bowl.
Blend the powdered spices into the oil in a medium bowl. Beat
the molasses and egg into the oil mixture. Alternating with the
hot water, add the flour mixture to the molasses and oil blend.
Beat well. Stir in the lemongrass and ginger root. Pour into a
greased and floured 8-inch square pan and bake at 350°F for
45 minutes.

Extra Dark Chocolate Brownies with Mint

½ cup flour

⅓ cup sugarless cocoa powder

¼ teaspoon baking powder

¼ teaspoon salt

½ cup butter, softened

¾ cup medium honey

2 eggs

1 teaspoon vanilla

2 ounces high-quality baking chocolate, 85–99% cacao,
broken into small chips

1 teaspoon dried peppermint leaf, crumbled

Sift together the flour, cocoa powder, baking powder, and salt
in a small bowl. Cream the butter and honey together, then
add the eggs, one at a time, beating well after each. Beat in
the vanilla. Stir in the chocolate pieces and the peppermint.
Spread in an 8-inch square pan and bake at 350°F for 20–25
minutes.

Majestic Summer Trifle

   2 cups whole milk, plus a few tablespoons

   ½ cup light honey, plus 2 tablespoons

   Pinch salt

   2 tablespoons cornstarch

   2 egg yolks

   1 teaspoon vanilla extract, plus a few drops

   1 package store-bought ladyfingers (between 10 and 14,
      depending on their size)

   ¾ cup brandy

   4 ripe peaches

   1 teaspoon lemon juice

   ½ teaspoon ground cloves

   6 fresh lemon verbena leaves, finely chopped

   10 fresh *Melissa* leaves, finely chopped

   1 cup heavy whipping cream

   2 tablespoons powdered sugar

   2 cups fresh raspberries

   ½ cup slivered almonds

First, make the vanilla pudding. In a heavy-bottomed sauce-pan over a low flame, gently heat the milk with the honey and salt. When it is just too hot to touch, put one ladleful into a cup, sprinkle on the cornstarch, and whisk thoroughly, then return this to the saucepan and continue stirring until it begins to thicken and is nearly boiling. Remove it from the heat. Beat the egg yolks in the same cup and add a few tablespoons of cold milk to it, whisking all the while. Then, add a ladleful of the hot milk mixture, continually whisking. Pour this egg yolk mixture back into the saucepan, always whisking, and return the saucepan to low heat. Stir constantly until it is thick and smooth, about two minutes, then remove from the heat and stir in the vanilla. Let cool.

Now, leave the ladyfingers in a dish with the brandy to soak.

Peel the peaches and slice them into a bowl. Add the lemon juice, 2 tablespoons of honey, the ground cloves, the chopped verbena, and the *Melissa*, and stir to blend.

Whip the cream and, just at the end, add the powdered sugar and a few drops of vanilla extract.

Now assemble the trifle. In a wide glass bowl or trifle dish, arrange the soaked ladyfingers to cover the bottom and partway up the sides. Layer on the peaches, then the pudding, and then the raspberries. On top of it all, spread the whipped cream. Chill for several hours. Just before serving, sprinkle the slivered almonds over the top.

Resources

Brunning, Andy. "Chemical Compounds in Herbs and Spices." Compound Interest. March 13, 2014. https://www.compoundchem.com/2014/03/13/chemical-compounds-in-herbs-spices/.

Segnit, Niki. *The Flavour Thesaurus: Pairings, Recipes and Ideas for the Creative Cook*. London: Bloomsbury, 2010.

It's Okay to Be Bitter

❧ by Emily Towne ❧

Most of us do not initially think of bitter as an appealing flavor, nor do we generally seek it out. There is a certain ick factor associated with bitter that tends to put us off. The mere mention of it can cause a visceral reaction, sour face, pursed lips, or clenched jaw. It's been theorized that our aversion to bitter might serve as a protection against consuming toxic substances, but not all bitter substances are toxic, and not all people can even taste bitter flavors, so there is still much to learn about why we react as we do. With rational thought and purposeful behavior, we are, however, capable of overcoming our aversion to bitter and learning to like it and even crave it. But why would we want to? Well, it turns out there are plenty of excellent reasons to invite bitter into our lives!

History of Bitter

Bitter flavors come from fruits, vegetables, plants, barks, roots, berries, flowers, leaves, and stems. Bitter has been used medicinally in China, Europe, India, and the Americas going back five thousand years or more. Ancient Egyptians were known to have utilized bitter flavors in healing modalities. The forerunner of modern cocktail and digestive bitters originated with those ancient preparations. Many bitter herbs were employed during the Middle Ages to treat various ailments as well. Paracelsus, a Swiss physician, is credited with developing an herbal tonic in the early 1500s that inspired many subsequent versions across Europe.

I imagine that many medicine women and men, hearth keepers, healers, and ancient foragers knew of a variety of go-to bitter herbs and botanicals for healing and whole-ing. Whether eaten raw, cooked in a pot, or extracted by way of tea or tincture, herbal bitters are intrinsically interwoven with human survival the world over. Modern science is just now catching up to them to validate their wisdom.

The wide range of bitter flavors found in plant-based foods and beverages has long been associated with myriad health benefits, including stimulating of the appetite and nervous system, improving digestion, adding balance and dimension to other flavors in a meal, mitigating dietary overindulgence, and improving metabolism, to mention a few. Bitter foods also contain important minerals, trace elements, vitamins, and compounds that protect us from carcinogens and increase our overall health.

Bitter has been used throughout the ages for these reasons, so what's not to love about it? And why do we not utilize bitter as fully as we do the other elements of taste? Our modern palate has largely lost the once-commonplace desire for bitter flavors. But with a little finesse, we can welcome them back to our palate.

As our food system has become more industrialized over time, sweeter and milder flavors have won out over those that are bitter. A number of vegetables, including eggplant and brussels sprouts, that were historically more bitter in flavor have had the bitter bred out of them to appease our more, shall we say, delicate modern palates. As we have increasingly sated our appetites with highly processed, sugar-laden foods, bitter has become a relic of times past. Simultaneously, our health and our satisfaction with our food have declined, leaving us with cravings, binge eating, obesity, diabetes, and other diet-related health issues. As modern science delves into the world of bitter, we are learning that these cast-aside bitter foods may well be an important factor in bringing balance and health back into our lives.

How We Taste Bitter

While bitter is a flavor that is detected on our taste buds, it is much more nuanced and complex than we might initially realize. We have bitter receptors in our airways and throughout our digestive system. These interactive receptors send messages to our bodies as we eat and drink. Smelling, sipping, chewing, and swallowing bitter flavors sends messages that activate processes that improve our digestion, our satisfaction with food, and eventually, positively impact our gut.

Bitter, Genetics, and Taste

To date, research has identified as many as a hundred different bitter compounds in food. Each of our taste buds has several dozen receptors to these compounds. The bitter in coffee is detected by some receptors, while the bitter flavor in say, arugula, is detected by others. The number of taste buds each person has also varies, all of which affects how individuals experience bitter. Approximately 25 percent of people are highly sensitive to a bitter chemical called 6-n-propylthiouracil (PROP), a treatment for hyperthyroidism, and are considered "super tasters," while 25 percent do not taste bitter at all and are considered "non-tasters." Approximately 50 percent find PROP only mildly bitter and are considered normal tasters. These are genetic factors that we are just now beginning to understand.

In spite of our genetic predisposition, which affects how we experience bitter, taste is malleable to a certain degree. Taste happens in the brain as well as on the tongue, and we are capable of training our brain to be more, or less, amenable to flavors through practice and habit. How we experience flavors—sweet, sour, salty, bitter, savory (umami)—is formed and affected by an orchestration of factors that includes our culture, diet, and genetics. The first time we sipped coffee or snuck a swig of beer from an adult, we probably were not impressed and may have wondered what was so great about these bitter beverages. But over time, we may have developed an affinity, and even cravings, for bitter, as evidenced by our ritual of cup of morning coffee or tea, both of which are full of bitter flavonoids. It is in this manner of repetition that we can train ourselves to perceive bitter flavors differently and welcome them into our repertoire of acceptable, desirable, and even craved flavors.

Bitter Benefits in the Modern Diet

Bitter flavors are no less important today than they were thousands of years ago. And in fact, bitter may be even more important than ever, considering the declining quality of our industrialized food system. Some of the packaged, preserved items on grocery store shelves today are food-like substances that our bodies may not even recognize as food. Our disconnect from the origins of real food parallels with our disconnect from bitter flavors. The ability of bitter to help us reconnect our bodies with a healthy food system is empowering.

Many bitter foods, such as arugula, dill, kale, brussels sprouts, dandelion, and burdock, can be either grown in a backyard garden or foraged locally. Make use of what's on hand and enjoy experimenting.

Smelling and tasting bitter initiates biological actions within our bodies. They make us pucker, but they also prime the digestive tract by initiating the release of digestive enzymes and bile (acids) that facilitate the breakdown of food and stimulate our nervous system. They stimulate motor activity of the stomach and intestines, improve vitamin and nutrient absorption, and ease common digestive ailments such as bloating, belching, and gas. They trigger the release of hormones that control the appetite and affect our sensitivity to insulin. Bitter flavors quell cravings for sweet flavors, which, if left unchecked, promote gluttony and obesity. Disrupting the cycles of sugar cravings and consumption can regenerate our gut flora, which impacts our immune system. Clearly, bitters are a valuable flavor element to include in our daily lives. The ancients who valued and employed bitter may not have known or understood the science behind it, but they certainly benefitted from wise usage of the bitter flavor.

Training the Palate for Bitter Foods

Bitter foods and beverages are available in a staggering variety of shapes, sizes, colors, textures, and flavor profiles, including fruits, vegetables, greens, and other plant components. Grapefruit, coffee, tea, spirits, hops, beer, arugula, bitter orange, amaranth, wormwood, ginger, cardamom, dandelion, lamb's quarters, sage, broccoli, kale, bitter melon, and endive are just a few of them. The list is long and varied, with something to appeal to even the most selective palate.

If you are not already a bitter eater and the idea of it seems somewhat daunting, don't be dismayed. It's been observed that there is somewhat of a learning curve for the palate when introducing bitter into the diet. Initially, it can seem quite unpleasant, but with repetition, it can even become more tolerable and even become a craving. One of the quickest and easiest ways to introduce bitter flavors into our daily diet is through teas and salads.

Many bitter elements can be foraged, and many can be grown in a backyard garden. In general, wild botanicals, herbs, and heirloom varieties of fruits and vegetables contain more bitter compounds than modern-day hybrids. Look for those at your local farmers' market, or seek out seeds to grow your own when possible. I found bitter melon at my local farmers' market. It came with several recipe ideas and cooking advice from the Indian women who staffed the booth.

Bitter Aperitifs and Digestives and Cocktails

Bitters have been used as both aperitifs and after-meal digestifs throughout history. Like tonic water, which started out as a medicine for malaria and evolved into the modern gin and tonic cocktail, the bitters used to flavor modern cocktails, such as Peychaud's and Angostura, started out as patented tonics ages ago. They contain potent bitter ingredients such as gentian, herbs, spices, roots, fruit peels, botanicals, seeds, bark, and flowers along with sugar and alcohol. Many brands are available commercially, and they can also be made at home. Spirits that are considered bitter are an entirely fascinating subject of their own. Many of them originate from old-world recipes and stood the test of time.

Bitter aperitifs and digestives are grouped into two categories: **potable** and **nonpotable**. The potables are those that are designed to be consumed as a drink or cocktail. The nonpotables are bitters that are to be added in smaller amounts to a beverage or cocktail or taken in small doses, such as a dropperful. **Aperitifs** are consumed at the beginning of a meal to prime our digestive system and whet the appetite. They typically contain a classic bitter spirit such as vermouth, Campari, Aperol, Cynar, Fernet-Branca, Chartreuse, or one of the Italian Amari and can be used for pre- or postmeal cocktails. A Negroni is an iconic Italian aperitif which contains one part gin, one part vermouth rosso, and one part Campari, garnished with an orange slice, and can easily be made at home.

Urban Moonshine produces a line of organic bitters available in health food stores and online that are promoted as both an aperitif and digestif. **Digestifs** are consumed post-meal and help balance the richness of a meal, ease fullness, and facilitate digestion. They can be an after-meal spirit, a cocktail, or herbal bitters. Experiment with some of these options to see what works best for your palate and lifestyle. The small bottles of digestive bitters are easily tucked into purses and travel bags and so are a great option for on-the-go eating.

From aperitifs to digestifs, and all the wonderful bitter foods in between, bitter has a place at the table. The artful use of bitter flavors allows the creative cook to successfully incorporate them into daily meals. Start small and develop your repertoire through experimentation. The idea with bitters is to include the flavor often, on a regular basis, in order to continuingly reap the benefits. Once bitter is on your radar, it becomes a fun challenge to discover new ways to incorporate it. Your palate and your liver will thank you.

Dandelion Tea

Make this tea in a teapot or quart canning jar. I recommend you forage and dry your own dandelion roots too!

Add 2 teaspoons of dried, chopped dandelion root and 1 teaspoon of mint for every 8 ounces of water. Add other dried flowers and aromatic leaves of your preference (optional).

Pour boiling water into tea pot or jar, cover, and steep for 5–10 minutes.

Strain into cups with a tea strainer. Add honey to sweeten.

Radicchio and Shiitake Sauté

Here's an easy one-dish side that has bitter taste plus umami from the shiitakes. Radicchio is a member of the chicory family and comes from Italy. This bitter green has been cultivated from the wild, like arugula, and has maintained its appealing bitter flavor over time. The most commonly available variety of radicchio is Chioggia, but any of the radicchios will serve for this recipe. With a bit of finesse, you can grow this radicchio in your garden, or look for it at farmers' markets and health food stores. It looks like a miniature deep red cabbage head.

1 head Chioggia radicchio

6–8 shiitake mushrooms

Olive oil

Butter

Salt and pepper to taste

Cut the leaves away from main stem of the radicchio and cut them into narrow strips. Remove the stems from the mushrooms and chop them into small cubes.

Heat a medium skillet with a few tablespoons of olive oil and butter. Sauté mushrooms in the fat until soft and browned, about 5–7 minutes. Add salt and pepper to taste. Remove from pan and set aside in a bowl.

Add more olive oil and butter as needed (a few tablespoons) to the pan and sauté the radicchio until soft, about 4–5 minutes.

Add the mushrooms back into the pan with the radicchio and stir until mushrooms are heated through. Add salt and pepper to taste. Serve hot as a side dish. Makes 4 servings.

Bitter Green Salad with Creamy Dressing

This recipe is a powerhouse of nutrition and bitter pungency. Use it as a template and feel free to substitute other greens that you may have available. The pea microgreens are a sweet base and act as a counterpoint to the bold bitter elements. Use organic ingredients when possible. Dress with oil and vinegar, or indulge with a creamy dressing, shared here.

For the salad:

- 1 cup arugula, woody stems removed, chopped into 1-inch pieces
- 1 cup dandelion greens, woody stems removed, chopped into 1-inch pieces
- 2 cups pea microgreens, chopped into 1-inch pieces
- 1 cup basil leaves, stems removed, cut into chiffonade
- 1 shallot, chopped
- 1 large tomato, chopped

Toss all ingredients together in a large bowl, dress, and retoss. Makes 4 servings. May be doubled easily.

For the dressing:

- ¾ cup high-quality mayonnaise (I like certified organic Sir Kensington, made with sunflower oil.)
- 2–3 cloves garlic, finely minced
- 2 tablespoons dill, very finely chopped
- 2–3 tablespoons apple cider vinegar
- Salt and pepper to taste

Place all ingredients in a glass jar (I use a pint-size canning jar), screw on the lid, shake the jar until the ingredients are thoroughly mixed, and pour over salad. This recipe makes almost 1 cup of dressing and will keep in the fridge 1 week.

Bitter Sweet Glazed Asian Ribs

This is a super easy rib recipe with great flavor that tastes like you spent a lot more time on it than you actually did! It's great for a main dish, or you can serve it as an appetizer. It's also excellent the next day. It's messy finger food, so put out plenty of napkins. I use organic ingredients when possible.

¼ cup soy sauce

½ cup hoisin sauce

3 tablespoons molasses or agave nectar

2–4 cloves garlic, finely minced

1 tablespoon peeled and chopped fresh ginger

1 tablespoon apple cider vinegar

2 tablespoons Angostura bitters (or substitute homemade or other brands of bitters)

1 tablespoon freshly squeezed orange juice

1 tablespoon coconut sugar

1–3 teaspoons sriracha sauce, to taste and heat tolerance

¼ teaspoon Chinese five spice powder

Pinch of Celtic sea salt

3–5 pounds pork spare ribs

Mix all ingredients except the ribs in a large bowl deep enough to accommodate the ribs. Remove ¼ cup sauce and set aside. Place the ribs in the bowl to marinate in the sauce in the refrigerator for a minimum of 1 hour, up to 6 hours. Turn occasionally to evenly coat with sauce.

Preheat oven to 400°F. Place ribs on a foil-lined baking sheet and bake for 45–55 minutes. Halfway through roasting, turn the ribs and slather generously with the reserved sauce. Roast until ribs are browned and tender. Bone should wiggle easily but not slide away from the meat.

Turn the oven to broil and let broiler get up to temperature. Place ribs under a preheated broiler for approximately 5 minutes, until charred but not burnt. Slice ribs into segments between each bone. Serve and enjoy!

Selected Resources

"Digestive Health with Bitters." Healthy Hildegard. Accessed March 15, 2019. https://www.healthyhildegard.com/digestive-health-and-bitters/.

Lu, Ping, Cheng-Hai Zhang, Lawrence M. Lifshitz, and Ronghua ZhuGe. "Extraoral Bitter Taste Receptors in Health and Disease." *Journal of General Physiology* 149, no. 2 (February 2017): 181–197. https://www.ncbi.nlm.nih.gov/pmc/articles/PMC5299619/.

McLagan, Jennifer. *Bitter: A Taste of the World's Most Dangerous Flavor, with Recipes.* Berkeley, CA: Ten Speed Press, 2014.

Nabhan, Gary Paul. *Why Some Like it Hot: Food, Genes, and Cultural Diversity.* Washington, DC: Island Press, 2004.

Parsons, Brad Thomas. *Amaro: The Spirited World of Bittersweet, Herbal Liqueurs, with Cocktails, Recipes, and Formulas.* Berkeley, CA: Ten Speed Press, 2016.

———. *Bitters: A Spirited History of a Classic Cure-All.* Berkeley, CA: Ten Speed Press, 2011.

"The Bittersweet Truth of Sweet and Bitter Taste Receptors." *Science in the News* (blog), May 03, 2013. Harvard University. http://sitn.hms.harvard.edu/flash/2013/the-bittersweet-truth-of-sweet-and-bitter-taste-receptors/.

Chutneys and Tapenade

≈ by Dawn Ritchie ≈

When the dips come out, a festive event is about to begin. Chutneys, relishes, and tapenades are featured condiments on party tables and are all about abundance. Abundance in the harvest, in flavor profiles, and in relationships.

It's curious that while we all enjoy a good chutney or tapenade at an event, they tend not to be part of our everyday dining experience. Packed with flavor and a stiff kick to the taste buds, they predictably elicit *ooh, ah,* or *yum!* responses. So, why on earth do we deny ourselves these delights daily?

It's time to change all that. The following recipes can be thrown together quickly, and they are a sophisticated

prelude to any meal. Setting aside an afternoon for a marathon preparation session can be a party in and of itself. Bring wine.

Mint Chutney

My kitchen smells like summer. Fresh mint, cilantro, limes, and garlic fill the air with piquant freshness. I'm making mint chutney. It's a dressing that is so easy to throw together it can be done in small batches for single use. It's also a wonderful way to consume the two herbs that grow prolifically and can take over a garden if you don't continue harvesting them regularly. I have a lot of mint and cilantro in my garden and need to get rid of it. You can only drink so many mojitos.

Mint chutney is a must-have for lamb and fish and as a condiment for samosas or crispy papadums. Use a blender, toss in all ingredients, and let 'er rip. A mint chutney dressing for a plate of lamb ribs turns an ordinary dish into a culinary experience. It helps to ameliorate that muttony aftertaste. Use also as a dip for savory wafers and chips.

1 bunch fresh mint (8 ounces compressed leaves)

1 bunch fresh cilantro (8 ounces compressed leaves)

6 fresh garlic cloves

2 shallots

3 tablespoons fresh squeezed lime juice

1–2 tablespoons olive oil

2 tablespoons ice water

½ teaspoon cumin

Pinch of salt, to taste

Strip leaves from the stems of the mint and cilantro. Discard stems. Peel garlic and shallots. Add all ingredients to a blender. Blend on medium to emulsify. Done!

Condiments Are the Spice of Life

It's early September, in the mad throes of the fall harvest, and I find myself in the kitchen of my dear friend Rachel. We are attacking a batch of chutneys and tapenades in a team effort. The kitchen is overflowing with hot red peppers, corn sliced fresh off the cob, glistening black olives, ripe mangoes, fresh ginger, and bottles of organic cold-pressed olive oil. A canner is bubbling away with anticipation of hot jars ready to be preserved, and a food processor is already purring. We are drinking delicious honey-laced green tea and laughing . . . a lot.

The main work ahead is peeling and chopping. Do your prep work in advance. Then the food processing and cooking down are quick and easy. We start by assembling a series of bowls and chopping boards. The countertops look like the stuff of a cooking show.

We have four dips to prepare. Try your hand at these recipes and remember to experiment a little on your own. Add a favorite spice or remove one from the recipe that you dislike. Experiment, always.

Here's a fall table relish, a sweet chutney, a hot jelly, and savory tapenade.

Mango Chutney

First up is a mango chutney, something every cook should have in their refrigerator. It's sweet, spicy, and not just a condiment for Indian food. Mango chutney complements any meal and can often be the saving grace when you've made a chicken that's a little dried out. Smear a spoonful of mango chutney atop a slice of poultry and all is forgiven. A dollop on a pork chop will excite. It is also useful as a sandwich spread, topping for appetizers, table condiment, and a tasty glaze for ham in the final stages of roasting.

As with all these recipes, the best practice is to use a heavy-bottomed pot on the stove. Mango chutney takes a bit more time than the other recipes offered here. So, pace yourself and enjoy the luscious aroma that will soon fill your home.

2 large mangoes (more on the unripe side)

½ cup water

½ cup of cider vinegar

½ cup brown sugar

½ cup granulated sugar

1 garlic clove, peeled and pulverized to a paste

¼ cup peeled and finely minced fresh ginger

5–7 peppercorns

¼ teaspoon dried chilies (or crushed flakes)

¼ teaspoon cumin or ½ teaspoon roasted cumin seeds

4 cardamom pods

Pinch of ground nutmeg

1 cinnamon stick (or ¼ teaspoon ground cinnamon)

¼ teaspoon salt

1 teaspoon lemon juice

Optional additions:

> ½ teaspoon nigella seeds or black onion seeds
>
> ¼ cup sultanas
>
> ½ apple
>
> ¼ teaspoon cloves

Chop all ingredients in advance. Peel and slice the mangoes into rough-size portions. I would say cube the mangoes, but

I've never square-cubed a fruit or vegetable since a Zen chef told me they should be cut at odd angles to encompass the full energy and spirit within each piece. I don't know if this is true or not, but the fruits and veggies certainly are more attractive and feel less industrialized.

Next, bring water, cider vinegar, and sugar in a heavy-bottomed pot to a boil. Add the garlic, ginger, and spices (peppercorns, chillies, cumin, cardamom, nutmeg, cinnamon, and salt).

Cook until the sugar dissolves, then add the mangoes. Bring to a full rolling boil.

Boil for 2–3 minutes, stirring all the while. Lower temperature and simmer for approximately 20–25 minutes, stirring frequently. Do not let the bottom caramelize. Keep it moving. The fruit will soften and some of it will break down. You want to reduce the fluid considerably and have some of the mango still hold its structure. Remove cinnamon stick and cardamom pods as the sauce starts to thicken. Squeeze in the lemon juice.

Remove from heat just before fully thickened. It should be just slightly runny. As the chutney cools, it will continue to thicken.

To preserve, fill hot jars, leaving ¼ inch of space, and process in a water bath for 15 minutes. It will keep for months. Makes 1 pint.

This is a warm and spicy chutney with crunchy little ginger pieces and a complexity of flavors. There is just the slightest hint of heat. A perfect complement to a savory dish. Serve warm or at room temperature.

Olive Tapenade

A traditional Provençal tapenade is a tasty puree consisting of olives, capers, anchovies, and olive oil that is served as a topping for crudité or crackers. It can also be utilized as a stuffing for chicken or fish. It is ubiquitous in French and Italian cooking, and you'll often find it as a precursor to a meal at fine-dining establishments.

Tapenade is a perfect appetizer topping, especially paired with cream cheese. Top with a sprig of parsley, chives, thyme, or fresh veggies. Try also as a topping for homemade pizza or as a stuffing for poultry and fish. Tapenade is fabulous to take to a potluck as an appetizer, surrounded by crackers or crostini. The appearance may give pause to unadventurous or picky eaters, so tell your guests what they are sampling by labeling a cheese marker.

Prep time is a mere 10 minutes.

2 teaspoons capers

2–3 garlic cloves

1½ cups pitted kalamata olives, drained (can be substituted with black or green olives or any mixture you so choose)

2 anchovies (rinse for less salt)

Juice of ½ lemon

1 teaspoon lemon zest

½ cup extra-virgin olive oil

2 teaspoons minced parsley

Optional additions:

Sun-dried tomatoes to taste

Fresh chopped onion to taste

In a blender or food processor, add the capers, garlic cloves, olives, and anchovies. Puree. Squeeze in lemon juice and lemon zest. Pulse a few times to incorporate. Oil is added at the end.

Pulse a few times to finish. You don't want the oil to emulsify. It is more of a base for the olive and caper mix to swim in. Use a spatula to scrape into a bowl. It will keep for 1 week, refrigerated. Makes about 1 cup.

To Use as a Bread Dip

Spoon a generous portion of tapenade into a shallow bowl and drizzle more olive oil on top to loosen the paste and restructure it. Sprinkle finely minced parsley to garnish, and freshen with a squirt of lemon and bit of lemon zest. You can also add chopped walnuts or chopped tomatoes to the mixture as well. Presentation, presentation, presentation!

Carnival Corn Relish

Have you ever munched on a raw ear of corn? It's scrumptious. Sweet, crunchy, and juicy all at once. So why do we boil it to death? All you end up with is texture. Corn on the cob should never be cooked longer than three minutes. But if you must, then make it into a relish.

Grow your own non-GMO corn. The rows of kernels will be imperfect, but the flavor, superior. Buy seed from organic seed catalogs. Plant squash around the corn. The prickly leaves keep squirrels at bay.

Carnival corn relish, a Southwestern favorite, can be prepared as a preserved, cooked relish or as a cold, uncooked relish. It's a great sandwich topping, especially paired with a tomato. Wonderful on burgers and hotdogs and beautiful on fish. Use as a side condiment for any meal.

Since fresh corn is best at autumn, follow this cooked recipe to enjoy it year-round on your hamburgers, on your sandwiches, and as a side condiment to cold meats. The relish will mellow in the jar. It will keep two weeks after opening.

For the cooked version:
   5 ears of fresh corn
   2 red hot serrano peppers
   ¼ cup green bell pepper
   ½ cup red onion
   ¼ cup cilantro
   3 cloves of garlic
   1 cup cider vinegar
   ½ cup lemon juice
   ½ cup light brown sugar (compressed)
   ¼ teaspoon cumin
   1 teaspoon pickling salt
   ½ teaspoon black pepper

Slice the corn off fresh cobs. Clean and finely chop peppers, onion, and cilantro. Mince garlic. Heat vinegar, lemon juice, and sugar in a heavy-bottomed pot on medium heat. Once the sugar is dissolved, add all the ingredients and spices, except for the cilantro. Cook until most of the liquid evaporates, around 20 minutes. Stir frequently. Add cilantro at the end.

Sterilize preserving jars. Ladle relish into hot jam jars, leaving ¼ inch of room at the top. Seal with lids and process in a hot water bath for 15 minutes. Makes about 4 cups, depending on the size of the vegetables.

For the uncooked version:

Use the same ingredients as for the cooked version, but add chopped tomato, substitute white vinegar for cider vinegar, and reduce garlic to 1 clove. It becomes more ceviche-like.

Hot Pepper Jelly

If you're looking for more heat, this is the recipe for you. Hot pepper jelly has the gorgeous appearance of stained glass. Divine on chicken, fish, a ham sandwich, or simply on a cracker.

    6 red hot chili peppers, seeds and all
    3 long peppers (red and orange)
    ½ cup lemon juice
    1 cup apple cider vinegar
    5 cups sugar
    2 packets liquid pectin (Certo), 3 ounces each

Mince all peppers to a fine consistency. No hunks! Add lemon juice and vinegar to a heavy-bottomed pot. Heat, adding the sugar slowly. Bring to a rolling boil, stirring constantly. Add liquid pectin. Keep a close eye to ensure it has a nice rolling boil. It looks like roiling lava. Cook until a gel stage has been reached. Check for a jam-like consistency with the back of a cold spoon. Skim any foam on top. Makes about 3½ cups, depending on the size of the peppers.

Process in hot jars in a water bath for 15 minutes.

Bon appétit!

Vivacious Vanilla

≈ by Elizabeth Barrette ≈

Vanilla is a spice so subtle that its name has become a synonym for "nothing" or "normal." This is easy to understand if you have encountered the thin, flat taste of artificial vanilla flavoring. However, the real deal is a flavor of symphonic complexity. It's just not as loud as, say, cinnamon, which can easily overpower everything else in a dish. Vanilla is the spice that binds everything else together.

Growing Vanilla Vines

Vanilla comes from the pods of the flat-leaved vanilla vine, *Vanilla planifolia*. It belongs to a genus of around 110 species in the orchid family. Members of the genus grow in tropical and subtropical habitats around the world, from the Americas to southern Asia and parts of western Africa. Several species even grow as far north as the United States, all of them in the southern tip of Florida. Native to Mexico, the vanilla vine has been transported to other tropical regions for use as a cash crop. Today, Madagascar is the leading producer.

The vines can grow over a hundred feet tall, although domesticated ones tend to be shorter and require a host tree or post to climb. Oblong leaves sprout alternately from the narrow stem. Flowers appear in voluptuous bunches of twenty to a hundred. Large and complicated, they may be white or tinted greenish or yellowish. They give off a sweet scent. A challenge for vanilla farmers is that each flower only opens for a few hours—if it doesn't get pollinated then, it falls off without fruiting. In Mexico, it has its own pollinators, but elsewhere it requires laborious hand-pollination every day during the blooming season.

Vanilla is the only orchid that bears edible fruit, often called "vanilla beans" although they are not true beans. The pods take eight to nine months to ripen. They turn black and release a potent fragrance. A pod holds thousands of tiny black seeds. Both the seeds and the leathery pod can be used for various purposes. The central flavor comes from **vanillin**, but many other phytochemicals contribute to its characteristic flavor and aroma.

Because the vines require a tropical climate, few people can grow them outdoors. If you live in a warm, moist place, however, you might want to try it—especially in the tip of Florida. Farther north, people put them in big pots so they can be moved according to the weather or grow them in greenhouses.

Growing your own vanilla is very challenging, but if you're bored with other houseplants, give it a try. It's not that much harder than other orchids or plants like gardenia and jasmine, and people manage to grow those. First, you need a pot at least twelve inches wide, filled with orchid mix. Then you need a sturdy support for the vine to climb, preferably a rot-resistant wood such as cypress or cedar. It requires bright but indirect light. Hot sun will burn the delicate leaves, while deep shade will retard growth. Keep humidity high and temperatures between 70 and 90 degrees Fahrenheit. Vanilla can tolerate somewhat cooler temperatures than that, but growth slows down. Water both the support and the potting medium, allowing the pot to dry slightly in between. Fertilize with a balanced product, and consider using one of the orchid mists designed to promote flowering.

Producing blooms is the real challenge. The vines must reach three to five feet high before they will bloom at all, which typically takes three years. When the vine reaches the top of its support and begins to drape down, that tends to trigger flowering. Each flower spike will open slowly, most often one blossom per day. These are easy to hand-pollinate with a cotton swab or toothpick, and the flowers are self-fertile, but you must be able to reach them while they're open or you'll get nothing except the flowers themselves.

If you do it right, long green pods will form. They are ready to harvest when the tip turns yellow. Then they require a complex maturation process. To cure them, scald the pods in 93-degree water for three to four minutes. To sweat them, spread the beans on mesh racks in strong sunlight for two hours a day for five to six days. To dry them, spread them on racks in an airy room for three to four weeks. To condition them, bundle the dried pods in buttered paper and store them in wooden boxes for three months. Mature pods have intense fragrance and good flavor.

History and Lore

Vanilla was discovered long ago, and control of it has changed hands many times over the centuries. The first known users were the Totonac people of Mexico. They called the vine *Tlilxochitl* and learned how to use its pods. Later the Aztecs moved in and defeated the Totonac, taking over the vanilla vines. The Spaniards came, invaded the Aztecs, and then shipped vanilla beans to Europe in the early 1500s. At first, the precious spice cost so much that only the rich and powerful could enjoy it. Gradually, its use spread, and vanilla became popular throughout much of Europe, although it remained expensive.

In the late 1700s, Thomas Jefferson served as ambassador to France. There he encountered vanilla in the cuisine. When he returned to the United States, he brought vanilla beans with him. Thus began its spread in America.

Artificial vanilla is bland.
Genuine vanilla is a rich, complex flavor.

Although people managed to grow the vines, they had great difficulty in producing pods. It took almost three hundred years before the Belgian botanist Charles François Antoine Morren discovered the missing piece to the puzzle in

1837: the stingless *Melipona* bee, native to Mexico, pollinated the flowers. Then in 1841, hand-pollination was invented by Edmond Albius, a twelve-year-old boy enslaved on the island of Réunion. From this French colony, vanilla vines were exported around the French Empire along with instructions for hand-pollination. This enabled France to dominate vanilla production.

Because of its expense, genuine vanilla retains associations with luxury, despite its artificial knockoffs being the epitome of all that is common. For many people, its warm milky odor brings up happy childhood memories of baking in the family kitchen. In perfumes, it creates a gentle and nurturing connotation.

Orchid flowers in general symbolize beauty, charm, fertility, love, refinement, and thoughtfulness. White orchids stand for reverence, humility, elegance, and purity. Yellow orchids evoke friendship, joy, and new beginnings. Green orchids symbolize health, nature, and longevity. Vanilla customarily blooms somewhere in that color range. In ancient Greece, orchids represented virility—in particular, large roots related to a baby boy while small ones related to a baby girl. In Victorian England, people displayed vanilla orchids as a sign of wealth, opulence, and fine taste.

Ups and Downs of Vanilla

The world supply of vanilla pods can't come close to meeting the massive demand. Around the world, about eighteen thousand products advertise themselves as vanilla flavored. This causes a number of problems. As more manufacturers respond to the growing consumer demand for genuine and sustainable ingredients, some of these problems are getting worse.

Around 98 percent of commercially used "vanilla" is artificial, either wholly synthetic or manufactured from sources other than vanilla pods. Natural materials used to produce vanillin include clove oil, lignin, pine bark, and rice bran. Compared to real vanilla, this type of vanillin has a thin, flat flavor. It appears on labels as "vanillin," "vanilla flavoring," or simply "natural flavors." Vanillin can also be synthesized from the petrochemical precursor guaiacol. It often has a pronounced metallic or chemical flavor. It cannot be listed as natural, appearing on labels instead as "vanilla flavored" or "artificial vanilla." This accounts for about 85 percent of vanilla flavoring today. Most of the remainder comes from lignin. At least one company produces its artificial vanillin from genetically engineered microbes.

These artificial flavors perform very poorly as solitary flavors, which is why vanilla ice cream or yogurt often tastes bland or fake. When mixed with other flavors, as in baking, they perform somewhat better. Even vanillin derived from natural sources has less ability to do one of true vanilla's best tricks, knitting other ingredients together, because its much lower complexity provides fewer avenues of connection. However, naturally derived vanillin is still much better than petrochemical vanillin.

Because cultivated vanilla comes from cloned plants, just a few cultivars make up the vast majority of crops. That leaves them vulnerable to pests and diseases. Caterpillars of the moth *Lobesia vanillana* eat the pods. Other insects and also slugs opportunistically eat the leaves. Madagascar already suffers from root rot, a fungal disease that attacks vanilla vines from the ground up. Once established, it is impossible to eradicate with current technology. Another fungal disease in the

Pacific Islands, anthracnose, causes blotches on leaves and can defoliate a vine. Vanilla necrosis virus also defoliates vines until they die.

For these reasons, vanilla production is precarious. Thieves often sneak onto farms and steal the vanilla beans just before they ripen, selling them to black-market dealers. This sometimes drives farmers to harvest pods early. Unfortunately, pods picked too soon have inferior flavor and intensity compared to ripe ones. Some companies have responded by reaching out to farmers, offering protection from thieves and guaranteed contracts. This may improve the security and quality of the vanilla harvest.

Culinary Uses

Vanilla is most famous for its potential in the kitchen. If you're going to cook with it, pay up for pure vanilla extract or a vanilla bean. Substitutes are inferior. Vanilla extract should be dark amber to brown, containing only vanilla bean and alcohol—additives such as high-fructose corn syrup just taint the flavor and make it prone to spoiling. A vanilla bean should be large, plump, dark brown to black, and slightly oily. You can make all kinds of exciting recipes with these ingredients.

Produced in commercial quantities by a handful of countries, vanilla comes in several varieties, each with its own flavor profile and ideal uses. By far the most common is Madagascar vanilla, often considered the best. It has a smooth, sweet, rummy flavor with a mellow feel and plenty of staying power. It goes well with rich foods, but people use it for all kinds of things. Mexico, the birthplace of vanilla, still produces a modest amount for export. It has a creamy base with spicy notes. Mexican vanilla pairs well with chocolate or with warm spices such as cinnamon or nutmeg. Tahiti is one of the few places that uses a different type of vanilla vine, *Vanilla tahitensis* 'J. W. Moore', which has a unique flavor. Tahitian vanilla has a floral and fruity character with notes of cherry and anise. It's popular in pastries stuffed with fruit or in other desserts, such as sorbet and fruit toppings, along with yogurt.

In recipes, vanilla acts as a culinary bridge. It connects other flavors together and enhances their positive qualities while downplaying negative ones. It adds creaminess, reduces bitterness or acidity, and rounds out sweetness. This makes it an important complement for things like caramel, chocolate, coconut, marshmallow, coffee, and strawberry. Consider some of the things you can do with it . . .

Vanilla Extract

You can make your own vanilla extract. You'll need a glass bottle, 1 or more vanilla beans, and some high-proof alcohol. You have two options. Choose a clear, minimally flavored one like vodka or moonshine if all you want to taste is the vanilla. Choose a rich amber one like rum or brandy if you want to harmonize the flavors. Do not buy cheap, lousy alcohol; buy a decent middle grade so it tastes good. If you wouldn't drink it, don't cook with it. Smoky and peaty notes are a great match for the leathery notes of the shell if you've used the seeds for something else. If you want to release more flavor, you can slit the beans or chop them into short segments, but it's okay to leave them whole. Put the beans in the bottle and cover completely with alcohol. Seal it tightly. Shake it twice a week. It takes about 8 weeks to mature. Store it out of direct light.

Often you can reuse the beans from this if you put them in liquid to simmer the last flavor out. Consider using them to make ice cream, or you can float one in mulled apple cider or wassail.

Vanilla Sugar

This is one way to double the bang for your buck. Stick a vanilla bean in a jar of sugar and leave it there for two weeks. Every day, gently turn and shake the jar to redistribute the sugar, so that it takes on the vanilla flavor. At the end of that time, you can take out the vanilla bean and use it for another purpose. If you wish, add a dash of cinnamon to the vanilla sugar and sprinkle over toast.

For more intense flavor, slit the pod open and mix its seeds into the sugar. In white sugar, this will leave obvious dark flecks, which not everyone likes. However, they disappear pretty well into brown sugar. Save the pod for another use.

Vanilla Ice Cream

For this recipe, you'll need an ice cream maker.

3 cups half-and-half

½ cup white sugar

1–2 teaspoons pure vanilla extract

Combine the ingredients in a large bowl, whisking gently until the sugar dissolves. Turn the ice cream maker on, pour in the batter, and then churn for about 30 minutes. Transfer to a container and store in the freezer. Makes about 3½ cups.

To make a lighter variation, replace 1 cup of half-and-half with whole milk. To make it richer, replace 1 cup of half-and-half with heavy whipping cream. If you have vanilla sugar, use that instead of plain sugar. This is great over warm pie, or you can top it with hot fudge or caramel.

Frozen Vanilla Custard

- 2 cups heavy cream
- 1 cup whole milk
- ½ cup white sugar
- Pinch of salt
- 1 vanilla bean
- 3 egg yolks

In a medium saucepan, whisk together cream, milk, sugar, and salt. Slit the vanilla bean and squeeze the insides into the mixture. Drop the pod in too. Simmer over low heat—be careful not to let it boil.

Put the egg yolks into a medium bowl and whisk until smooth. Slowly add 1 cup of the hot cream to the egg yolks, whisking to combine. Pour the egg mixture into the hot cream, whisking gently. Simmer 5–10 minutes until the custard thickens enough to coat the back of a spoon. Remove the vanilla pod and squeeze to remove any remaining insides; save the shell for a craft use if you wish.

Let the custard cool to room temperature, stirring frequently. Then pour it into a bowl and press plastic wrap over the surface to prevent a skin from forming. Chill in the refrigerator for at least an hour. Turn an ice cream maker on and pour in the custard. Churn for about 30 minutes. Transfer to a container and store in the freezer. Makes about 3½ cups.

Try a few variations: Add any warm spices, such as cinnamon or nutmeg, for a holiday flavor. A little rum extract makes it into frozen eggnog. Or you could add apple pie spice and apple pie filling.

Medicinal Uses

Vanilla has a variety of health benefits. Chinese medicine uses the orchid to soothe coughs and lung diseases, aid stomach deficiencies, and treat problems of the kidneys and eyes. Some people find that it soothes stomachaches and other digestive problems, hence the popularity of cream soda or vanilla ice cream at such times.

The smell of vanilla eases stress and anxiety. It soothes and calms by reducing the startle reflex. This works in animals as well as humans, so it's not purely coming from positive childhood associations. In aromatherapy, vanilla can revitalize energy and encourage happy thoughts. It is widely used in situations that require a "universally pleasant" scent.

Vanilla has antibacterial properties, making it useful in herbal medicines. It can help heal burns, cuts, and other minor wounds. Use vanilla oil in essential oil blends, or add vanilla extract to preparations with an alcohol base. It also has a high amount of antioxidants. The active ingredient vanillin promotes cardiovascular health by lowering cholesterol. It reduces inflammation too. Vanilla appears in many body care products, as it benefits the hair and skin.

Craft Uses

Vanilla has a variety of craft uses. For most of these, you will want to use vanilla extract or oil. Use vanilla to help combine other scents in potpourri. If you make holiday ornaments out of cookies, you can add an extra drop of vanilla to enhance the aroma. Sprinkle it on cinnamon sticks for crafting to add a mellow note. In perfume or essential oil blends, it adds a sweet middle note.

You can also make crafts with vanilla pods, not just fresh ones, but also ones already used to put the flavor into other products. After simmering a pod, you can dry it out. Put one vanilla pod amidst a ring of cinnamon sticks to make a decorative band around a candleholder. Chop up an empty pod to include in the stuffing for dream pillows. Vanilla powder makes a good ingredient for incense, although it has a more woodsy aroma than the usual creamy one.

A Valuable Herb

Vanilla has been used for nearly a thousand years. People have spread it around most of the tropical parts of the world, with varying degrees of success. Despite the challenges of growing it, vanilla remains a valuable herb with many important uses in cooking as well as health care and crafts. Genuine vanilla is tastier and healthier than synthetic, and it supports the livelihood of vanilla farmers. Try to find real vanilla from sustainable, fair-trade sources. It's worth every penny.

Selected Resources

Lubinsky, Pesach, et al. "Origins and Dispersal of Cultivated Vanilla (*Vanilla planifolia* Jacks. [Orchidaceae])." *Economic Botany* 62, no. 2 (2008): 127–38. http://plantbiology.ucr.edu/faculty/Lubinskyetal(EB08).pdf.

Martin, Laurelynn, and Byron Martin. "Growing a Vanilla Bean—The Coveted Culinary Spice." Logee's. Accessed February 6, 2019. https://www.logees.com/grow_vanilla.

Swift, Liya. "The Little-Known History of Vanilla." The Chef Apprentice School of the Arts. January 20, 2015. https://www.casaschools.com/the-little-known-history-of-vanilla/#nav.

Medina, Javier De La Cruz, et al. "Vanilla: Post-Harvest Operations." Food and Agriculture Organization of the United Nations. June 6, 2009. www.fao.org/fileadmin/user_upload/inpho/docs/Post_Harvest_Compendium_-_Vanilla.pdf.

Health
and
Beauty

Marie Antoinette's Makeup Box: Eighteenth-Century Botanical Beauty

⁂ by Natalie Zaman ⁂

What beauty product do you swear by? I have a favorite purple shampoo that keeps my real white and faux-blonde pixie shiny and bright, a cry-proof mascara (tested multiple times), and a cream that erases (or covers!) creases. This is nothing new. Beauty-enhancing products have been around for thousands of years, with time, trial and error, and technology making improvements in efficacy, toxicity (important, this), and, it has to be said, odor (an American Colonial moisturizing face mask was simply strips of bacon . . .).

Every era has its signature look and fashion icon. None defines the eighteenth century quite like Marie Antoinette. After seeing Sophia Coppola's glossy, '80s music–laced *Marie*

Antionette, based on Antonia Fraser's *Marie Antionette: The Journey*, I became somewhat obsessed with Marie herself, but perhaps more so with high, powdered hair, floral essences, curved court heels, and rouge—a beauty (?) item that was an obsession with all classes. Ranging in hues from pale pink to almost black (different colors for different occasions and times of day as well as skin tones), the wearing of rouge was a status symbol rather than a means of color and contour. How one wore rouge was very exact: two round circles applied to the cheeks. Non-aristocratic women and men would rouge their cheeks with wine in an attempt to be like "their betters." What people won't do to be fashionable!

Wanting to know more, I started devouring biographies: Fraser's book, quite different from the Coppola film, and *Georgiana: Duchess of Devonshire* by Amanda Foreman. Georgiana Cavendish was an icon in her own right and a lifelong friend to Marie Antoinette; their lives and tastes paralleled each other in many ways. While the lives of these women and the political intrigues that swirled around them made for fascinating reading, it was the day-to-day details of their lives that drew me in, and just like many of us today, they used products to enhance their charms.

Thanks to primary sources such as account books, letters, personal journals, and newspaper advertisements and editorials, we know much about eighteenth-century beauty and grooming routines: the products that were used, the people who made them, and some intriguing and still useful formulas.

Keeping It Clean

Bathing habits had certainly improved by the eighteenth century, although folks still didn't bathe as regularly as we do today. Marie Antoinette was, technically, a foreigner in the French

Court; she was Austrian, and, as noted in many sources, bathed more often than most—which didn't add to her popularity. Her bath time was quite the ritual: she wore a special sheer bathing gown (she was never alone), and in addition to using scented soaps, she sat in the tub on a cushion filled with pine nuts, sweet almonds, and linseed—the oils of which seeped into the water to soften and scent her skin. For the record, Versailles was not a pleasant-smelling place. Palaces were still vacated periodically to be cleansed of pet as well as human waste.

Whatever her French counterparts thought of her habits, keeping clean in the eighteenth century meant keeping healthy. Bathing kept the spread of disease in check to a degree, but it was also necessary to cleanse the skin of the dangerous cosmetics used to achieve the still-ideal luminous white complexion. Face powders and creams often contained toxic ingredients such as arsenic. A part of Marie Antoinette's regimen included a cleanser called *Eau Cosmetique de Pigeon*, which contained, as the name suggests, pigeons—seventeen of them, stewed and fermented. Where's that soap?

In addition to flower and herbal waters (more on these later), wash balls (the predecessor of our modern day bath bomb) were available, but more humble ingredients were used for bathing the face and body: barley, rice, and bran. From a dietary standpoint, these grains have multiple beneficial qualities as antioxidants and antibacterial and anti-inflammatory agents. Ingested, they lower cholesterol and blood sugar.

Heavily influenced by the writings of Rousseau, Marie Antoinette had an appreciation for the simple life. A skincare regimen utilizing wholesome ingredients must have appealed to her personally. Once she scored the Petit Trianon as her private escape, she invited close friends to share in farm-to-table meals as well as beauty treatments such as ass-milk baths as a means of refreshment and relaxation.

To wash her face, Marie Antoinette used an exfoliating sachet made from herbs and bran wrapped in muslin—much more appetizing then her pigeon-infused antiaging product. The sachet is simple to make, and the pouch can be used in the shower or bath and on the face and body.

Because many of the recipes that follow call for the use of herbs, be sure to check with your physician before applying anything to your skin!

Exfoliating Sachets

Muslin cut into four 12-inch squares

2 cups of bran, barley, or rice

½ cup of your choice of herb or combination of herbs (Marie Antoinette is thought to have used thyme and marjoram in her bath sachets.)

Twine or cotton string

Blend the ingredients thoroughly. Place ¼ cup of the mixture on each square of fabric. Gather the square into a small pouch and secure it with twine. Toss the sachet into the bath or under warm water to soften, then rub it over the skin to cleanse and exfoliate.

Powder and Pomade

The incredibly fashionable Georgiana, Duchess of Devonshire, is credited with creating the "hair tower." Increasing a lady's height by about three feet, the hair tower was constructed by combing and securing the hair over a fabric roll called a *pouf* (sometimes adding false hair was necessary) and then powdered. Depending on the occasion, decorations were added; flowers, spangles, scenery (idyllic farm scenes were popular) and themes such as life events like the birth of a child, or the launch of a ship or balloon.

The hair towers were impractical and therefore short lived. (Women who braved this fashion found it hard to ride in coaches, as their hair made it impossible for them to sit on the seats.) Powder, however, had more staying power.

Until I discovered dry shampoo, I wondered why people would powder their hair, but even 200 years ago, its use started from a practical need. **Hair powder** acted as a degreaser and refreshed locks that probably weren't washed that often. Powder was also used to hide bald spots and gray hair. **Pomade** (also called pomatum) was made with a combination of animal fats, spices, and floral essences and massaged into the hair to condition and style it. Once every hair was in place, powder was blown on; the pomatum also acted as a fixative. As can be imagined, it was a messy process. Powdering rooms were designated for the purpose, and those powdering and being powdered wore robes and masks. A snootful of hair powder couldn't be pleasant, nor was it proper to have one's hair powder dusting one's fine clothes.

Powders were made from a combination of starch, orris root (which adds a bit of a floral scent), and ground-up mutton or cuttlefish bones. Different minerals and metals were added to the powder to color it. Blue, popular with Whig politician Charles James Fox, was made by adding crushed lapis lazuli to the powder, making it very expensive. Pink and red shades were achieved with the addition of iron oxide. Powder makes for a wonderful temporary fix if you'd like to try something a bit daring. Here is a basic recipe for hair powder and some suggestions for color:

Hair Powder, Dry Version

> 2 cups starch (Arrowroot works equally well.)
>
> ¼ cup orris root (for scent)
>
> ¼ cup powdered calcium (standing in for the bones!)
>
> Colored powder: ultramarine for blue, iron oxide for red, yellow ochre powder for yellow (available in craft shops or online)

Simply mix the ingredients together, adding the colors a bit at a time until the desired hue is achieved. This is closest to eighteenth-century recipes.

Hair Powder, Wet Version

> 2 cups starch (Arrowroot works equally well.)
>
> 3–5 drops essential oil of choice for scent
>
> Food coloring
>
> 1 cup water
>
> Metal bowl

Mix all the ingredients in a metal bowl until well blended. Eliminate all clumps of powder; more water can be added if necessary. Add the food coloring until the desired hue is achieved, remembering that you can mix colors to create new ones (e.g., blue and red to make purple or lavender). Let the mixture dry overnight. You can also place the bowl in an oven on low heat to speed up the process. Once it's dry, break the now-solid mixture out of the bowl and pulse it in a food processor until powdered. Apply the powder to your hair with a shaker—then get ready to party like it's 1777!

Scents and Sensibility

By the eighteenth century, perfumery was a booming industry—perhaps not the branded one we know today, but one of strong single essences and signature scents. Marie Antoinette had scents made for those close to her; the one she had created for her lover, Count Axel von Fersen, was heavy with tuberose—very romantic!

While the creation of *eau de toilette* and *parfum* is a complex science, flower waters are relatively easy to make. Marie Antoinette favored orange flower water. These essences were used for personal scents well as for scenting linens and, depending on the ingredients, as astringents, refreshers, moisturizers, and antiseptics. The methods below can be used with just about any flower or herb to create a water essence.

Flower Water

> Heat-tempered glass bowl
>
> Lidded pot that will accommodate the bowl with room to spare around the sides
>
> Leaves, buds, and/or flower petals of your choice
>
> Distilled water
>
> Ice cubes
>
> Bottles or jars for storage
>
> Funnel
>
> *Optional:* Vodka or witch hazel (acts as a preservative)

Place the glass bowl in the pot. Place the leaves, flower petals, or buds around the bowl (not in the bowl); do not pack the plant material. Cover the plant material with distilled water. Put the pot on the stove on low heat.

When the water starts to simmer, put the lid on the pot, upside down so that it is concave on top. Place ice cubes on top of the lid. You will notice that water will condense and collect on the lid of the pot and drip down into the bowl—*that* is your flower water. Keep an eye on the pot and keep placing ice cubes on the lid until the bowl has the desired amount of water in it. Allow the whole apparatus to cool before pouring the water into storage jars or bottles. You can add a little vodka or witch hazel to the water to help preserve it, or store it in the refrigerator.

A simpler method is to boil the herbs, petals, or buds and steep them like tea. Allow them to cool, then strain off any plant material before pouring the waters into jars for storage and use.

In addition to perfume, eighteenth century women used flower waters such as these for skincare and self-care:

Rose water acts as an astringent, tightening the pores; it is also antibacterial and an anti-inflammatory and can fade scars.

Lavender water is cleansing and relaxing—a spritz on your pillow will help promote sleep.

Rosemary water is an antiseptic and disinfectant for the skin and hair.

Mint water is an anti-inflammatory that can help control acne and soothe insect bites.

Lemon balm water is also an anti-inflammatory and a natural astringent that can be used to heal acne.

Hands-On Beauty

Marie Antoinette was something of a glove addict (she bought about eighteen pairs a month). While most courtiers wore white, she opted for pastels and soft grays, all made especially for her by her perfumer, Jean Louis Fargeon, who also scented them. Fargeon used violets, hyacinths, and jonquils to perfume them, stipulating that the flowers be picked in dry weather, after dawn and before dusk, to avoid dealing with any kind of moisture.

You can employ his methods to scent your gloves or other personal articles (including paper and notebooks!).

Scenting Gloves

Scented flowers of your choice

Large lidded box

Items of your choice to scent

Basically, you're bathing the items in flowers, or, more accurately, their scent. Layer the bottom of the box with flowers, being careful not to crush them. Do not pack them down—the idea is aeration, rather than volume. Place your items in a single layer over the flowers, and then cover them with flowers before lidding the box.

Fargeon placed his gloves directly onto the flowers. If you are scenting light-colored items, be aware of the potential for color transfer. If you wish, place a piece of tissue paper over the flowers, then set your items on top of it. Place another piece of tissue on top of your items before adding the second layer of flowers.

Fargeon left the gloves in this "bath" for about eight days, during which time they imbibed the scent of the flowers. The process can be repeated to refresh the scent. *La reine* simply ordered more gloves.

It should be noted that Fargeon's gloves were multitaskers: ungloved, a lady's hands were always on display and had to look their best. The inside of Marie Antoinette's gloves were treated with a mixture of wax, almond oil, and rose essence to soften her skin.

Resources

My evolving understanding of eighteenth-century beauty practices was enhanced by immersing myself in the lives of women and men who used them. The following biographies had a narrative flair in which I could lose myself and provided bibliographies rich with primary source material:

De Feydeau, Elisabeth. *The Scented Palace: The Secret History of Marie Antoinette's Perfumer.* London: I. B. Tauris and Company, 2004.

Foreman, Amanda. *Georgiana: Duchess of Devonshire.* London: Modern Library, 2001.

Fraser, Antonia. *Marie Antoinette: The Journey.* New York: Random House, 2001.

Weber, Caroline. *Queen of Fashion: What Marie Antoinette Wore to the Revolution.* New York: Henry Holt and Company, 2006.

Primary sources are also readily available online and provide recipies and formulas for a variety of beauty treatments. Peruse these titles on Google Books:

Buchoz, Pierre Joseph. *The Toilet of Flora.* London, 1772.

Le Camus, Antoine. *Abdecker: or, the Art of Preserving Beauty.* London, 1754.

The Toilette of Health, Beauty, and Fashion. Boston: Allen and Tinknor, 1834.

Adventures in Tea Soap–Making

⤜ by Linda Raedisch ⤛

Someone once asked me, "Why on earth would you put lye in soap?" The answer was easy: because without lye (sodium hydroxide) to bond with the oils, there is no soap. The question "Why put tea in soap?" is a little harder to answer. Tea is a stimulant and an antioxidant, though it's hard to say how much of these properties make it through the soapmaking process. There's no denying that tea, when handled properly, imparts a pleasant color to the finished bar of soap, that the ground leaves work as a gentle exfoliant, and that the word *tea* has strong label appeal.

There's also a precedent for applying tea leaves to the skin. Before it became a pleasure drink, the leaves of *Camellia sinensis* were used medicinally, both inside and out, and ancient Chinese physicians prescribed a paste of ground tea leaves to be spread over arthritic joints.

Traditional Tea

During the Shang dynasty (c. 1766–1050 BCE), the tea bush was still a wild plant, just one herb among the many in the ancient Chinese apothecary's cabinet. It was rarely taken by itself. Up through the Tang dynasty (618–907 CE), tea was cooked with a variety of other ingredients, including tree bark, dogwood berries, jujube, plum, orange, and other fruit juices, pastes, and peels—and even onions. It was only toward the end of the Tang that people started to enjoy their tea straight. Tea was domesticated during this era too, with the first "tea garden" appearing in 53 BCE.

The scholar Lu Yu was one of the first to encourage the mindful drinking of unflavored tea. He advised drinkers to heat the cake into which the tea leaves were pressed until it was "as tender as a baby's arm" before brewing, and to choose one's teacup carefully. Traditionally, the Chinese have preferred green teas over black, the latter being traded only to "barbarians." There are a handful of legends in which a batch of green tea leaves was either smoked for too long or allowed to grow moldy over the course of a long voyage. The foreigners who bought it loved it and quickly ordered more.

I must count myself among those "barbarians" because I am, at heart, a tea philistine. I drink ordinary orange pekoe all day long out of whichever cup happens to be clean. The subject of tea continues to fascinate me, however, and I do own one of those little unglazed pots that serious green tea drinkers use, though mine spends most of its time in the silk-lined box it came in. I have always kept some fragrant Taiwanese mountain tea on hand to offer to discerning guests, and I know that the first cup is to be discarded, not drunk. All this has earned me an undeserved reputation as a tea connoisseur. Now, whenever a friend, a friend of a friend, or even the in-laws of a friend of a friend travel to China, Japan, India, or Nepal, I end up with another pretty bag of loose-leaf tea in my kitchen. What to do with it all?

While I can read the Chinese character for "tea," I often have no idea what I have in my hands. Or do I? All tea, be it Darjeeling, bright green matcha powder from Japan, or that refreshingly soapy-tasting stuff you get at Chinese restaurants, comes from the same plant. Which leaves are plucked and when and what happens to them after is what makes one variety of tea different from another. The terroir or soil it's grown in also plays a role. My beloved orange pekoe is a "black" tea because the green tea leaves are fermented before roasting. The "orange" in "orange pekoe" has nothing to do with its warm reddish color; it refers to the royal Dutch House of Orange-Nassau and describes a high grade of tea leaves, one fit for the cups of the Dutch royals, I suppose.

Making Tea Soap

I became interested in soapmaking at about the same time I became unable to close the cupboard door on my overflowing collection of teas. What to do with it all? Make soap! My very first batch of soap was a tea soap made with an infusion of green tea leaves left behind by someone who had moved to Hong Kong. I was pleased with the result, and since there was already a goat's milk soapmaker in the area, I decided to make tea soaps my specialty.

If this is your first stab at soapmaking, start with the basic recipe below. You can use any tea you like, but know that if you use green tea it will turn brown when you add the lye. Always use distilled water to brew your tea. Use the cheapest grade olive oil you can find in the store—it works better than extra-virgin. Don't use aluminum pots or utensils, as they will react with the lye and ruin your soap. Also, once you have used a utensil for soapmaking, don't use it for cooking!

I recommend using Red Crown High Test brand lye because it's easy to find, but you can use any sodium hydroxide recommended for soapmaking. Open the windows wide when you add the lye to the tea: the fumes are caustic, but they will dissipate after a few minutes. When working with lye and raw soap (soap less than twenty-four hours old), wear rubber gloves and goggles.

All ingredients except the grapefruit seed extract and powdered tea must be weighed on a kitchen scale to insure accuracy. This recipe makes one pound of soap.

Basic Tea Soap

   5.25 ounces coconut oil

   10.5 ounces olive oil

   0.5 ounce castor oil

   5 ounces strong-brewed tea in a heatproof container, well chilled

   2.4 ounces lye

   1 teaspoon grapefruit seed extract (GSE), an antioxidant that will help your soap batter thicken and will impart a very light citrus scent

   ½ teaspoon finely ground tea leaves

Shoebox lined with freezer paper, shiny side up

Plastic wrap

In a double boiler or water bath, melt the coconut oil and keep it warm until needed. Measure olive and castor oils in a heat-proof bowl and set aside.

Carefully pour the lye into your chilled tea. Stir the solution to the best of your ability, but don't be a hero. After the fumes dissipate, you can return and stir until all the lye is dissolved.

Watch a few cat videos while your lye solution cools. When it's about 125°F or just cool enough that you don't have to pull your hand away when you touch the container, you're ready to make soap! Stir your coconut oil into the bowl with the other oils. Then, gloved and goggled, carefully pour the lye solution into the oils, stirring all the while. Add the GSE and keep stirring until the batter has "traced"—i.e., a dribble from the spoon lingers for a second on the surface before sinking. A stick blender comes in very handy, but I have made many batches of soap using a slotted wooden spoon. Your soap may trace in minutes or it could take upward of 45.

Once it has traced, stir in the ground tea thoroughly and pour your soap into the lined shoebox. (If it hasn't reached trace after an hour of stirring, pour the soap into the box anyway. It will probably set eventually.)

Lay plastic wrap over the surface of the soap and place it in a warm place. An oven is ideal, as long as you remember not to turn it on while the soap is in there! If you have no warm place, lay a thick towel over the mold to hold in the heat. Leave it for 24 hours, after which, if it feels nice and firm, you can peel off the plastic and remove the loaf of soap from the mold. Peel off the freezer paper and leave the soap at room temperature for another 24 hours, exposed to the air. After that, it should be hard enough to cut into 8 bars. Leave the bars out in the open to cure for at least 4 weeks before using.

Once you have made the basic tea soap, you can get fancy. To retain more of the tea's natural properties and color, prepare 2 ounces of "slurry" (i.e., slushily frozen, strongly brewed tea). Dissolve your lye in just 3 ounces of distilled water and proceed as usual, adding your slurry just before you pour the soap batter into the mold.

You can make an indulgently fragrant soap by adding 2 milliliters jasmine essential oil after the soap has traced and scattering dried jasmine flowers over the surface before putting on the plastic wrap. Or try an Earl Grey tea soap with bergamot essential oil. Experiment with some of the ancient Chinese tea ingredients mentioned earlier in this article—but leave out the onions!

Because these soaps are all natural, they tend to get very soft when they have been in the shower for a while. Keeping your tea soap in a well-drained soap dish will help keep it firm and prevent it from becoming "as tender as a baby's arm."

Resources

Faiola, Anne-Marie. *Pure Soapmaking: How to Create Nourishing Natural Skin Care Soaps*. North Adams, MA: Storey Publishing, 2016.

Heiss, Mary Lou, and Robert J. Heiss. *The Story of Tea: A Cultural History and Drinking Guide*. Berkeley, CA: Ten Speed Press, 2007.

Hoh, Erling, and Victor H. Mair. *The True History of Tea*. New York: Thames and Hudson, 2009.

Herbs for the Heart

~ by Holly Bellebuono ~

As an herbalist, I've had the opportunity to use herbs for healing and supporting all the major body systems. The heart is the first organ to develop in a growing fetus in the womb; composed of the heart, the blood, and the vessels, the cardiovascular system is the longest-working system in our bodies. The heart is the seat, in various traditions, of power, courage, and love, and it is both wondrous and completely natural that the heart responds so well to the green herbs around us.

Whether you're interested in supporting the long-term health of your heart; you're dealing with issues of the heart muscle, vascular health, or cholesterol; or you need emotional support due to an open heart or a broken heart, herbs can help. Maintaining a healthy diet by eating lots of dark green, leafy vegetables, getting enough dietary fiber, and keeping salt and sugar to a minimum is important too. Exercise, of course, and not smoking are equally important. But when it comes to herbs—to botanical remedies that satisfy both the physical and the emotional heart—we are drawing upon an incredible tradition that is truly supportive.

There is a wide range of herbal actions that can affect the heart—both positively and negatively. **Cardioactives** are herbs that exert a very strong action upon the heart, such as foxglove and lily of the valley. These herbs contain powerful cardioglycosides, making them very effective at stimulating the heart muscle to contract, but they are unpredictable and so powerful that they can be dangerous, and I discourage herbalists from using them. **Cardiotonics**, on the other hand, are milder and more reliable, providing medicine that can be used long-term and with well-anticipated results. Tonics generally support an organ or system of the body, and in this case, heart tonics or cardiotonics can be relied upon to gently and effectively support the ongoing health of the heart; these remedies are particularly useful for someone concerned about high blood pressure, heart attack, or stroke.

Here, we will explore eight herbs that are traditionally used for the heart—and many of them have been the subjects of recent scientific study confirming what folk healers have known for centuries. We will focus on their medicinal actions and also on each herb's emotional effects, including the symbolic natures of these herbs along with visualizations you can use to support your own emotional health when you need it.

Rose, *Rosa rugosa*, *Rosa* spp.

Rose is one of humanity's most beloved flowers, and it's no wonder it is an herb of the heart. Both its scent and beauty are lovely, and it has long represented love in many cultures.

Cardio

On a purely physical level, rose petals are an extremely mild cardiovascular tonic, supporting the heart and the vascular system. Rose hips are high in vitamin C, which supports immune function.

Emotional/Symbolic

The scent of a rose is healing; its lovely fragrance is calming and can bring on feelings of relief and relaxation. Use rose petals in teas, syrups, attars, essential oils, spritzers, massage oils, foods, and much more; the stronger the rose scent, the better. I like to use roses when someone is feeling out of sorts, confused, or sad and especially when someone is grieving or suffering a loss. In this way, roses are a wonderful heart remedy, helping both the mind and heart release those gnawing feelings of grief and emptiness. Even more, roses sport thorns—some branches boast small triangular jabs while others are covered in piercing needles. Symbolically, these thorns can help us protect our heart—supporting us as we learn to set boundaries and enforce personal limits. Many of us need to grow thorns and embrace the sharper sides of ourselves; planting rose bushes can help us remember how growing our own hedges can be very beneficial in setting our boundaries.

Visualization

Picture yourself feeling balanced, perfectly balanced. In one hand, you hold the soft pink petals of a very delicate rose, and you feel gentle, at peace, and loving. In the other hand, you hold a single sharp thorn, and you feel strong and protected, knowing you hold a barrier to defend yourself if you should need it. You have boundaries, and yet you are also generous and giving. No one takes advantage of you, and you are comfortable loving others because you confidently love yourself.

Hawthorn, *Crataegus* spp.

Hawthorn is a tree that thrives in deciduous forests; its creamy white flowers grow in sprays among very long spiny thorns. The flowers give way to berries, called haws, thus the name *hawthorn*. I first met hawthorn in the mountains of North Carolina and was drawn to Euell Gibbons's colorful description of the countless species of this remarkable tree. As a relative of rose, it makes sense that it would have similar heart effects, but the hawthorn is much stronger—acting as a reliable cardiotonic that supports many various heart conditions, including hypertension (high blood pressure).

Cardio

Hawthorn (its leaves, flowers, and berries) is considered cardiotonic. Hawthorn contains flavonoids that are believed to dilate the coronary arteries, increasing blood flow throughout the body and thereby reducing pressure on the heart. Those dealing with cardiac insufficiency, congestive heart failure, cardiac dyspnea, or fatigue as well as those with irregular heartbeat may consider consulting their health care provider about using the leaves, flowers, and berries of hawthorn as a tea or tincture.

Emotional/Symbolic

Again, due to its long spines, we have an herb that is symbolically excellent for protection. While roses are covered in nasty needles, especially the lovely *Rosa rugosa*, or beach rose, that perfumes the sand dunes around Martha's Vineyard, hawthorn is covered in long, spear-like spines that reach out to entangle your hair when you're walking through the rich woods of the southern Appalachian Mountains.

Visualization

Think of hawthorn as a walking stick—a strong support when you're traveling an unknown path. You can pick up this walking stick and carry it with you anytime. Think of hawthorn as a fence rail—those long horizontal pieces of a country fence that form a barrier and let nothing pass. You can lean against this long, sturdy fence knowing that it is a solid boundary and your heart is protected. Think of hawthorn as a porch post—a tall column that stands firm and supports the roof, keeping its wide, shady porch clean and inviting. Imagine yourself sitting in a porch chair on this wide, shady protected porch, knowing it is well-supported and you are welcome, welcome, welcome.

Linden, *Tilia ×europaea*

Another tree that is wonderful for the heart is linden. Also called basswood or tilia, linden is often planted in cities because it grows in a compact and beautiful form that graces sidewalks and parks. Like with hawthorn, we can use the flowers, leaves, and seeds as medicine, and in this case, it is a dual medicine for both the heart and the nervous system.

Cardio

Linden is considered a hypotensive herb, meaning it lowers blood pressure. It makes a lovely tea, very mild, almost honey-flavored, and is easy on the tongue and throat. As a nervous system tonic, linden is wonderful for stress and anxiety, helping ease tensions in the body and soothe the wandering, chattering mind. It's a great herb to use at bedtime, especially for someone who can't sleep due to a tense body or a tense heart. Try making a strong linden tea, sweeten it with a touch of honey, and freeze it in ice cube trays for a welcoming, soothing treat on a hot day. Or make a linden syrup and add it to sparkling grapefruit juice or seltzer.

Visualization

Whenever you need a little sweetness in your life, imagine yourself sitting under the branches of a linden tree, its wide trunk and bright green leaves rustling in the cool breeze above you. The air is scented with honey, and soon other people you love dearly are there under the tree with you. The shade is comfortable, and you can spend all day there in the sweet company of those you love.

Oats, *Avena sativa*

Long a staple of many a kitchen, oats are heart-strengthening plants. The same grass and cereal grain that provides our morning oatmeal also gives us milky oat tops (the immature floret) and oat straw (the stalk), and all three are high in calcium. When prepared or cooked, it is indeed milky and is used both internally as a demulcent and nutritive and externally as a lotion.

Cardio

Considered a cardio-restorative and a nervine tonic, oat is a mineral-rich and nutritious plant. Calcium is indispensable in the body: not only is it needed for proper bone density, it is also required for proper heart-muscle action, stimulating and regulating the electrical function necessary for the heart to beat and contract. Raw oats are high in soluble fiber and contain 8 percent of the daily recommended value of calcium, along with lots of iron, vitamin B_6, and magnesium. For the heart, this means stronger electrical function, and for the vascular system, the soluble fiber leads to lower cholesterol, opening up the vessels and reducing blood pressure. Herbalists use oats to support those with atherosclerosis (fat or plaque in the arteries) and arteriosclerosis (hardening of the arteries).

Emotional/Symbolic

Oats are a soothing nervous system tonic, bringing on feelings of steadfastness, steadiness, and feeling grounded. Eating oatmeal or taking milky-oat tincture on a regular basis can help one feel calmer and more relaxed. Many of my students and clients report that oats help them deal with anxiety and stress. Juliette de Bairacli Levy, herbalist, forager, mother, and author, suggested oats for anger—especially for children and teenagers who feel out of control, angry, and irritable. She recommended taking the oats as food and tea and also in the bath because the lotion made from oats in water is soothing, creamy, and soft. I find oats cooling (especially helpful for hot, inflamed conditions and emotions), and they combine well with other cooling herbs, such as lavender, chickweed, and spearmint.

Visualization

When you're feeling angry or irritable, imagine yourself stepping into an old-fashioned claw-foot tub. The water is lukewarm and creamy with lotions and scented oils poured there just for you. You have nothing to do but sit back and enjoy. Whenever you swish around in the tub, the creamy water rolls over your skin in smooth waves; you can dip your hair in the water, and your hair feels cool and soft.

Hibiscus, *Hibiscus sabdariffa*

Cool and tart, iced hibiscus tea is enjoyed by many of us on a hot day. Its deep strawberry color and punchy flavor belie an interesting fact: hibiscus can be used medicinally. This plant is also called Jamaica, sorrel, or roselle; its deep magenta calyces (sepals) near the flower are harvested and made into sour drinks. This plant is different from *Hibiscus rosa-sinensis*, which boasts a larger flower and is in the Malvaceae family.

Cardio

Hibiscus is a lovely herb for nervous system support, helpful for easing the mood, and is also cardiotonic. Clinical trials show that hibiscus reduces cholesterol and hypertension.

Emotional/Symbolic

The deep red color of hibiscus is pulsing and vibrant, full of life and the beat of the heart.

Visualization

Imagine the deep crimson-red color enriching your vessels and heart. Picture your red blood cells as healthy cells freely traveling inside clean, expansive red vessels and arteries. Your vessels and arteries are happy! Red, pulsing, healthy, and vibrant, they will support your wonderful body for years to come.

Silk Tree (Mimosa), *Albizia julibrissin, A.* spp.

A lovely small-to-medium-size tree native to China, mimosa produces fluffy clouds of pink blossoms; these flowers, leaves, and the bark of the tree have been used for centuries in Traditional Chinese Medicine for depression and insomnia.

Cardio
Albizia indirectly supports the physical heart as it directly nurtures the emotional heart, supporting those experiencing grief and heartache.

Emotional/Symbolic
With its soft, feathery blossoms and delicate fern-like leaves, this tree invites us to open up to our softness. This tree also cautions us to be careful and protective of our hearts, opening enough to experience love but not enough to recklessly abandon our heart's integrity.

Visualization
Discard any irritability and let your anger float heavenward. Picture the pink blossoms fanning your negative emotions away from you, and see the leaves opening and closing to push away negative thoughts.

Garlic, *Allium sativum*
We're all familiar with garlic as a food and condiment, and we are increasingly aware of its beneficial effects on the heart.

Cardio
In addition to being a prime antibacterial and antifungal that I, along with many others, use frequently throughout the winter to keep colds at bay or to fight the flu, garlic is an excellent heart herb. The bulb, high in the sulfur compound allicin, is being researched for its powerful effects against high blood

pressure and atherosclerosis, particularly lowering cholesterol levels in the blood. Eat garlic raw or lightly cooked, preferably one to two cloves per day.

Emotional/Symbolic

Garlic is a root medicine. Imagine your flighty, fluttery, weak heart rooting toward the earth. It gets grounded, stable, and secure. A garlic bulb is also made up of many cloves; imagine dedicating your love and your heart to many people, animals, causes, and needs and still feeling whole. Your heart is limitless; there is always more love.

Motherwort, *Leonurus cardiaca*

Perhaps one of my favorite herbs, and one that I learned quite late in the game, is motherwort. This is a small herb or a little shrub, depending on how happy it gets in your garden. Motherwort blooms tiny pale blue flowers on stalks that get quite prickly, and the leaves are resoundingly bitter on the tongue. It's a bitterness I find appealing, and chewing a leaf will often dispel feelings of panic, fear, or worry. It's long been used for three specific body systems, which is why I call it a "trinity" herb: the nervous system, the cardiovascular system, and the digestive system.

Cardio

As herbs for the heart go, motherwort is one that proudly displays its "overlap" effects, supporting the cardiovascular system while also supporting the rest of the body. It is cardiotonic and gently lowers blood pressure. The Latin genus and species names indicate it provides the heart with the strength of a lion. As a nervous system herb, it is renowned for helping a person let go of blinding fear or sudden panic, especially that horrible feeling of overwhelm often experienced by harried and exhausted mothers of young children, hence its name. Its ability to stimulate digestive juices due to its bitter principles increases its value to the heart; only when we properly digest food do we relieve the heart and the entire vascular system (and the lymph system and the liver) of an unnecessary burden. Good digestion is the "heart" of health, and bitter plants in moderation have great benefit; they stimulate your immune system and initiate the release of hydrochloric acid to make certain that digestion is complete and thorough—this may be because, as animals and human evolved, a bitter flavor indicated the presence of poison, and our bodies adapted to minimize any chance of damage. Better digestion, better excretion, and better elimination all lead to a stronger and healthier heart.

Emotional/Symbolic

It's easy to go to a strong visualization with a roaring lion protecting your heart or in control of vast territory. And while that image may resonate, also consider the image of community—people coming together from all walks of life with children of all ages—to support one another. This image of motherwort is sustaining and, for me, evokes the cyclic images of maiden, mother, and crone. If we are lucky enough to experience each of these stages of life, we can take a deep breath and feel our hearts at ease.

Visualization

Imagine a living room or a front porch or a summertime backyard with many, many loving, supportive people, each helping one another, watching kids peacefully, eating from a table laden with plenty of food, and laughing and telling each other stories of past and present. They are always here for you; they are your siblings, your silly cohorts, your wistful friends. You are nurtured in this circle that has no end.

Resources

Hudson, Tori. "Hibiscus, Hawthorn, and the Heart: Modern Research Supports the Use of Traditional Plants." *Natural Medicine Journal* 3, no. 7 (July 2011). https://www.naturalmedicinejournal.com/journal/2011-07/hibiscus-hawthorn-and-heart.

Romm, Aviva. "Bitter Plants: The Ultimate Paleo Food." Aviva Romm. August 24, 2016. https://avivaromm.com/bitters-for-digestion/.

Myth-Information: Deciphering Fact from Fiction in Food and Nutrition

❧ by Mireille Blacke ❧

In my career as a registered dietitian-nutritionist, university professor, and addiction counselor, numerous patients, colleagues, family members, and friends have come to me confused, irritated, and frustrated about recurring trendy diets, media-hyped "super-foods," Himalayan sea salt, coconut oil—you name it! Perhaps it's the skeptic in me, but the ability to discern science from sales pitch seems to fly out the window if Dr. Oz or a celebrity famous for being famous endorses a nutrition-related "miracle product."

That was one reason I decided to write this article, but I have another. I specialize in working with patients in the bariatric surgery process, arguably

the most stigmatized and misunderstood in terms of public misinformation and accepted half-truths: consider the common public perception that weight loss surgery is "the easy way out." The simple truth is that no bariatric procedure is the easy way out of morbid obesity, no surgery is a magic bullet, and weight does not stay off without significant effort on the part of the patient. Patients can and do gain weight back.

Maybe writing this to address common questions will foster some open-mindedness as well.

I will not be discussing the following diets: alkaline, apple cider vinegar, Atkins, blood-type, egg, food-combining, grapefruit, high-protein, Jenny, juicing, ketogenic, low-carb, low-fat, Master Cleanse, moon, NutriSystem, paleo, raw food, sea buckthorn, soup, South Beach, WW, or Zone! Are you as exhausted as I am reading that list? Some of those will drop scale numbers (not the same as weight loss), but the average person won't be able to stick to them long-term. Further discussion would require an entire article itself! However, see the resources list for additional information about these diets.

Food and Nutrition Myths

Get comfortable and grab yourself some coconut water and a gluten-free snack, because this might take a while. Here we go.

Myth #1: Organic produce is more nutritious than non-organic/conventional.

I get asked about this a lot, and there's really a simple way to determine how to spend your food dollars when it comes to organically or conventionally grown foods. Though there are numerous people who believe the term "organic" is used to con consumers out of hard-earned dollars, the term actually refers to foods that are farmed without the use of pesticides, herbicides, growth hormones, or genetically modified organisms (GMOs). Some people prefer organic on that basis alone, which is fine. Others believe that organic food has substantially higher levels of antioxidants or other health-promoting compounds compared with conventionally grown foods. However, there is no peer-reviewed research to support the claim that eating organic will lead to improved health compared to non-organic, and any differences found in nutritional composition between organic and conventional foods have been statistically insignificant (meaning unlikely to influence the health outcomes of people who buy organic).

Bottom Line: I can fully understand the desire to avoid pesticides! To assist you with this, I suggest you check out ewg .org/foodnews/dirty-dozen.php. The Environmental Working Group puts out annual "Dirty Dozen" and "Clean Fifteen" reports, which you can use for making organic-buying decisions.

Myth #2: Detox diets (cleanses or fasts) are necessary to clear toxins from your body.

Proponents claim a "detoxification diet" is necessary periodically to cleanse toxins from your body that accumulate from environmental pollutants and unhealthy diets. Such detox diets include several days of juice fasts, short periods of vegetable and water regimens, or more invasive colonic irrigations. (I suppose you could toss the maple syrup-based Master Cleanse diet in here too.) But the body has its own system of organs to do that—the liver, spleen, and kidneys—and there is no scientific evidence to suggest that any detox diets assist or improve these organs in performing the same tasks.

Bottom Line: For healthy adults, living on vegetables and water for a few days won't likely do any harm, but it doesn't top your own body's natural detoxification system either. Consistently eating nutrient-dense foods, drinking plenty of calorie-free fluids, following a recuperative sleep schedule, and getting regular physical activity are the core pillars in optimizing your body. No detoxes or fasts needed!

Myth #3: Eggs raise cholesterol and are bad for your heart.
Egg yolks contain dietary cholesterol, but this form of cholesterol has little to do with the cholesterol linked to clogged arteries and heart attacks, which is **serum cholesterol**. In other words, the cholesterol in food (eggs or otherwise) doesn't directly raise our serum (blood) cholesterol because our bodies will adjust accordingly by manufacturing less. Instead, problems with serum cholesterol and heart disease are scientifically linked with intake of saturated and **trans fats** (aka trans-unsaturated fatty acids). From that perspective, one egg provides a very low two grams of saturated fat and zero trans fats.

Numerous studies have concluded that there is no relationship between egg consumption and heart disease risk, and additional research has indicated that eating unfried eggs for breakfast could assist with hunger control and decrease overall daily caloric intake. For more egg nutrition research than you can imagine, as well as some great recipes, stop by eggnutrition center.org.

Bottom Line: Most people can eat one egg per day without negative health consequences. For those with a history of heart problems or diabetes who wish to limit dietary cholesterol intake, cap your egg intake at roughly two per week.

Myth #4: A gluten-free diet will benefit anyone.

Unless you've been diagnosed with celiac disease or gluten intolerance, gluten itself isn't unhealthy for you. Gluten is a protein found in wheat, barley, and rye. With celiac disease, the body cannot digest gluten, and eventually nutrient absorption is compromised. If celiac is ruled out, gluten intolerance may be diagnosed based on recurrent abdominal distress and fatigue after gluten consumption.

Would a person without either condition benefit from going gluten-free (GF)? Possibly. Gluten is an ingredient in many empty-calorie, high-carbohydrate foods: think of the bakery section of the biggest supermarket chain in your town. Following a GF diet means you're cutting that stuff out; doing so often results in weight loss and less bloating. But with all the food manufacturers coming out with GF products now, I don't think the trend of GF for weight loss will continue long-term.

One controversial discussion about GF diets involves autism. Some families of children with autism and gastrointestinal problems have reported improvement of symptoms when the child followed a gluten-free diet that also eliminated casein, a milk protein. However, objective research hasn't supported these results.

Bottom Line: Unless you have a medical reason (diagnosed celiac disease or gluten intolerance), there is probably no benefit to either avoiding gluten or going gluten-free (GF). If you suspect you have a problem with gluten, consult a medical professional; do not self-diagnose. Objective clinical studies do not show significant effects of a gluten-free, casein-free diet (GFCF) for people with autism spectrum disorders. But based on reports of children with autism and GI problems, parents might consider consulting with a registered dietitian-nutritionist (RDN) for medical nutrition therapy (MNT) to identify and manage any related issues.

Myth #5: Coconut oil is incredibly healthy.

Coconut oil is a **saturated fat**, which means it's the type associated with heart disease and high cholesterol. There is evidence to suggest that the saturated fat in coconut oil might be metabolized differently from other saturated fats, meaning it may not negatively impact serum cholesterol and general cardiovascular health. Coconut oil, however, does lack the essential fatty acids found in unsaturated fats that foster heart health ("good cholesterol") and the fat needed by our bodies. The American Heart Association suggests using heart-healthy mono- and polyunsaturated cooking oils, such as olive, safflower, soybean, and sunflower. If you have the extra cash, splurge for avocado oil!

Bottom Line: Until there is conclusive evidence otherwise, use unsaturated, heart-healthy plant-based oils for cooking instead. Use coconut oil for skin and hair (sparingly).

Myth #6: And then we have coconut water.

Supposedly it is healthier, keeps us "better hydrated," and has more beneficial effects than regular plain or bottled water. I now present you with the facts:

Fact: Coconut water does not hydrate you better than plain water. Though coconut water is rich in potassium, relatively low in calories, and fat and cholesterol free, there is no evidence that it is actually better than plain water for simple hydration. *Fact:* Coconut water does not have anti-aging properties. Plain water will help you feel and look just as good by maintaining adequate hydration levels. *Fact:* Coconut water should not be considered a "heart-healthy beverage." There is no evidence to suggest it helps prevent stroke and heart attack. *Fact:* Coconut water does not speed up your metabolism. When dehydrated, anything you drink will keep your metabolism going. *Fact:* Coconut water is not an ideal post-exercise drink. Sports drinks are meant to replace fluids, supply energy, and replace sodium and potassium lost through perspiration during intense physical activity; individuals in this category will need more than coconut water provides. Similarly, the benefit to the average person (after light-to-moderate physical activity) between coconut water and plain water would be negligible.

Bottom Line: Save your money. Drink plain water instead of coconut water.

Myth #7: Vegetarian and vegan diets are healthier than animal-based diets.

Nutritionally speaking, choosing a vegetarian or vegan diet means avoiding animal-based food products that contain saturated fat and adverse health effects that come with such overconsumption. However, if you replace the meat and dairy in your diet with refined carbohydrates and sweets, being a healthy vegetarian or vegan is not likely! Whether or not vegetarian or vegan diets are healthier than animal-based diets completely depends upon which foods are being selected and eaten. A diet of potato chips and chocolate would technically rank as vegetarian but hardly healthy!

For some, vegetarianism and veganism are lifestyles. I have worked with some individuals who label themselves vegan while wearing leather, smoking a pack of cigarettes daily, and slamming back several shots of vodka with veggie burgers and fries most nights of the week. Overall, not a healthy lifestyle! I've also worked with vegans who walk the walk, and do so with a lot of effort and consistency, with great results.

Bottom Line: For those individuals making healthy choices, vegetarianism or veganism are considered nutritionally sound, environmentally friendly, and more sustainable than animal-based diets. Even shifting to a vegetarian or vegan eating plan for two days per week will likely make a difference in your lifestyle and health as well as positively impact the environment.

Apple cider vinegar is not a miracle elixir for weight loss, curing diabetes, lowering cholesterol, stabilizing blood pressure, or preventing cancer. It does, however, make a fantastic all-purpose cleaner!

Myth #8: Snacking between meals is a bad idea.

Eating smaller portions with two sensible snacks a day is actually healthier and more conducive to weight loss than eating three huge meals every day. Planned snacking also helps to prevent blood sugar and energy crashes between meals.

But what exactly are your snack foods? Make smart choices and select nutrient-dense snacks that help you feel full for a while: avoid empty calories in sugar-packed, processed foods (cookies, candy bars, pastries), and choose a lean protein with a healthy (unsaturated) fat to enhance satiety. Examples include a low-fat mozzarella cheese stick and a palm-sized serving of almonds, a handful of granola, a slice of apple with a (level!) spoonful of peanut butter, or plain low-fat Greek yogurt with your own added fruit.

Bottom Line: Two protein-based snacks of around a hundred calories each per day will assist with weight loss goals, satiety, blood sugar control, and optimal energy throughout the day.

Myth #9: Sea salt is a healthier version of regular salt.

Both regular (table) salt and sea salt contain roughly 2,300 milligrams of sodium per teaspoon. Regular salt is mined, while sea salt results from evaporated seawater. Sea salt contains the minerals magnesium and iron but only in trace amounts. That means you'd have to ingest a dangerous level of sodium to make those minerals count. In contrast, ordinary table salt is fortified with iodine, which is critical to the body's hormone regulation. There is almost zero iodine in sea salt.

Bottom Line: Sea salt (no matter its color, region of origin, etc.) has no significant nutritional benefit over regular (table) salt. Regular salt is fortified with iodine, which aids in hormone regulation. Any trace nutrients found in sea salt are negligible. The extra cash you've wasted is not!

Myth #10: Vitamin water is the best thing ever!

This goes to show you how strong marketing campaigns can be. Most of the micronutrients (vitamins) contained in the current brands of vitamin waters are rarely needed because most individuals ingest more than enough with food. Excess amounts of water-soluble vitamins (any of the B vitamins, for example) are excreted through urine. Avoid vitamin waters containing vitamins A or E, as these fat-soluble vitamins may be harmful or toxic when consumed in large amounts.

Bottom Line: Vitamin waters are a waste of your money. Drink plain water, or flavor plain or seltzer water with cucumber, mint, basil, lemon, lime, strawberries, or orange slices for extra zing.

Myth #11: "Trans fat–free foods" are actually trans fat free.

Foods with **trans fats** (foods containing "partially hydrogenated oil") have conclusively been linked with heart disease, so it's no surprise that trans-fat intake should be eliminated or extremely low: limit to approximately 1 gram for every 2,000 calories. According to the FDA, food is considered "trans fat free" if it contains 0.5 grams of trans fat per serving or less. Considering that the food package is allowed to read "trans fat free" but in reality each serving may have almost half a gram per serving, you may exceed that limit each day without realizing it. Pay attention to the ingredients!

Bottom Line: Avoid all foods with trans fats (or "partially hydrogenated oil") on their nutrition labels or ingredients lists.

Myth #12: Doctors are nutrition experts.

Despite what you might see on television (Hi, Dr. Oz!), doctors receive very little nutrition education in med school. MDs are not RDNs, who are considered nutrition experts. Nutritionists are not RDNs; however, RDNs are certified nutritionists. There is a difference—a lot of education and training! When seeking accurate nutrition advice, please find a local RDN in your area or visit eatright.org/find-an-expert.

Bottom Line: As a consumer, always look for potential bias and self-interest, no matter how many credentials the spokesperson has.

Nutrition Myth Rapid-Fire Quick Bites

Dark chocolate is good for you.

The healthy polyphenols in dark chocolate that help lower blood pressure and decrease stress hormones are mostly lost in chocolate processing. To ensure health benefits, your dark chocolate must contain at least 70 percent cacao on the nutrition label. Otherwise, it's just candy!

While we're on the subject, chocolate does not cause acne. Research has shown conclusively that there is no connection between eating chocolate and developing acne or skin problems.

Bottled water is superior to tap water.

Bottled water is not more hydrating, more pure, or healthier than tap water, but public perception indicates those hefty marketing dollars are working to convince you otherwise. The hard truth is that most people can't distinguish between bottled or tap in taste tests, and there are no legitimate health reasons to purchase more plastic bottles you'll need to recycle anyway.

Oatmeal is good for you.

This statement is true if you make the oatmeal from scratch and add a bit of fruit for sweetness. But most people buy instant oatmeal packets, which consist of corn syrup solids, cornstarch, and trans fats, mixed with highly unnatural-sounding "creaming agents." Take the extra time to make your steel-cut oats and your body will thank you.

Celery has negative calories.

The "negative calorie" concept is simple: certain foods are supposedly so low in calories that chewing and digesting them burns more calories than the body absorbs, resulting in a calorie deficit. Celery tops the "negative" list at only ten calories, though digesting a stalk requires only a half calorie. Therefore, if you're eating, you're consuming calories. Even "negative calorie" foods like celery aren't fast solutions for instant weight loss.

Fresh produce is healthier than frozen.
The fruits and vegetables you find in your grocer's freezer are usually frozen right after ripening at harvest, prior to any deterioration, which helps to preserve nutrients. While fruits and vegetables are at their most nutritious when freshly eaten, going with frozen versions is an easy and reliable way of getting your five recommended servings per day without sacrificing nutrition for convenience.

Consumer Crossroads

In writing this article, I realized that food and nutrition myths are created and resurrected, even in the face of persistent scientific evidence, because many people prefer to contemplate the too-good-to-be-true possibilities even when instinct tells them they're fiction. Scientific, proven facts are dull and boring, with results that require work and effort, while myth-information is glamorous, easy to obtain, and instantaneous! I find it ironic that it's often the same people who chastise patients in the bariatric surgery process for "taking the easy way out" who have no insight into their own investments in "quick-fix miracle" foods or nutrition plans.

Recommendations for a balanced (individualized) diet, adequate fluids and sleep, and increased physical activity just aren't as exciting as some of the empty promises wrapped in shiny packaging. Maybe it's easier to believe that "eating healthy is too expensive" than to actually sit down, budget your food dollars, and see that it actually isn't. Facts are easy to check, but readiness to change, personal accountability, and lifestyle changes take consistent effort and persistence over time. Whether a person believes a nutrition myth and eventually accepts the truth, or begins with the facts, most people ultimately end up on the same path toward sustained health. I will continue to work with people who choose that path and seek guidance, even though it's much harder and gleams with sweat instead of glitter.

Resources

Bennie, Maureen. "Gluten Free/Dairy Free Diet for Autism: My Experience." Autism Awareness Centre Inc. February 9, 2017. https://autismawarenesscentre.com/my-experience-with-the-gfcf-diet/.

"Healthy Cooking Oils." American Heart Association. Last modfied April 24, 2018. http://www.heart.org/en/healthy-living/healthy-eating/eat-smart/fats/healthy-cooking-oils.

Kimball, Molly. "Protein Primer: How Much We Need, Why We Need It, How to Get It." *The (New Orleans) Times-Picayune*. October 2, 2018. https://www.nola.com/healthy-eating/2018/10/protein_primer_how_much_we_nee.html.

"Learn about the Benefits in 5 Minutes: Cacao Polyphenols and Cacao Protein." Meiji. Accessed September 29, 2018. https://www.meiji.co.jp/chocohealthlife/en/efficacy/.

"Nutrition Fact or Fiction." UCLA Center for Human Nutrition. Accessed September 29, 2018. https://www.uclahealth.org/clinical nutrition/nutrition-fact-or-fiction.

Piwowarczyk, Anna, Andrea Horvath, Jan Łukasik, and Hania Szajewska. "Gluten- and Casein-Free Diet and Autism Spectrum Disorders in Children: A Systematic Review." *European Journal of*

Nutrition 57, no. 2 (March 2018): 433–40. https://doi.org/10.1007/s00394-017-1483-2.

Wolfram, Taylor. "Coconut Water: Is It What It's Cracked Up to Be?" Academy of Nutrition and Dietetics. Last modified July 2017. https://www.eatright.org/food/nutrition/healthy-eating/coconut-water-is-it-what-its-cracked-up-to-be.

A Rainbow of Herbal Health

by Autumn Damiana

One of the most popular health trends right now is to "eat the rainbow." What this means is that as long as you have at least four or five colors of food on your plate, you will get a variety of vitamins and minerals and therefore have enough nutrients in your diet to be healthy. This "eat the rainbow" phrase is especially prevalent in schools and among those with children, because the idea is that if you promote healthy eating at an early age, it will carry over into adulthood as children mature and begin making healthy choices for themselves. The "color" theory of eating is not a bad one, as it is usually fresh fruits and vegetables that help make up the color eating palette. However,

there is new evidence to support the idea that herbs and spices can also be part of this strategy.

Food scientists, doctors, nutritionists, and dieticians are investigating the health benefits of herbs and spices. These were once thought to contribute little in the way of nutrition, because they existed simply to flavor or visually enhance different foods. And yet, even that has become a recognized health benefit, because adding many different herbs and spices to food will, in fact, make food healthier because you can cut down on sugar, fat, and other empty calories without losing taste. Although herbs and spices are often eaten in small quantities, adding them often to meals will make them effective over time as more and more are ingested.

Polyphenols and Antioxidants

All plants, including herbs and spices, contain nutrients called phytochemicals. **Polyphenols** are a group of over five hundred phytochemicals recognized for their health benefits, mostly because they have antioxidant properties. Polyphenols are also responsible for giving plants their color. Herbs and spices, especially if they are dried, have high levels of polyphenols when compared with fruits and vegetables, because drying causes the polyphenols to become concentrated. Antioxidant-rich foods have long been known to have anti-inflammatory, anticancer, and antimicrobial properties, as well as the ability to improve certain conditions, like asthma, diabetes, and high cholesterol.

There have been few studies done on the overall effects of herbs and spices as they relate to health, since they are usually consumed on such a small level. Some herbs and spices, however, are receiving a lot of media attention because of their healing properties. For example, the capsaicin found in red chilies, chili powder, and paprika is said to be effective for weight loss. Curcumin, which is the active component of the yellow spice turmeric, is being touted as a miracle food because of its anti-inflammatory action on arthritis and chronic pain. All green herbs contain chlorophyll, which is loaded with vitamins and minerals and is thought to purify the blood. And let's not forget the purple flower echinacea, which wards off colds and flu and stimulates the immune system. Just like with fruits and vegetables, herbs and spices of various colors, when combined, will contribute to overall health. Here is a short list of the rainbow of herbs and spices available:

Pink/Red: Cayenne, chilies/chili pepper, hibiscus, paprika, rose, saffron, sumac

Orange/Yellow: Asafoetida, calendula (pot marigold), cumin, dandelion, fenugreek seeds, mace, turmeric

Green: Too many to name here; some examples are basil, bay, chives, cardamom, cilantro, dill, fennel, green onions, lemon verbena, mint, oregano, parsley, rosemary, sage, tarragon, thyme

Blue/Black: Cornflower, juniper berries, nigella seeds, poppy seeds

Purple: Echinacea (coneflower, different from "cornflower" above), lavender, purple basil, purple sage, violets

Brown: Allspice, cinnamon, cloves, nutmeg, star anise, tons of others

White: Chamomile, garlic, ginger, horseradish, jasmine, sesame seeds, sweet woodruff

Multicolored: Mustard (yellow, black, brown), pansies (pink, red, orange, yellow, blue, purple, white), peppercorns (pink, green, black, white), salt (pink, red, blue, black, white, even gray!), tea leaves (green, black, white)

Get the Most Benefit from Herbs and Spices

Herbs and spices can be used dried or fresh. Dried are more concentrated in flavor—a general rule is that one teaspoon of dried herbs and spices is equal to one tablespoon fresh. The general shelf-life for dried herbs and spices is one to three years: usually one or two for ground or chopped and two or three for whole. Dried herbs and spices never spoil, but over time they do lose aroma, flavor, and (theoretically) nutritional value, so buy accordingly and date/label the jars. Because whole spices last longer than ground ones, it is a good idea to grind them yourself. This can be done using a spice grinder, a coffee grinder, or even a mortar and pestle. I personally recommend that you to invest in a good Microplane or other similar small grater. They are easy to clean and can be used on anything from cinnamon and nutmeg to garlic and ginger (as well as citrus zest, hard cheese, chocolate, etc.).

Fresh herbs taste wonderful and can really elevate a dish from ho-hum to *wow*. Sometimes the fresh herb is one of the main ingredients itself—for example, what would margherita pizza or caprese salad be without basil? In addition to flavor, scent, color, and texture, fresh herbs do add nutrients to any meal for the simple reason that they are, well . . . vegetables. The same is true of edible flowers. While these are often used for decoration or color (think candied violets or rose petal lemonade) they also have nutritional value. Growing your own herbs can be a fun and worthwhile pursuit, but if this is not an option, then you can maximize the health benefits from fresh herbs in other ways. Try to get herbs, just like vegetables, when they are in season and are at the peak of both freshness and flavor. Opt for locally grown herbs whenever possible. Often the region's culinary heritage determines the herbs being grown in the area, like cilantro and oregano for Mexican cuisine.

Regardless of what fresh herbs you use, try to plan your meals around them, because they will fade fast, even in the refrigerator. Keep your fresh herbs in the "high humidity" drawer, where you would also keep lettuce. Put them in a plastic bag with a napkin or paper towel, which will soak up the condensation, and change this often or the herbs will rot. When the herbs start to wilt, they can still be used as long as they are not yellow, brown, or slimy. To preserve the herbs, lay them on a cookie sheet and freeze them, and then transfer them to a container you can keep in the freezer. As an alternative, you can pack an ice tray with chopped fresh herbs, fill it with water, and then freeze it. The resulting herb ice cubes can be put in a plastic bag until you want to thaw them for use. Keep in mind that freezing most herbs will change their composition, rendering them limp or mushy, but they will retain their flavor.

Tea Blends

Tea usually starts with white, green, or black tea leaves. However, herbal tea combinations exclude the tea leaf altogether and use only noncaffeinated ingredients, like herbs, spices, flowers, and fruit. Whatever your tea preferences, you can easily create your own blends. Start with a common base, such as tea leaves, mint, or chamomile, and then add in a complimentary herb or spice, such as ginger, hibiscus, or lavender. From there you can keep building layers of flavor, color, and complexity.

It's best to use dried or dehydrated ingredients in your tea blends because they have more concentrated flavors that are unlocked when you add them to water and brew the tea. To become more adept at making your own blends, taste each ingredient on its own and become familiar with the flavor so you can figure out what pairs well with what. One readily available blend I enjoy is spicy chai, containing green cardamom, black tea, brown cinnamon and clove, white ginger, and multicolored peppercorns; another is the lightly floral Evening Repose, made from pink rose petals, green lemon verbena and peppermint, blue cornflowers, purple lavender, and white chamomile.

Ramen "Hacks"

Look up this phrase online and you will be inundated with recipes, instructions, and ideas on how you can elevate the lowly instant ramen noodle into something more palatable or even delicious. This can be really important for anyone who is on a budget and needs to get by sometimes with this cheap meal option. The herb and spice suggestions will not only impart a better flavor, but they will also add some much needed nutrition if you include a variety. This is a DIY meal: there are so many protein, vegetable, sauce, and seasoning variations, that it's impossible to give a real recipe. So here are some of the best herb and spice options for you to try:

Red: Chili flakes (crushed red pepper) or chili powder

Orange/Yellow: Cumin (powder or seeds)

Green: Cilantro (fresh or dried), chives (best used fresh), green onion flakes, tarragon (dried)

Blue/Black: Poppy seeds

Brown: Cinnamon (use sparingly), star anise (add whole to the broth—gives it a Chinese five spice flavor)

White: Garlic powder, ginger (grated, which is very strong, or powdered), onion powder, sesame seeds

Multicolored: Basil (any varietal fresh or dried), peppercorns/pepper (any color), salt (use garlic or celery salt, or try something gourmet, like Himalayan pink or French gray)

Go easy adding your herbs and spices (especially salt) if you are using any of the enclosed ramen seasoning packet. If you would like to skip the seasoning packet all together, that's even healthier. Plain, unflavored ramen is like a blank canvas that on which you can paint any colors and flavors you like.

Moong Dal with Panch Phoran

This is adapted from a simple vegetarian Indian recipe that tastes wonderful and satisfies even a meat-and-potatoes kind of person like my husband. It uses hulled and dried split mung beans (*moong dal*) as its base, but whole or sprouted mung beans will work, or you can substitute lentils of your choice.

Panch phoran, sometimes called "Indian five spice," is the real star of this dish. You can make it yourself by combining equal parts of these seeds: yellow cumin and fenugreek, green fennel, brown mustard, and black nigella. (Just so you get the right spice, nigella is also called *kalonji* in India. In English-speaking countries, it goes by a number of misleading names.) Funky, skunky, sulfuric yellow asafoetida is traditionally used in this recipe, and if you are feeling brave, I highly recommend that you try it. Once cooked, it has a really deep, complex umami flavor, and I don't think the moong dal recipe tastes nearly as good without it. Look for it labeled as *hing powder.* The recipe also calls for orange turmeric and optional red saffron-flavored rice.

Moong Dal

1 cup mung beans (or lentils)

¾ teaspoon salt

3 cups cold water

2 teaspoons ghee (or use vegetable oil)

¼ teaspoon asafoetida (or substitute garlic powder and onion powder mixed together to make ¼ teaspoon)

½ teaspoon panch phoran

1 large tomato, peeled, seeded, and chopped

¼ teaspoon turmeric

In a bowl, rinse the beans well and pick out discolored grains. Drain in a strainer and put into a pot with the salt and water. Stir to mix and bring to a boil. Reduce heat to low and simmer as per bean (or lentil) package directions.

Stir occasionally, especially near the end, to prevent sticking. When the beans are almost done, heat the ghee in a small pan over medium-high heat. Add the asafoetida and panch phoran. Stir until the spices sizzle and pop, about 30 seconds. Add the tomato and turmeric. Mash the mixture together with a wooden spoon to puree.

After 3 minutes, add the tomato mixture to the cooked beans. Simmer for a few more minutes. Serve over bowls of saffron rice (or use turmeric to flavor the rice, which will compliment the recipe). You can also eat the moong dal with naan or pita.

DIY
and
Crafts

Crafts in the Name of the Rose

≈ by Diana Rajchel ≈

Perhaps it's a bit cheesy, but my favorite flower is the rose. Everything about it delights me, from the flower's history to its fragrance. Learning ways to extend the life of this enjoyment led me from easy-to-make beauty products to arts and crafts. The following crafts are all suggestions for ways to continue the joy of the rose—whether it's the scent, the texture, or simply a reminder of a beautiful day. Not all are simple, but all are well worth the effort if you love roses.

Rose Beads

Most Catholics know about the rosary, a beaded string with a crucifix that is both an expression of faith and a tool of prayer. The earliest of these prayer chains came from beads made of rose petals, crafted by devoted nuns. The original process for making the beads was arduous—after the petals were dried, nuns ground the petals into clay by hand. Now, thankfully, we have blenders and stovetops to ease the process. You will need:

1 cup rose petals

Pot

Frying pan (optional)

Strainer

Blender

Wooden spoon

Cheese cloth or coffee filter

Rose fragrance oil if you wish for the beads to retain the rose scent (optional)

Toothpicks

Parchment paper or wax paper

Cookie sheet

Metal cooling rack in grid form, slightly smaller than the cookie sheet

White glue

Small paintbrush

Place the rose petals in a pot and pour enough water over them to cover them. Gently simmer over low heat until the petals appear translucent. Remove from heat and allow to cool to room temperature. Once cooled, strain the roses (you may wish to set aside the resulting tea for home beauty or fragrance products) and transfer the petals to the blender. Blend into a paste, adding water if needed. The resulting mixture will appear runny. To form beads, it needs a clay-like consistency. You can speed the drying process a small amount by lightly frying the rose petal mix over low heat to encourage evaporation. Even after this, it can still take about a day for enough water to dissipate from the rose petal mix.

When ready to leave the mix to dry, place a coffee filter over your strainer, and place the strainer inside the cooled pan used to boil rose petals. Pour the mixture over the filter. Leave to dry overnight. The remaining water should have dripped to the bottom. The mixture should feel and behave like clay.

Rose petals lose their fragrance in the cooking process—if you want fragrant beads, at this point you may wish to add a few drops of a rose-scented oil or spray.

Preheat your oven to the lowest setting (usually 200°F).

Set the drying rack on top of the cookie sheet and lay the parchment paper on top of the rack.

Also, grab a dish towel for your hands, as this process gets messy. Take a dime-size amount of clay and roll it into a ball. If it can't hold its shape, it needs longer to dry. Slide this ball onto the toothpick. Place the toothpick with the shaped bead onto the rack, piercing the parchment paper. Repeat, placing beads about two or three grid squares apart.

Place the filled rack in your oven at the lowest heat setting and allow to dry for four to six hours. When you remove the beads, they may still feel soft. You can reshape them slightly so that they are rounder or more the desired shape. Allow them to air dry overnight, under a fan if possible.

The new beads can still melt in water, so it's good practice to add an element of water resistance. When firm to the touch and still on the toothpick, paint each bead with white glue. Standard Elmer's glue dries clear. You may also want to mix a few drops of scented oil into the glue for extra fragrance. When finished, leave the beads to dry overnight again.

When the rose beads are fully dry, gently remove them from the toothpicks. If a hole feels too small, you can poke around with the toothpick to widen the pathway for any string. They are ready for your next bead project!

Rose Petal Potpourri Vacuum Powder

Aromatherapy methods such as candles and incense have long since usurped potpourri and sachets. Even so, none of them do what a good powder can do: eliminate bad odors while leaving a nice one behind. You can enjoy the lovely fragrance of rose petals and more while removing that smelly dust and dirt. Once you stir your ingredients, all you need do is shake it on the carpet or couch and vacuum it along with the debris. Both your carpet and your vacuum end up smelling better because of it! You will need:

1 cup dried rose petals

Coffee grinder

Glass bowl

½ cup cornstarch or arrowroot powder

½ cup baking soda

Essential oil (optional)

Old spice jar with a shaker top

Make sure your coffee grinder is clean and dry. Pack in as many dried rose petals as possible; grind them into a fine powder. You may need to dump out the petals and regrind a few times periodically, adding further petals. When powdered, pour the rose petal powder in the glass bowl and mix thoroughly with cornstarch and baking soda. If desired, add up to 5 drops of your favorite essential oil. Do not exceed 5 drops—you do not want oil stains on your carpet! Scoop or funnel the mixture into the old spice jar and close the lid tight. Make sure you label the jar. When ready to use, sprinkle this on carpets and furniture before vacuuming, or even toss a pinch on your mattress when you change the sheets on your bed.

Pressing Flowers
The following crafts combine the art of pressed flowers, the art of decoupage, and the love of books into one. Whether you simply want to beautify a reading experience—or you need a way to prove the copies of Sandman comics your sibling always borrows belong to you—this simple craft adds a bit of Victorian delight to one of the most pleasurable of introvert experiences.

To press the roses, strip the petals from the rose. Place a wax sheet inside the book and spread the rose petals evenly over the page in one layer. Place a second wax sheet on top of the petals and close the book. You can do this over several pages. While usually the weight of the book is enough to press the petals flat, you may wish to stack a few books on top of the first. Leave the book in a cool, dry place for a week. At the end of the week, you can remove the sheets and flowers. It's recommended you use the pressing book as storage until ready to apply the flowers in the next medium.

Pressed Flower Book Plates

> 2 × 2-inch or larger square adhesive blank labels
>
> Calligraphy pen or marker
>
> Dried pressed rose petals
>
> Scissors or pen knife

To make the book plates, write your book dedication on the label using the calligraphy pen or marker. Place the rose petals around the text. You may want to trace the border with stick glue to hold them in place. Apply the packing tape over top of the label—you may need to use one or two strips. When you're ready to place the book plate in your book, take scissors or the pen knife and cut around the edges of the packing tape. Peel the label and stick it inside your book!

Pressed Flower Bookmarks

> Dried pressed rose petals
>
> Blank index cards cut in half longways
>
> Packing tape
>
> Scissors or a pen knife

Arrange a few of the flattened rose petals on the cardstock strips. Measure out the packing tape so that it extends about ¼ inch beyond the edge of the index card. Place the tape over top of the petals and run your fingers down the length of the card to further flatten the petals.

Carefully fold the tape back over the back edges of the bookmark and use the scissors or pen knife to trim away any excess.

Preserved Roses

Often people want to save wedding bouquets or other flowers as mementos of special occasions. You can do more than just make a rose to keep in a box; preserved roses make wonderful Christmas ornaments, additions to door wreaths, or focal points in shadow boxes.

Traditionally, flowers are air-dried and then sprayed with a preservative or dipped in wax. In modern times, glycerin and silica gel are also popular preserving options. A lesser known option—because it is trickier—is crystalizing roses by suspending the flowers in a borax solution.

Of these options, the traditional wax preservation is probably the best. You do not need to use petroleum-made paraffin wax—any white-colored wax can work as a rose preservative, and soy wax or beeswax is recommended. You will need the following:

Parchment paper

Cookie sheet

Double boiler fashioned from a deep pot and a coffee can

Wax

Candy thermometer

Fresh or dried roses (fresh is easiest)

Lay the parchment paper over the cookie sheet and set them next to the double boiler on your stove.

Pour water in the base pot and place the wax in the coffee can. Clip the candy thermometer in the wax. Melt enough wax to cover the entire flower bloom when dipped. Do not allow the wax temperature to exceed 150°F. Dip the bloom into the wax and immediately remove it; allow the wax to drip back into the wax pot. Gently lay the rose on the parchment paper and move on to the next flower. When finished, allow the waxed flowers to dry and cool. Then, holding by the blossom (or using tongs if you prefer), dip the stem end into the wax.

You may need to trim the stems to fit the pot. When finished, lay the rose back on the parchment paper and allow to dry.

When cooled and ready, pack them in boxes in between cotton batting and wax paper until ready for display.

A dozen roses are a dozen opportunities to make more beauty. Whether you want to grind up the petals and scatter them on your carpets or dip them in wax and give them away as keepsakes, you now have both a generous gift of love—and new methods of continuing to share that love.

Aquaponics: Fish and Garden at the Same Time

⤙ by JD Hortwort ⤚

Do you remember, as a child, growing a sweet potato vine from a tuber, carefully suspended in a glass jar? The spud was delicately dangled about halfway in water, held up by toothpicks poked horizontally in its sides. You probably didn't realize you were experimenting with hydroponics.

Perhaps you tried your hand at raising goldfish or brightly colored neon tetras as your first pets. If so, you were dabbling in aquaculture.

If you combine these two concepts, you have a bright new idea—aquaponics. According to Peg Godwin at the North Carolina Cooperative Extension, "aquaponics is defined as a food production system using the recycling of fish wastes to provide nutrients to support plant growth. The system has two products: fish and plants." You might be old enough to remember a novelty gift from the 1980s—a decorative large glass vase with a Siamese fighting fish circling in the water. A peace lily (*Spathiphyllum*) was the plant of choice suspended overhead, held in a mesh basket at the top of the vase, roots dangling in the water. This is a very small example of an aquaponics system.

The History

Actually, calling aquaponics "new" is a bit deceptive. It's a new concept in the modern agricultural community, but it's not new to the world. Land-based aquaponics systems were known to Central American natives and Asian cultures that used systems of canals fed by nearby rivers to irrigate their various crops. If you're letting water in from a river or stream, it's bound to have fish in it.

The waste produced by the fish nourished the surrounding crops. As for the folks who worked the fields, did they eat the fish that were wiggling around their legs? Of course they did! They might not have bragged about their skills in aquaponics, but they had a hearty dinner each night. When efforts were made to move these farming practices from canals to self-contained water systems, aquaculture and hydroponics parted ways for a while.

The concept of controlled hydroponics is a bit more modern. It first emerged in the 1930s as researchers began growing plants in water, gravel, rock wool, perlite or some other loose material (anything but soil) while supplementing with nutrients via drip irrigation or frequent drenches.

Enterprising farmers and researchers combined the two ideas in the 1980s and aquaponics was born.

In Practice

My first encounter with this intriguing idea was when I learned about a young man in my area who wanted to get into growing crabs commercially. As a business reporter for a local newspaper located four hours from the coast, I must say I was curious and maybe just a bit amused.

But as the young entrepreneur explained his plan to me, I was amazed. A recently discharged military serviceman, he had come home with a Southeast Asian bride. As they shared their cultures, he learned that her family farmed a special type of crab in the Indonesian islands. I believe it was the black or mud crab, *Scylla serrata*.

This crab grows quickly to an extraordinary size, larger than North American crabs. Not only is this crab content to live in a contained aquaculture system, it is said to be very tolerant of high nitrate and ammonia levels in the water.

According to my young businessman, it reaches a mature, marketable size in roughly six months, a fraction of the time it takes an Atlantic crab to get to the same size. Foodies were just beginning to discover its delicate flavors, he said. At the time I was working on the article, the meat could sell for upwards of twenty dollars per pound.

Obviously, he couldn't grow South Sea crabs outdoors in Piedmont North Carolina. This businessman had found a vacant warehouse. He intended to set up commercial tanks inside with climate controls. He had the aquaculture part of this down pat.

To generate money while the crabs were growing, he planned to grow salad greens for area restaurants. These would float in special trays in the crab ponds. Most salad greens come to maturity in six weeks. With coordinated schedules, he expected to harvest crabs at least three times a year and salad greens pretty much continuously all year long.

Aquaponics is a self-sustaining form of agriculture that combines plant and fish cultivation. As of 2018, the largest commercial aquaponics operation in the US was in North-field, WI, where operators expect to harvest 30,000 heads of lettuce daily and 160,000 pounds of fish annually.

Sadly, his backing fell through before his dream came to fruition. That doesn't mean the idea isn't very doable, even if you only want to produce fish and plants for your immediate family.

How It Works

I once heard a joke in which one person asked where the superhero Aquaman went to the bathroom. Fortunately, the conversation took a turn before the discussion got too graphic. But it does raise an important point central to aquaponics.

Fish, like all animals, have to relieve themselves in the very water they swim in. Why don't they die in a toxic sludge?

According to researchers, fish can survive due to the volume of water and a complex relationship between them, plants, and the beneficial bacteria in the water. This relationship works even in standing water, such as in ponds or enclosed bay areas. A simple explanation of what happens goes like this:

A key component of all animal waste is **ammonia**. Land animals excrete this in urine in ways I'm sure everyone is familiar with. Fish excrete ammonia through their gills. Once in the water, bacteria eventually turn ammonia into **nitrates**. Plants use nitrates. In a balanced, natural setting, the nitrates are mostly used up by plants on stream banks or pond shores or by plants living in the water. When everything is in balance, this is a perfect setup.

When it gets out of hand, we see algae bloom and overgrowth on the banks at water's edge. You have probably seen a farm pond covered over with a green coat of algae and scum. But let's not dwell on the negative. When the system works, fish produce a by-product that can be used by plants and we, as humans, can be the beneficiaries.

Do It Yourself

Aquaponic systems come in all shapes and sizes. My entrepreneurial friend was interested in building long troughs that would have plant trays floating on top while his crabs matured in recirculated water below. That's why he wanted to rehabilitate an old warehouse that had plenty of light and plenty of space.

Some large systems maintain the fish in a separate container and pump the water through nearby stacks of plant trays. For a time, our local community college taught aquaponic classes that used large tubs, roughly forty inches tall and about eight feet across. I discovered this while working on a different business article. In this setup, the plants removed the nitrates they needed for growth. The water was filtered to remove any impurities that might harm the fish. It was then sent back into the fish container.

Obviously, this can be done on a large enough scale to become a half- or full-time business or just large enough to keep a family stocked in produce and fresh fish.

However, there is a simple way for a homeowner to benefit from aquaponics, and it doesn't entail a huge vat of fish. It involves a ten-gallon fish tank, a soil-less growing medium, a plant tray, and small produce sets or seeds. In this case, you'll be enlisting the fish as laborers to provide most of the nutrients your plants will need to grow. I suppose you could eat the fish, but they probably wouldn't even make a mouthful after cleaning and gutting them. Better to head to your local sushi restaurant if you have a hankering for raw fish.

To develop this project, I started with the instructions from an industry journal and modified them to fit my goals.

The first task is to set up your fish tank.

For the fish tank:

10-gallon tank

Enough fish tank gravel to create a 2–3-inch thick layer at the bottom of the tank

Water pump that moves roughly 75 gallons of water per hour. This is a little larger than what you would need if you were just sitting up a fish tank because it has to pump water up and into the plant bed.

4 feet of plastic tubing that will fit onto your water pump

Small fish (no more than 10)

Set the fish tank up according to the instructions. Wash the gravel before putting it into the tank. Nothing says you can't also put any decorative items into the fish tank, like plastic plants or little underwater castles. It won't interfere with the production of produce, and the fish might like the diversion.

Fill the tank with water. My father was an amateur fish hobbyist with a 20-gallon tank. He always advised letting the water set for 24 hours before adding fish.

Attach the plastic tubing to the water pump and nestle it into the bottom of the tank. One source recommends using an air pump to aerate the water, but most of my sources didn't. Whenever my father set up his tank, sometimes he used an air pump; sometimes he didn't. I opted to go without.

Now it's time to take care of your plants.

For the plants:

Plant tray

Soilless medium like perlite or vermiculite. I've tried growing plants in pea gravel but I find it too heavy.

Plants grown in a soilless mix. You can purchase plants grown in soil, but you will need to wash the soil away, thoroughly cleaning the roots, and reset the plant in your soilless mixture.

The plant tray should be a couple of inches wider than your fish tank and just a little shorter in length. It will balance on top of the tank. It should be at least 6 inches deep. To be safe, wash it thoroughly before you begin.

Before adding the growing medium, measure 3 inches in from each side of the tray. Drill multiple holes with a ⅛ bit into the bottom of the tray. The bottom should look like a colander with a solid 3-inch border all around. This will allow water to drain back into the fish tank without running outside the tank. On one end of the tray, measure up at least 3 inches from the bottom and drill a hole big enough to accommodate the plastic tube you attached to the fish tank water pump.

Thread the tube into the plant tray. The tube should loop like a long U shape, running to the end of the plant tray and back up to where it starts. If the tube is too long, cut it back to fit. Bend the end of the tube over and use a small alligator clip or strong rubber band to keep it crimped. Notice where the tube comes into the tray. Beginning about 10 inches from that point, carefully make a hole in the tube about every 2 inches. This is how the water will be feed into the plant tray. The water will flow back into the fish tank through the holes you drilled in the bottom of the tray.

Set the plant tray on top of the tank and fill with the soil-less mix. Run your system for a day to make sure nothing leaks. Then you can add the fish and plant your tray. The number of plants will depend on the type of plant. Lettuce plants can grow closely together, spaced about 2 inches apart. Herbs will need more space, approximately 4 inches apart.

Monitor the system daily. Over time, you will need to add water because the plants will take up some. Harvest will take a little time, but you should be ready for your first salad in about 4–6 weeks!

Plant and Fish Varieties

What kind of plants can you grow in an aquaponic garden? Just about any kind you can imagine. For this fish tank aquaponics project, it's best to stick to small produce like lettuce, spinach, and other greens. For herbs, try chives, basil, parsley, dill, and savory. From my experience, it's best to stay away from herbs that like especially well-drained, low-humidity conditions like rosemary, sage, or ground cover thymes.

The fish you grow can be varied as well. I prefer goldfish, but koi are perfect for this project. You can also use zebra fish, guppies, or my father's favorite, neon tetras—really any freshwater fish you find at your local pet store will thrive in an aquaponics system.

Common Pitfalls

As with any gardening project, I have to caution people not to assume this is a hands-off endeavor.

You have to monitor the system. This means testing the water periodically to manage the pH levels and to control for possible bacterial infections. If you purchase plant sets from a nursery, it is still possible to accidentally contaminate your system.

Filters need cleaning and changing from time to time. This is especially critical in small systems like our fish tank. Periodically, you will need to break down and clean the system, doing so with gentle cleaners that won't harm the fish.

Your plants will get the necessary nutrients from fish waste but you still have to feed to fish! This should be done daily.

A small, ten-gallon aquaponic fish tank is usually set up indoors in a home or classroom, so climate control probably isn't a problem, especially for the fish. What will become a problem is light quality. Even salad greens need sufficient light to grow in the winter or in low-light conditions. You may find it necessary to add a plant light over your indoor garden.

Disease and insect control on the plants shouldn't be a problem either. However, should that come up, treat plants early with an organic control approved for use around fish. For example, a mild soap insecticide will take care of aphids with little danger of harm to the fish. A control like neem oil is safe for plants but could be harmful to the fish, so read labels before you apply anything.

Aquaponics Supplies and Resources

You can buy most of the items for a small fish tank aquaponics project at any garden center or big box department store. Farm supply stores can be another beneficial resource.

In North Carolina, our cooperative extension service has put a lot of resource material out there for small and large aquaponics operations. These can be accessed at ces.ncsu.edu. Or you can explore what is available at your own extension office by going to outreach.usda.gov/USDALocalOffices.htm and clicking on "USDA Cooperative Extension System Offices."

Finally, as with most industries, there is an association for that. In this case, you will find information at the Aquaponics Association website aquaponicsassociation.org. This can lead you to other state and regional organizations.

Aquaponics can be a fun project for students or for those like the elderly who can't get out to garden as much as they might like. For the rest of us, not only is aquaponics a self-sustaining form of agriculture, it's a great way to extend the growing season throughout the year.

Selected Resources

Bradley, Kirsten. "Aquaponics: A Brief History," *Milkwood* (blog), January 20, 2014. https://www.milkwood.net/2014/01/20/aquaponics-a-brief-history/.

Nelson, Rebecca. "Build a Mini Aquaponic System." Nelson Pade. Accessed September 17, 2018. https://aquaponics.com/build-a-mini-aquaponic-system/.

Sawyer, Tawnya. "Aquaponics: Growing Fish and Plants Together." Colorado Aquaponics. Accessed March 15, 2019. Slideshow, 72 slides. https://www.scribd.com/document/351734340/Tawnya-Aquaponics-Intro#fullscreen&from_embed.

All the Thyme in the World

by Mickie Mueller

Thyme is an herb that seems so simple and unassuming, doesn't it? This is a very common kitchen herb with a very interesting history and a rich amount of options for irresistible puns as well, so apologies for that. You can purchase this herb just about everywhere—even the smallest grocery store stocks thyme. Its savory flavor is a basic staple in roasted dishes, and it's included in simmering pots of soups and stews nearly as often as we find salt and pepper. Thyme plays along in harmony in jars of Italian herb blends and the French classic blend *herbs de Provence*. It's one of the first herbs to appear at the garden center in the spring, and if you plant this little evergreen

perennial in the right spot in zones 5 through 9, it's likely to last year after year. In Missouri I've even harvested a bit in the dead of winter. Thyme doesn't even mind being stepped on. Many people use varieties of it in gardens between pavers, sweetening the air as people walk. Would you ever imagine that this low little ground cover has been associated with pharaohs or brave knights of old? Sometimes there's more than meets the eye, and this sweet little herb is no exception.

In ancient Rome, thyme was not just eaten with meals for its flavor, but it was also believed to be an antidote just in case a disgruntled kitchen worker decided to slip something toxic into the *domina*'s dinner. We do know that it's not a cure for all poisons, but modern research suggests that thyme does have natural food preservative properties, protecting against some forms of foodborne bacteria that can cause illness, so maybe the Romans had something there. Soaking in a tub with thyme sprigs was also a popular practice thought to protect the health of the bather from toxins either ingested or contracted elsewhere.

The protective energy of thyme was also used by both the aristocracy in Rome and its soldier classes. Thyme sprigs were sometimes carried or worn as talismans of protection and also gifted from one soldier to another as a sign of respect and an emblem of that soldier's courage in battle. The Egyptians used thyme as one of the herbs in their embalming ceremonies, inspiring bravery and offering protection to the honored dead as they journeyed through various trials in the afterlife. The idea of thyme sprigs as a symbol of bravery continued into the Middle Ages, when knights either carried it hidden within their armor or wore it visibly to represent honor, strength, and courage. Ladies would also embroider a blooming sprig of thyme and a bee onto fabric "favors" for their knights.

The folklore involving protection, healing, and strength in the face of mortality that surrounded the little thyme plant was embraced during the time of the Black Death. The plague ravaged Europe, and thyme was one of the many herbs that people carried, strewed about, and fumigated with in hopes of staving off infection or "pestilent humors" during the worst epidemic in human history.

Victorian nurses sometimes soaked bandages in thyme solutions before applying them to patients' wounds; at one point it might have been looked on as a mere folk remedy, but more and more modern research points to the herb's antiseptic properties. Thyme is also well known as being a plant associated with fairies. Fanciful children in the Victorian era must have gazed over patches of wild thyme in hopes of catching a glimpse of the revelries of little people from the fairy realm.

Thyme has a history and folklore as vibrant as its lovely green foliage. From cooking staple, to remedy, to symbol of courage, this little herb has found its way through the ages and is finally being looked at with a scientific eye. What are some ways that we can use this tiny-leafed wonder in big ways to benefit our everyday lives? Here are a few ideas I've whipped up for you.

It's Thyme to Clear the Air

Many people use incense or burn sage bundles to clear the air and raise the vibrations of their space. Sometimes it seems like we always use sage as a go-to, but there are other herbs that you can burn to purify your area, and thyme harkens back to the ancient Greeks and Romans. According to Merriam-Webster, the name *thyme* comes from the Latin and Greek words for a burnt offering or smoke. Thyme smoke creates a lovely scent and fills your space with vibes of good health, positivity, courage, and healing for your heart. It can be really fun to experiment with various herbs, and often the ones that we think of as being quite common can yield wonderful results. Years ago my husband and I ran a New Age/metaphysical shop in St. Charles, MO, and we carried a variety of herbs and resins that could be burned on a charcoal block for cleansing and purification. We still laugh about the time that we fired up a charcoal block at home and proceeded to go through every herb we could get our hands on to test the scent while burning. We found some great herbal incenses and smoked up the house significantly in the process.

Thyme Incense

To make a simple thyme incense, you can do just what we did, in moderation of course. Only use the round charcoal disks made specifically for burning indoors; never use barbecue charcoal indoors as it releases deadly carbon monoxide. You can find the safe charcoal disks at your local metaphysical shop, but you can also find them in any store that carries shisha, which is a flavored tobacco smoked in a hooka.

Simply place the charcoal disk with the depression side up in a fireproof dish that's filled with sand or gravel. I like to additionally place the dish on a trivet for extra protection against heat. Light the edge of the charcoal. It contains potassium nitrate, so it's self-igniting; orange sparks will dance across the surface. Let it heat up for about 3–5 minutes and carefully spoon ¼ teaspoon or so of thyme right into the depression. It will begin to smoke and fill your space with lovely natural incense. You can add more but take heed from the lesson my husband and I learned: add it a little bit at a time.

Incense Herb Bundle

Another wonderful way to use thyme as incense is to create a dried herb bundle. Gather up some long sprigs of thyme from your garden; about 15–20 sprigs will do. If you don't grow thyme, you can purchase packaged fresh thyme sprigs in the produce section of your supermarket. Gather the stems together and line them up so that they're even across the bottom. If you have some sprigs that are a bit short, put them in the middle of the bundle with the longer stems around the outside to hold them all together.

Using some thin cotton twine about 2 feet long, tie the bottom of the stems together, leaving about a 1-inch tail of twine on one side. Next wrap the twine going up the bundle at about ½-inch intervals, wrapping the bundle tightly as you go. When you reach the top, begin wrapping your way back down again in the same manner but in the opposite direction until you reach the bottom. Tie off the ends together.

Now don't light that just yet—it needs to dry first. Hang it up in a cool dry place or on a drying screen and forget about it for 7–10 days. Once it's dry, you'll have a nice little thyme bundle to freshen up the air and boost the energy of your space. Just light the end and fan the smoke around. You can place it in a heatproof dish. If want to extinguish it to use the rest later, just put the smoldering end into a dish of sand. You can shake out the sand once it's done burning.

Tea Thyme

Seriously couldn't resist that one. Did you know you can brew thyme leaves to make a delicious tea? According to scientific studies, this earthy tea has antioxidant, antifungal, and antiviral properties that may bring health benefits. Lots of people use it alongside regular medications to help alleviate the symptoms of cold and flu; it tastes really nice. There are several ways to make thyme tea, but the one that produces the highest antioxidant properties is powdered thyme made in a similar fashion to matcha tea. I've tried two other methods, which I'll share with you.

Thyme makes a lovely savory tea. As always, take common-sense precautions and check with your doctor or health professional before using herbal supplements, including teas. You can add other herbs and flavors to either method shared here. Cinnamon is a nice addition, and so is ginger, lemon, or a bit of fresh fruit, such as blueberries or apple slices.

Fresh Thyme Tea

To make tea from fresh thyme, simply boil 15 ounces of water and pour it over 3–5 sprigs of thyme into your cup or mug. Cover it with a plate or coaster and allow it to steep for 5 minutes and enjoy. If you prefer not to have thyme sprigs floating in your cup, you can also roughly chop the thyme and add it to a tea ball. Fresh thyme renders a delicate, fresh-flavored tea, which I enjoy quite a bit.

Dried Thyme Tea

To make tea from dried thyme, boil 1½ cups of water and put ½ teaspoon of dried thyme into a tea ball. Place it in your mug and pour 15 ounces of boiling water over it. Allow it to steep 5 minutes. Using dried thyme is handy in the winter when a lot of fresh isn't available. The flavor is different from fresh thyme: I found it to have a somewhat richer, deeper flavor.

Mini Thyme Wreath

I love hanging herbs from my little garden in my kitchen to dry. It's a handy way to have home-grown herbs at your fingertips when you can't harvest fresh, but it also looks charming on my little rack on the wall. I devised a little fancier way to display herbs just to add interest to my hanging herbs. I love the look of this mini thyme wreath. It's really very simple to make, and this beautiful thyme circlet reminds me of the history of thyme as an emblem of courage, luck, and protection to the ancients.

You'll need 12 sprigs of thyme about the same length (5 inches or so) and about 2 feet of embroidery floss or kitchen twine. You can use a floss color that matches your kitchen decor, or you can match the color of the thyme to make it blend in—the choice is yours. Gather 3 sprigs and tie them together with twine about 2 inches above the base of the sprigs, leaving about a 2-inch tail at the end of your twine. Begin wrapping the twine around the sprigs, spiraling the string as you go about 1 inch apart. Halfway up the sprigs, stop wrapping and add 3 more sprigs, working the cut ends of the new sprigs inside the growth ends of your previous ones so that the leafy part covers the cut ends of the new ones you're adding.

Continue wrapping the sprigs together tightly. Continue adding three new sprigs as you reach the halfway point of the previous ones until you get to the end. Tuck the first set of thyme sprig stems inside the last bit of leafy ends, completing a hoop, and wrap tightly. Tie the end of the twine together with the tail from where you tied the first three sprigs together in a double knot.

You can now create a little hanging loop by tying each end around a kitchen spoon handle and then sliding the handle out.

If you want it to be a rustically shaped hoop, you can hang it up right away. If you prefer it to be a nice, perfectly even circle, you can slide it around something that it fits tightly on, such as a coffee can, cylindrical oatmeal box, and so on, and allow it to dry for about 5 days until it holds it shape, and then hang it up. You can keep it as a decorative piece as long as you like. You can also eventually crumble the leaves off of the wreath on a sheet of clean paper and then bottle them for whatever use you wish and make a new wreath from fresh thyme to replace it.

Thyme Facial Cleanser

Thyme has antiseptic, antibacterial, and antimicrobial properties, and since acne breakouts are caused by bacteria and oil having a party in your pores, this knowledge can be very helpful. Some scientists in Leeds, England, did a study in which they discovered that thyme actually had a stronger effect on the acne-causing bacteria than benzoyl peroxide, which is the main ingredient in most of those over-the-counter pimple remedies that dries out our skin so much. So why not add thyme to your skincare regimen to help manage bacterial and fungal skin conditions?

- ¼ cup hot distilled water
- 1 tablespoon dried thyme
- ¼ cup honey (Up your game by using thyme honey or natural local honey.)
- 2 tablespoons liquid castile soap

Boil the water and pour over thyme in a clean coffee cup. Cover with a small plate or clean coaster. Steep the thyme in the hot water for 15 minutes.

Strain the thyme infusion through a coffee filter. Mix it in with the rest of the ingredients and pour it into a clean container.

To use, pour a small amount about the size of a quarter into your hand, gently massage it into your skin, and rinse with warm water.

Thyme Surface Cleaner

Do you still have some of that castile soap from your facial cleanser recipe? Here's another quick and easy way to combine it with the power of the simple thyme plant and use its powerful properties to clean your kitchen or bathroom.

- 2 cups distilled water (Really, use distilled to prevent the castile from leaving a buildup.)
- 1 teaspoon dried thyme
- 2 tablespoons liquid castile soap

Boil the water in a saucepan, remove from heat and add 2 teaspoons dried thyme. Cover and allow to cool, about ½ hour. Strain through a coffee filter. Add the liquid castile soap and pour the mixture into a spray bottle and label. This formula is great for cleaning your counters, wiping up spills on your stovetop, and general cleaning.

I hope this and the other ideas inspire you to consider bringing the little thyme plant into your daily life. As we've discovered, it's for more than just soup. This dainty herb has a fascinating history and is a modern-day unsung hero offering so much to humanity, including courage, cleansing, healing, spiritual offering, protection, and happiness.

Resources

Dunn, Beth. "A Brief History of Thyme." History Channel. May 10, 2013. https://www.history.com/news/a-brief-history-of-thyme.

Gomez Escalada, Margarita. "Thyme for a More Natural Cure for Acne." Leeds Beckett University. November 18, 2018. http://www.leedsbeckett.ac.uk/news/thyme-for-a-more-natural-cure-to-acne/.

Nordqvist, Christian. "What Are the Medical Benefits of Thyme?" Medical News Today. Last modified August 23, 2018. https://www.medicalnewstoday.com/articles/266016.php.

Shealy, C. Norman. *The Illustrated Encyclopedia of Natural Remedies*. Boston: Element Books, 1998.

Merriam-Webster's Online Dictionary. S.v. "thyme." Accessed January 25, 2019. https://www.merriam-webster.com/dictionary/thyme.

Ushakova, Maria. "How to Make Thyme Tea." August 1, 2017. MariaUshakova.com. https://www.mariaushakova.com/2017/08/how-to-make-thyme-tea/.

Ideas for Seasonal Decorations

≋ by Charlie Rainbow Wolf ≋

How many times have you had a wonderful idea for a decoration to go with a particular season or holiday, only to find out that you should have started several weeks ago in order to have everything you need? Maybe you've thrown something together last minute, and while everyone else thought it was awesome, you kept thinking how much better it could have been if only you'd planned ahead. With a little forethought, you can produce stunning seasonal decorations for your table and other areas, and it doesn't have to break the bank either. It only takes organization— and, in my case, the ability to actually remember what it was I'd planned to do in the first place!

Planning

Let's start with the basics. It may be off-season now, but there's absolutely no reason why you can't curl up on a cold or wet day and plan out what you hope to achieve for future festivities. My daughter depends on a bullet journal to organize her thoughts. I have a large loose-leaf binder with subject dividers. We're both avid writers, though; if you're not, you might want to go with something more simple, such as a month-at-a-glance planner or even an app for your phone or tablet. There's no wrong or right way to do this part. The main thing is that you brainstorm your ideas out of your head and into a notebook or program where you can start to organize them.

Begin by writing down the occasions you wish to celebrate and how you're planning on theming them. Is this an indoor or outdoor event? That will make a difference, because the weather is never guaranteed.

Once you have listed the experience you're making the decorations for, it's time to conceptualize what you want to do with it. Consider colors, what's going to be available at that time of year, what's within your budget, whether you'll need to obtain unusual items or enlist the help of someone else, and more. Make notes of everything that might go wrong too, so that you're able to see where backup plans are necessary. There's nothing worse than planning an elaborate outdoor Halloween decoration focused on candles and jack-o'-lanterns, only to have it rain!

Now it's time to prioritize your lists. What is most important? What's absolutely necessary to pull this off? What's merely a cool addition but not part of the fundamental piece? Look also at what you can prepare beforehand so there's not so much pressure on you when it comes to putting your decoration together. Baked goods can be frozen; flowers and herbs can be dried. You might be able to purchase end-of-season things on clearance to be incorporated at another time or even the next year. For example, decorations that are appropriate for flag-centered or patriotic holidays might be purchased at one and used for another—they are the same colors, after all. The colors of Halloween spill over into Thanksgiving, perhaps even Christmas too. If you've made your lists and have them with you, then you'll always be ready to take advantage of the seasonal sales in the shops.

So, you have your list of celebrations, and those lists are broken down into things you need to purchase or acquire and things you need to make or do. The last step in the organizational process is to work out a time frame. What do you need to do a week before? A month before? Even more in advance? If you structure these into your planner, then you'll have your reminders so that nothing gets overlooked or forgotten. Just remember to keep checking your planner.

Seeds and Plants

One of the simplest ways to know you're going to have what you need when it's time to make your centerpiece is to grow it yourself! Obviously, you won't be able to plant a sapling and gather a bountiful harvest the same year, but it is possible to grow seasonal items such as herbs and flowers for future use. If you have a larger plot of land, think about making a raised bed dedicated to your decorations. Even if you live in an apartment or are unable to get out and garden, growing things in bags of potting soil or in pots on the windowsill isn't beyond reach.

Some grow-your-own ideas might be peppermint for Christmas, pumpkins and squash for Halloween or Thanksgiving, and daffodil bulbs for spring and Easter. These all have very different growing habits and their own needs. Mint creeps, but it's possible to contain it in a windowsill pot if needed. Pumpkins and squash are sprawling vines and need quite a lot of space. Daffodils are bulbs; they're planted in the autumn for the following spring but can be force grown indoors in pots.

Check what is available in your area and keep an eye on clearance. Often the companies marketing the seeds and bulbs—and trees and bushes, for that matter—sell them off at the end of the season for a fraction of their original price. This is all the more reason to have your planner handy; you never know what you might find on your travels. I've plopped many a five-dollar tree in a little postage stamp of land we lovingly call "the orchard." Yes, I've had to wait a year or three for maturity, but I'm now rewarded with plentiful colored blooms and fruits that are welcome additions to both decorations and culinary delights.

Foraging

If you're not able to grow your own, maybe you can get outside and forage, collecting things that you wish to include in your setting. Nature's bounty makes a lovely addition to a table setting or centerpiece. In many parks and rural areas, it's possible to gather nuts, seed pods, cones, bark, fallen branches and twigs, and more. Do your research beforehand and make sure you're not collecting from a protected area.

Don't dismiss what others might consider to be a weed. One definition of a weed is a plant growing where it's not wanted, but that doesn't detract from either its beauty or its usefulness. Many so-called weeds are quite beautiful and grown as cultivated flowers in other areas. Milkweed pods, pokeweed, teasels, mullein stalks, and the hips from wild roses all make very welcome additions to topical centerpieces.

Seasonal Themes and Thoughts

This is where your planner will come in really handy, because very often you need to get started on one season's decorations weeks before that season even starts—sowing seeds in the spring for autumn's project, for example. Ideas for spring tables include seeds and other items that represent renewal and rebirth. Even plants that you've started indoors for future use might be included here, for nothing says spring like young seedlings bursting forth from the soil after the long winter's sleep.

Spring

Spring is the time for planning and planting. If you've got the area to till up a bit of soil, do this as soon as the ground is soft enough to work. The more you aerate it and add well-rotted compost, the better your plants will grow. For perennials, I like wild roses and berry bushes. The flowers of both are decorative, plus the flowers of the wild rose are also edible. The hips from the rose and the berries from the bushes make nice ingestible additives to centerpieces and place settings. If you have a dehydrator, the berries can also be dried for future use.

If your growing space is limited, look for things to start indoors. Seasonal bulbs such as daffodils and tulips might be started in plant pots and grown on windowsills. Many low-growing herbs are also suitable for indoor gardening. A fun idea might be to make a Scarborough Fair–themed piece, growing your own parsley, sage, rosemary, and thyme.

Even if you've nowhere to grow, nature will provide—although you might have to venture out into rural areas to do your gathering. The early days of spring are ideal for collecting twigs and branches to use for your future pieces. Add some sphagnum moss (available from florist suppliers) and even some seasonal fabric to make a one-of-a-kind place setting for your table.

Summer

Concepts for the longer days and warmer weather in summer embrace themes of relaxation, sunshine, and growth. The seeds that were planted in the spring are now taking hold and stretching, and that's a metaphor as well as a gardening observation! There are many wildflowers blooming at this time of year. Don't overlook things like wild rose, Queen Anne's lace, or beautiful ditch lilies when initially planning your piece. Many of the wildflowers are also edible—but some aren't, so make sure you double-check before creating an edible decoration.

Summer is often a bit of a paradox because there's a lot of outdoor work to do for the farmers and other people who depend on seasonal income, but there's also the lure of lazy days, when it's too hot to do anything but breathe and when water and picnics and outdoor recreation extend an invitation to slow down to the speed of life.

When you're planting the garden, keep an eye out for items that have more than one season. For example, gourds and squash have beautiful (and edible) summer flowers as well as the autumnal fruits. Another summer favorite that has many uses is the humble sunflower. There are dwarf varieties if your outdoor space is limited, or you can grow the traditional giants if you have the room.

Autumn

As the wheel turns into autumn, the seedlings of spring have grown through the summer and are now bearing fruit—which is perhaps another metaphor. If you planted pumpkins or squash, they'll be ready for carving into jack-o'-lanterns or making into breads and pies. Other autumnal activities that also make nice additions to centerpieces and decorations include putting up preserves and drying herbs and flowers.

One of the things we used to do on the farm was forage for the odd few cornstalks that harvest left behind and put them into stooks—bundled up and stood on end. This made a nice backdrop for other items and arrangements. Smaller versions might be placed on the table for an imposing centerpiece. Theme it with a few ears of dried corn. In the past, we've even grown the colored grains specifically to use as decoration. Keep an eye out for heirloom varieties such as big horse spotted corn, Cherokee white eagle corn, and glass gem corn, all of which belong to the flint corn species (*Zea mays* var. *indurata*).

Autumn is also the time of year when flowers that bloomed in the summer might be dried to add to your arrangements. Think of hydrangea heads or my favorites, sea holly (*Eryngium*) and globe thistle (*Echinops sphaerocephalus*). Look for vegetation in your area that is going to seed and add that abundance of texture and color to add to your theme. Even if you don't need them this year, you might want to gather some seed pods and winter them over for future additions.

Winter

It may be hard to find growing things for the colder weather, but if you've outlined everything beforehand and used your planner throughout the year, you will find you've got a plethora of items just aching to be turned into something tantalizing. Look for bark that trees may have shed, fallen twigs and small branches, cones and seeds from evergreens, and nuts from nut trees. Bushes such as holly (*Aquifoliaceae*) have evergreen leaves and bright berries that you could add to a wreath or decorative bough. Mistletoe (*Viscum album*) is another seasonal favorite. It is usually purchased, but perhaps in your locality you'll find it growing wild on a host, such as an apple.

La Noche de los Rábanos is a tradition from Oacaxa, Mexico, celebrated around December 23. Radishes and other root vegetables are carved to represent saints, animals, the nativity scene, and more. The radishes for this festival are huge and not to be eaten.

You have to plan ahead a bit for your winter flora, but it's not impossible. Here at our little smallholding, we even have hellebores that are frequently in bloom under the crabapple tree at this time of year, and of course, inside it's the time for the Christmas cactus (*Schlumbergera*) to put on its show of color. Other ideas include thyme (*Thymus vulgaris*) to accompany a traditional Yule log, or even growing some radishes to carve in the spirit of La Noche de los Rábanos for a different twist on the usual trimmings. Before we moved to the country, we used to "first foot," a tradition where the first person over the threshold of a home in the New Year would take a gift of a coin, a lump of coal, or a piece of bread. The coin represented wealth, the coal represented warmth, and the bread represented food. I would harvest herbs from my windowsill garden, herbs that resonated with plenty (thyme), health (rosemary), and success (basil), bake them into a loaf, and share the bread around the neighborhood to get the year off to a good start.

For most of us in the Northern Hemisphere, winter is the time of year when everything slows down and sleeps. Themes include rest, sharing, and finding things to occupy your time in preparation for the coming spring. Those who know me know that this is the knitting season, sat cozy by a fireside. It's possible to include pleasures like that in your table settings too. If you knit, sew, crochet, bead, paint, or whatever, consider making small tokens to go on seasonal wreaths, name cards, or place settings. Don't forget the traditional wreath, either! While usually thought of as a door decoration, with a bit of ingenuity, a wreath makes a unique and beautiful centerpiece for a table or sideboard too.

Paper Projects for All Occasions

There are several easy ways to make your own paper and so many permutations for putting it to use. You can find full instructions for homemade paper online or in *Llewellyn's 2017 Herbal Almanac*. You just need a few simple tools, most of which you can make yourself with common household items, which I recommend here.

Gather a bowl or dish, some window screen or plastic needlework canvas, an old picture frame, some kind of a blender (I got mine from the thrift store), a soft sponge (mine is a car wash sponge from the dollar discount store), and some scrap paper. Don't use the shiny kind that advertisements are often printed on. Newsprint is the best, and if you use the packing kind that hasn't been inked, that's even better. I'm not fond of adding bleach into the process so that the paper isn't dull.

Paper Additives

Once you've shredded your scrap and created the sloppy pulp needed for making paper, it's time to include interesting additives. What do you have in your garden, or what have you gathered from previous seasons to throw into your pulp and really make it ring with the occasion that this piece is going to honor? Inclusions can be fresh or dried; let your imagination run wild! It's best to introduce smaller items; you don't want your finished paper to be too lumpy and bumpy!

Consider ornamental grasses and flower petals for spring, flower petals and dandelion seeds for summer, corn husks and fallen leaves for autumn, and evergreen needles and dried spices such as cinnamon or ginger for winter. This is the time to add a drop of essential oil too, should you want your piece to be fragrant. If you plan on carrying your decoration over from one season to the next, think about putting flower seeds into your paper so that when you recycle it in the earth, they might bloom and grow for your next project. The only limitation is your imagination—although some things do work better than others! Remember to keep inclusions small and fine; you don't want great whacking lumps of vegetation in your finished paper.

Homemade Paper Decor

There are many ways to incorporate your homemade paper into seasonal decor. Garlands, paper chains, and streamers are all ideal for hanging. When it comes to your table, perhaps cut interesting shapes to add to your wreaths and centerpieces. Placecards made of your own paper and embedded with seeds make a nice gift for your guests to take home with them. It's all about creating a lasting memory—what do you want to say in the way that you create your trimmings?

Seasonal Inspiration

I hope this article has inspired you to look at what is local and readily available to you in order to plan your festive decorations. Use your imagination when it comes to what you want your centerpiece or place settings to look like, and then fuel your ideas with seasonal colors, scents, and other inclusions.

- Tie homemade paper tags with words of inspirations to a summer wreath made from grapevine, or attach them to winter boughs of evergreen branches.

- Decorate your picnic area or your Christmas tree with paper chains and hand-rolled beads.

- Arrange seeded cards on your table and let your guests take them home to plant them.

- Add some fragrant candles, a colored table cloth, some celebratory food, and you'll have an ambience that sets the mood whatever you are choosing to honor.

Your planner is your friend, and a little forethought will go a long way to creating an atmosphere that is decorative, enjoyable, and unforgettable for years to come.

Suppliers

Baker Creek Heirloom Seeds
Mansfield, MO
www.rareseeds.com

Baker Creek provides a mail-order service for rare heirloom seeds.

Seed Savers Exchange Heirloom Seeds
Decorah, IA
www.seedsavers.org

This is a seed exchange dedicated to conserving endangered plant life by collecting, saving, and sharing plant starts and seeds.

Wooden Deckle
Twin Lakes, WI
www.woodendeckle.com

The Wooden Deckle is a well established source for paper-making supplies. They also have an informative and very helpful blog.

Recommended Resources

Farmer, James T. *Wreaths for All Seasons*. Layton, UT: Gibbs Smith, 2012. A useful handbook for making wreaths throughout the year.

Neddo, Nick. *The Organic Artist: Make Your Own Paint, Paper, Pigments and Prints from Nature*. Beverly, MA: Quarry Books, 2015. This is book is full of both practical and inspirational ideas for making paper and more using what nature provides.

Norman, Edle Catharina. *Beautiful Wildflowers: Wedding Bouquets, Arrangements, and More from Nature's Seasonal Abundance*. South Portland, ME: Sellers Publishing Inc, 2014. A collection of ideas for using wildflowers in different arrangements.

Edible Art: Tricks and Tools for Mastering Centerpieces. Atglen, PA: Schiffer Publishing, 2006. This book is full of interesting ideas for making all kinds of unusual shapes and displays from fruits and vegetables.

Plant
Profiles

Plant Profiles

This section features spotlights on individual herbs, high-lighting their cultivation, history, and culinary, crafting, and medicinal uses. Refer to the key below for each plant's sun and water needs, listed in a helpful at-a-glance table.

Key to Plant Needs	
Sun	
Shade	—
Partial shade	☀
Partial sun	☀ ☀
Full sun	☀ ☀ ☀
Water	
Water sparingly	◗
	◗ ◗
Water frequently	◗ ◗ ◗

USDA Hardiness Zones

The United States is organized into zones according to the average lowest annual winter temperature, indicating a threshold for cold tolerance in the area. This USDA Plant Hardiness Zone Map uses the latest available data. For best results, plant herbs that can withstand the climate of their hardiness zone(s) and bring less hardy plants indoors during colder weather. Seek additional resources for high summer temperatures, as these can vary within zones.

It is helpful to keep track of temperatures and frost dates in your neighborhood or check with a local gardening center or university extension for the most up-to-date record. Climate change and local topography will also affect your growing space, so compensate accordingly.

US Plant Hardiness Zone Map

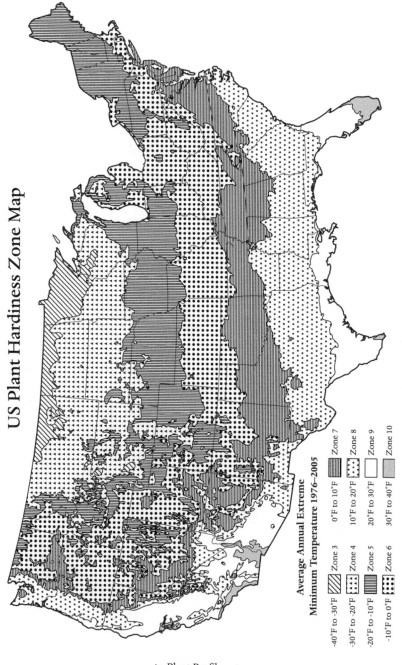

**Average Annual Extreme
Minimum Temperature 1976–2005**

-40°F to -30°F	Zone 3	0°F To 10°F	Zone 7
-30°F to -20°F	Zone 4	10°F to 20°F	Zone 8
-20°F to -10°F	Zone 5	20°F to 30°F	Zone 9
-10°F to 0°F	Zone 6	30°F to 40°F	Zone 10

US Plant Hardiness Zone Map (Cont.)

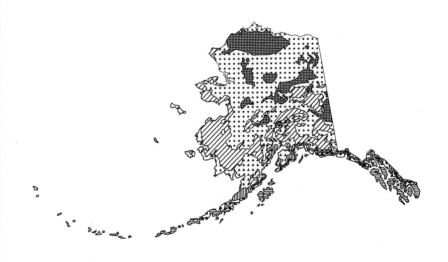

Average Annual Extreme
Minimum Temperature 1976–2005

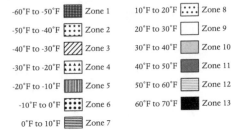

-60°F to -50°F	Zone 1	10°F to 20°F	Zone 8
-50°F to -40°F	Zone 2	20°F to 30°F	Zone 9
-40°F to -30°F	Zone 3	30°F to 40°F	Zone 10
-30°F to -20°F	Zone 4	40°F to 50°F	Zone 11
-20°F to -10°F	Zone 5	50°F to 60°F	Zone 12
-10°F to 0°F	Zone 6	60°F to 70°F	Zone 13
0°F to 10°F	Zone 7		

Lemongrass

Notext by Anne Sala Notext

When I'm grocery shopping with my children, we often linger by the cooler where the "rare to us" fruits and vegetables are stored and imagine their purpose. Lemongrass once was one of those exotic-seeming offerings, but now it has become as much a staple as carrots and potatoes.

During my research process for this almanac, I was surprised by how quickly I started to rely on lemongrass during my meal prep. For months, I had pieces of lemongrass stowed in my crisper and freezer. The longer it stayed there, the more often I used it, oftentimes to simply stand in for lemon in a recipe or just to add an extra, mysterious facet of flavor.

Lemongrass	
Species	*Cymbopogen citratus*
Zone	9–10
Needs	☼☼☼ ◑◑◐
Soil pH	5.0–8.0
Size	3–4.5 ft. tall

If I was throwing together a vegetable soup, I'd toss in a piece of lemongrass. I sliced it into simple syrups of water and sugar to make flavored soda water. While making iced tea, I'd boil the water with lemongrass before adding the teabags. Just knowing I had some lemongrass in the house made me feel as if I had a load off my shoulders.

Lemongrass's scientific name is *Cymbopogon*, which comes from the Greek description of its simple flower: *kymbe,* "boat, and *pogon,* "beard." This genus represents a family of over fifty-five aromatic grasses in the Poaceae family. They grow in tropical areas of the Asian Pacific, India, Africa, and Australia. Usually, *Cymbopogen citratus*, or West Indian lemongrass, is the one used in the kitchen. Its lemony flavor is strongest when fresh, but it can also be dried and used to make tea or added to soups and curries. It is used heavily in the cuisine from Thailand, but it also finds its way into recipes around the globe.

Its close cousin, *C. nardus*, is known as citronella grass and is used medicinally and as an essential oil to make insect repellent and perfume. Another relative, *C. martini*, is also known as palmarosa or Indian geranium, and its leaves smell of roses.

Growing Lemongrass

Growing in a clump, lemongrass is a half-hardy perennial and does not die back in tropical regions. A scallion-shaped bulb sprouts a green stalk, sometimes with a reddish-purple streak. This supports long, grayish-green, strap-like leaves that can stand as tall as four and a half feet. The leaves' texture is rather rough and the edges are sharp. In temperate climates, the grasses don't live long enough to blossom. Instead, their leaves turn rust-colored when touched by frost.

Lemongrass is a fairly easy-going plant to have in the garden, no matter the climate. It can also flourish in a pot. All it needs, in either location, is lots of sun, nutrient-rich soil, frequent waterings, and good drainage. It doesn't like to dry out, so it may need to be watered daily.

In Jerry Traunfeld's cookbook The Herbal Kitchen, *he writes he has had "no luck growing lemongrass in the Pacific Northwest." So please keep that in mind if you live near Traunfeld.*

When nighttime temperatures start to drop to about 40 degrees Fahrenheit, it is time to take the plant inside. If the lemongrass is planted in the ground, dig out a handful of the bulbs, trim the leaves and upper stem, and put them in your freezer to cook with over the winter—freezing doesn't affect the herb's flavor very much—then transplant some other bulbs to a pot and bring indoors.

Keep the pot in a sunny window and allow the plant to go dormant: reduce the amount of water it receives and cut back the grass to about four inches above the stem. In the spring, as the days get longer, new leaves will appear, and the lemongrass can be replanted outside when the threat of frost is gone.

Herbal Remedies

In Eastern cultures, this herb is well known for its culinary benefits and also for its medicinal properties. According to herbalist Jekka McVickar, evidence shows the Persians were using lemongrass medicinally since at least 1 BCE. In many areas of the world, this herb is called "fever grass" because a tea made from it will cool a fever.

Ayurvedic and Traditional Chinese Medicine practitioners also recognize lemongrass tea for its ability to relieve indigestion and menstrual cramps, lower blood pressure, treat respiratory ailments, and clear up skin infections like ringworm and scabies.

Scientific studies have proven the herb to be antimicrobial and antifungal, as well as an insect repellent. Some studies also suggest the essential oil contains an insulin-like compound that may be helpful in treating diabetes.

Despite having such a fresh scent, the aroma of lemongrass is thought to be calming and sleep inducing. Dried lemongrass leaves are often used in sleep pillows along with mugwort and lavender.

From a nutritional standpoint, lemongrass is quite beneficial. It contains vitamin A, vitamin B_1, vitamin B_2, vitamin B_3, vitamin B_6, and folate. It is also a rich in minerals such as zinc, iron, copper, potassium, and calcium.

Lemongrass Essential Oil

If your lemongrass plant grows like gangbusters over the summer, it might be fun to make an essential oil. Since there is a whole industry surrounding the extraction and use of lemongrass or citronella oil, it may seem unnecessary to learn how to make your own. However, if you're like me, when I look at a happy, healthy herb growing in my garden—and autumn is fast approaching—I want to use every last bit of it. With this method, all you really need is a crockpot and space in the refrigerator.

4–6 cups fresh lemongrass stalks (or as much as your plant produced) roughly chopped

1–3 gallons distilled water, depending on the size of the crockpot

Clean cheesecloth or hand towel

1 small blue- or amber-colored bottle with dropper cap

Ensure that the crockpot is in a stable spot where it can remain running undisturbed for 24–30 hours.

Place all the lemongrass into the crockpot. Pour enough distilled water into the crockpot to bring the level to about an inch below the top of the earthenware insert.

Place the lid on the crockpot. Some recipes suggest inverting the lid to help the steam condensation return to the pot, but I found that trick did not work well with my style of crockpot. It may work with yours, though.

Turn on the crockpot to the *high* setting and monitor the heating process. Once bubbles begin to form but the mixture isn't boiling yet, turn down the heat to the *low* setting.

Allow the lemongrass and water to simmer for about 24 hours. After that, unplug the crockpot, take off the lid, cover the crockpot with the cheesecloth or hand towel, and allow everything to cool for a few hours before placing the insert into the refrigerator overnight.

The next day, remove the crockpot from the fridge and examine its contents. You should see bits of congealed oil floating on top of what's left of the water. Scoop this oil out and place it in the small bottle, then discard the contents of the crockpot. Leave the bottle uncapped and covered with cheesecloth for about three days or more, to ensure any remaining water has a chance to evaporate. Afterward, cap the oil tightly and store in a cool, dark place.

Lemongrass Bug Repellent

After all that hard work, you might feel like hoarding the precious drops of oil you extracted, but if you are eager to put your fresh lemongrass oil to use, you can make homemade bug repellent. If you did not produce enough lemongrass oil to make the 20 drops needed in the recipe, use more drops of citronella oil to make up the difference. The vodka is optional, but it helps prolong the spray's shelf life.

Always spot test your skin's reaction to the spray before applying a large amount. Do not spray on your face, and avoid contact with eyes and mouth.

1 tablespoon witch hazel

½ tablespoon organic apple cider vinegar

½ teaspoon vodka

20 drops lemongrass essential oil

15 drops citronella essential oil

10 drops rosemary essential oil

5 drops lavender essential oil

8–12-ounce spray bottle

Distilled water

Place all ingredients in the spray bottle. Fill with distilled water. Shake vigorously before each use. Makes 1 spray bottle.

Cooking with Lemongrass

Just as lemongrass essential oil performs a distinctive role in the effectiveness of the above bug repellent, fresh lemongrass's role in the kitchen is just as remarkable.

Most cuisines have a certain ingredient combination that imparts a flavor profile, thus ensuring a dish "tastes" right—

like France's *mirepoix* of onion, carrot, and celery. According to cookbook writer Kasma Loha-Unchit, lemongrass is paired with galangal and lime leaves to create the bedrock flavor of Thai cuisine, the "Magical Three."

Loha-Unchit explains in *It Rains Fishes: Legends, Traditions and the Joys of Thai Cooking*, "Like the social Thai people, herbs like the company of other herbs, to create together wholesome harmonies in which the individual parts become almost inseparable." She goes on to explain how this "Magical Three" are the base flavors of *thom yum* soup, which is the first dish I ever had with lemongrass in it.

Another interesting tip I learned from Loha-Unchit's book is that cooks can be picky about what part of the lemongrass they use in a recipe. Even though the plant can grow over four feet tall, usually the only the bottom twelve or fifteen inches of the stalk are used in the kitchen and none of the grass "leaves." If you are making something that is going to simmer for a long time and the lemongrass piece will remain whole, use the woody, robustly flavored bottom section. If you need to mix the herb into the food and your guests will eat it, use the softer upper section of the stalk. The flavor of this part is milder, but it is easier to chop up.

Pearl Balls

This recipe is an example of when it is necessary to use the upper part of the lemongrass stalk because it will be chopped fine and eaten. If you are buying the lemongrass from a store and don't have a choice about what is on offer, just be mindful of how tough the outer layers of the lemongrass stalk can be and remove them before chopping.

1 pound ground pork

2 tablespoons garlic, minced (about 3 cloves)

¼ cup thinly sliced green onions, both the white and
   green parts

6 inches of lemongrass stalk, chopped fine

1 tablespoon ginger, peeled and chopped fine

1½ teaspoon fish sauce

1½ teaspoon light brown sugar

½ teaspoon ground black pepper

¾ teaspoon salt

1 egg, beaten

1 tablespoon chopped fresh cilantro leaves

1 cup short grain white or brown rice

Place all the ingredients except the rice into a large bowl. Use your hands or a large spoon to mix all the ingredients together. Chill in the refrigerator for about 15 minutes.

Place the rice into a small bowl.

Wet your hands, scoop out about 1½ tablespoons of pork mixture, and carefully roll it into a ball. Then gently roll the ball in the rice until it is completely covered.

After rolling, set each rice ball on a lightly oiled metal steamer or in a double bamboo steamer lined with baking paper. Leave plenty of space between the balls because the rice will expand.

Pour water into a wok large enough to hold the steamer. Turn the heat to high until the water begins to boil. Place the steamer basket in the wok and cover with the steamer's lid or with the lid of the wok. Once that is done, turn down the heat until the water is at a low, steady simmer. Steam for about an hour. Add more hot water to the wok if the level gets low.

Serve with a sweet chili dipping sauce. A simple recipe for this is to combine ½ cup Thai sweet chili sauce, ½ cup soy sauce or tamari, and a splash of rice wine—or more—to taste. Makes about 20 balls

Lemongrass and Ginger Panna Cotta

While looking through one of the cookbooks I've owned the longest, I came across a recipe for lemongrass and ginger cheesecake. Due to my son's egg allergy, I usually steer clear of this dessert; however, this recipe made me think of the "quick" cheesecakes my mother used to make with gelatin— and that made me think of panna cotta!

Below is a recipe I adapted from an exhaustive article on the chemistry behind a delicious panna cotta. I think this recipe hits the mark.

1 can (14 ounces) unsweetened coconut milk

2 cups heavy cream

5 tablespoons sugar

4 pieces lemongrass, 2–3 inches long and slightly crushed

4–5 slices of fresh ginger, ⅛-inch thick

Pinch of salt

1 teaspoon or more neutral-tasting oil, like grapeseed, for greasing

2 tablespoons water

1 tablespoon powdered gelatin

8–16 tiny Thai basil leaves for garnish

Zest from 1 lime for garnish

Place the coconut milk, cream, sugar, lemongrass, ginger, and pinch of salt in a saucepan over medium heat. Stir to dissolve the sugar. Once the mixture begins to simmer but isn't boiling, turn off the heat and steep for 20 minutes.

While the cream mixture is steeping, use a paper towel dipped in the oil to lightly coat the inside of eight ramekins, bowls, or wine glasses that are able to hold at least ½ cup liquid.

At about the 15-minute mark, pour the water into a large bowl and mix in the gelatin. Gently stir until gelatin softens.

After the 20 minutes are up, pour the cream mixture through a strainer into the bowl containing the softened gelatin. Stir to completely dissolve the gelatin. Discard the contents of the strainer.

Ladle the gelatin and cream mixture into the prepared bowls. Place a piece of cling film over the top of each of them, allowing the plastic to touch the mixture. This will prevent a skin from forming on the panna cotta while it cools. Place the bowls in the refrigerator overnight or for at least 4 hours.

To serve the panna cotta, you may eat it straight out of the ramekin, like my family does, or if you want to be fancy, set each ramekin in a shallow bowl of hot water for 30 seconds or so to loosen it. Then slide a butter knife around the inside edge of the container to further loosen it. With a quick motion, flip the ramekin upside down onto a serving dish to unmold it. Garnish with Thai basil leaves and grated lime zest. Serves 8.

In Africa, lemongrass is woven into the lower
sections of a home's walls to repel snakes.

Lemongrass is a beautiful, useful, and pleasant herb to have in your garden. Even if you only grow it as a landscape feature, the lemon scent released when the wind rustles its leaves is reason enough to grow it.

Resources

Bown, Deni. *The Herb Society of America Encyclopedia of Herbs & Their Uses*. New York: Dorling Kindersley Publishing, 1995.

Browning, Katie Rose. "Lemon Grass." Rebecca's Herbal Apothecary & Supply. Accessed September 10, 2018. https://www.rebeccas herbs.com/pages/herb-article-br-lemon-grass.html.

Emmons, Didi. *Vegetarian Planet*. Boston: The Harvard Common Press, 1997.

Harpham, Zoë, ed. *The Essential Wok Cookbook*. San Diego, CA: Thunder Bay Press, 2002.

"How to Grow Lemongrass." Grow This. June 4, 2013. https://www .growthis.com/how-to-grow-lemongrass/.

Loha-Unchit, Kasma. *It Rains Fishes: Legends, Traditions and the Joys of Thai Cooking*. Rohnert Park, CA: Pomegranate Artbooks, 1995.

Parsons, Russ. "3 Keys to Perfect Panna Cotta." *Seattle Times*, June 12, 2012. https://www.seattletimes.com/life/food-drink/3-keys-to -perfect-panna-cotta/.

McVicar, Jekka. *The Complete Herb Book*. Buffalo, NY: Firefly Books, 2008.

Traunfeld, Jerry. *The Herbal Kitchen: Cooking with Fragrance and Flavor*. New York: HarperCollins Publishers, 2005.

French Tarragon

≫ by Diana Stoll ≪

French tarragon, botanically known as *Artemisia dracunculus* var. *sativa*, is an aromatic herb with a fragrance akin to anise. It is a must-have herb in traditional French cooking and is used in making sauces, mustards, relishes, and flavored vinegars. Its distinctive licorice flavor is delicious with eggs, fish, meat, soups, stews, and *fines herbes* mixtures.

French tarragon is sometimes confused with Russian tarragon (*Artemisia dracunculus*), which may appear similar, but there are some notable differences:

- French tarragon doesn't grow as tall and isn't as winter hardy as Russian tarragon.

French Tarragon	
Species	*Artemisia dracunculus* var. *sativa*
Zone	4–7+
Needs	☀☀☀ 💧
Soil pH	6.0–7.0
Size	2 ft. semiupright

- French tarragon is propagated by cuttings; Russian tarragon is usually planted from seeds.

- The leaves of French tarragon are smoother, glossier, darker green and more fragrant than Russian tarragon.

- French tarragon offers a lot more flavor than Russian tarragon.

Although its common name is deceiving, French tarragon is native to western Russia and has been believed to draw venom from victims of snake and insect bites, cure bites from rabid dogs, aid digestion, cure colic, soothe stomachaches and toothaches, and treat everything from intestinal problems, nausea, flatulence, and bad breath to gout, arthritis, and rheumatism. With a medicinal repertoire like that, it is no wonder travelers once carried tarragon in their boots to aid them on long journeys!

The culinary use of French tarragon began in England in the sixteenth century. It didn't make its way to North America until colonists brought it in the 1800s. Today, the herb is widely grown throughout southern Europe and the United States.

Description

French tarragon typically grows eighteen to twenty-four inches tall but may reach as high as three feet, and it spreads up to eighteen inches wide. It is a well-behaved herb, spreading slowly by rhizomes instead of clambering about the garden and is incapable of scattering viable seeds.

The herb is not an unattractive plant, but it won't win a beauty contest in the herb garden either. Its long, slender, green leaves on thin, upright stems contribute fine texture to the garden. In overly rich soils, stems may flop. A small wire tomato cage or staking will discipline misbehaving stems.

If plants bother to produce any flowers at all, they bloom in mid to late summer with very small, insignificant yellowish- or greenish-white, drooping flowers.

Plants are winter hardy to USDA zone 4 but do not like hot summers. Although it is technically a perennial, it may tend to be transitory, moving out of the garden before its gardener is ready for its exit.

Planting and Care

Plant French tarragon in a sunny spot in the garden with very well-drained, average soil with a neutral pH. It can tolerate a position with part shade, can endure slightly acidic soil, can put up with periods of drought, and actually prefers poorer soil over soil too rich in nutrients. What French tarragon cannot survive is wet, compacted soil, which will cause its roots to rot, especially when plants are subjected to these conditions in winter.

Planting French tarragon in light shade in gardens with hot summers helps it handle the heat. In gardens with very cold winters, planting it in an area with protection from harsh, cold winter winds helps it fend off the cold.

Remedy adverse growing conditions by adding ample amounts of organic matter to the soil to improve the drainage before planting. Work a small amount of an organic, balanced, granular fertilizer into the top six inches of soil only if the soil is poor.

When planting, position plants at the same depth they were growing in their nursery pots. Water thoroughly after planting and keep the soil slightly moist until plants have established in their new homes. Once established, allow the soil to dry before watering.

French tarragon needs little, if any, fertilizer. In fact, its flavor may intensify in soils lacking nutrients. If fertilizing is required as plants grow, spray them with compost tea.

French tarragon rarely suffers assaults from insect pests or disease, but plants grown in an area where leaves are slow to dry after rainfall or morning dew may be more susceptible to powdery mildew.

After several hard frosts, cut plants back to the ground. Covering them with a light blanket of shredded leaves or other lightweight, well-drained mulch after the ground freezes may help those growing in dubious areas survive the winter. Cutting evergreen boughs from Christmas trees after the holidays and tossing them over the plants is another suitable option of winter protection. Mulch also helps moderate the soil temperature, decreasing the chance of plants being heaved from the ground during freeze-thaw cycles.

Growing in Containers

French tarragon can also be grown in containers if they are at least twelve inches in diameter and at least twelve inches deep to allow for adequate root growth. Use a light, soilless potting mix and be sure pots have several drainage holes to satisfy the herb's penchant for sharp drainage.

Container-grown French tarragon can be overwintered indoors. Cut the plant back after the first frost has blackened the foliage and position the pot in a sunny window. Reduce watering because the plants require less water indoors than they do in the garden. Fellow gardeners have been successful overwintering their French tarragon indoors; I have not. The plants in my house end up slouching and offering much less flavor. So instead, I take my chances on plants chilling in the garden for the winter and replace them in spring if necessary.

Propagating

The seeds of French tarragon (if plants produce any at all) are sterile, so new plants cannot be grown from seed. New plants can be started by taking six-to-eight-inch cuttings from stems in summer. Cut stems just below a node and remove a third of the lower leaves. Poke holes with a pencil in moist sand, vermiculite, or soilless potting mix and insert cuttings. Gently press the medium against stems.

Cuttings can be slow to root, as it can take up to six weeks for them to develop life-sustaining roots. And sometimes cuttings are stubborn and do not root at all. Dipping stems in rooting hormone before planting and misting them frequently may help.

The roots of French tarragon grow so aggressively they can become entangled. Plants need to be divided every few years to prevent them from declining. This presents an opportunity to get new plants by dividing established plants in spring as new shoots are forming. Dig up the plant when new shoots break through the ground and wash off the soil. Any shoots with roots attached can be replanted.

The easiest option for getting new plants is to simply sentence waning plants to the compost pile and replace them with new plants purchased at a local garden center.

Harvesting and Preserving

French tarragon is ready to harvest a couple of months after planting. The young leaves at the top of the plant have the best flavor. Continue to cut top growth whenever a recipe calls for it or at least several times during the growing season to help plants maintain a dense shape. The more you cut (within reason, of course), the more flavorful leaves they grow.

French tarragon is best when it is used fresh from the garden. If the leaves won't be used immediately after harvesting, they can be kept in the refrigerator for up to three weeks. Just wrap them loosely in a moist paper towel and put them in a plastic bag.

Make tarragon butter to use on French bread.
Combine 2 tablespoons finely chopped fresh tarragon
and 1 cup softened butter. Store in the refrigerator.

Freezing French tarragon ensures plenty will be on hand to enjoy in the winter. It couldn't be easier. Strip the leaves from their stems by running your fingers down the stem, beginning at the tip and working your way toward the base. Wash them, pat them dry between two kitchen towels, spread them out in a single layer on a tray, and put the tray in the freezer. When they are frozen, store them in a sealed container. Done! Be sure to label the container so you don't forget which tasty treat is inside.

French tarragon can also be frozen as herbal ice cubes. Whether you freeze the leaves whole or chop them finely before freezing depends on how you plan to use them later. If you want to use whole leaves in recipes, place a couple of leaves in each section of an ice cube tray and cover them with water or oil. Mix chopped leaves with water or oil before filling trays. Once the ice cubes are frozen, pop them out of the trays and store them in a sealed freezer bag. Again, remember to label the bag.

Drying is considered the least favorable method to preserve French tarragon because the herb loses a lot of its flavor in the process. If you would like to try drying the herb, harvest stems in August, when the leaves are less succulent and best for drying. Cut them in the morning after the dew has dried. Strip the leaves from stems and spread them out in a cool, shady location, inside or out.

Stems can also be hung (with leaves still attached) upside down in loose bundles to dry. Be sure they are hanging in a spot with good air circulation to prevent mold. To keep dust from settling on drying herbs, cover bundles with paper lunch bags, with holes punched in all sides for air flow.

Whichever drying method is used, it may take up to two weeks for leaves to dry completely. When leaves are dry, they will be brittle and break apart easily. Be sure to discard any moldy or spoiled leaves. If they were dried by hanging, stems will have to be removed too. Crumble leaves and store in airtight containers, out of direct light, to preserve the most flavor and fragrance.

The flavor of French tarragon can also be infused in olive oil. Crush ¼ to ½ cup of freshly harvested and cleaned tarragon leaves with a wooden spoon to release their flavor. Pour 2 cups of extra-virgin olive oil over the leaves and stir. Pour the mixture into a mason jar or other jar with a wide mouth, close tightly, and set it in a sunny window for a couple of weeks, shaking the jar once each day. Strain the mixture into an attractive bottle, cap tightly, and remember to label. Tarragon-infused olive oil, stored in a pantry, can last up to six months.

Health Benefits

French tarragon has been used throughout history to relieve toothaches. It is also said to aid digestion, soothe an upset stomach, and stimulate appetite. A nice cup of tarragon tea may relieve stress and help you get a good night's sleep. Rich in vitamin A, tarragon may benefit eye health.

Other possible health benefits of tarragon include lowering blood pressure, reducing blood sugar levels, and preventing heart attacks and strokes.

Cooking with French Tarragon

While French tarragon may not possess the vast medicinal qualities of some other herbs, it is indispensable when it comes to cooking, especially French cuisine. It is used to make traditional béarnaise sauce and tarragon mustard, and mixed with chives, parsley, and chervil, it creates *fines herbes*—an herb mixture essential to French cooking.

French tarragon enhances the flavor of fish, meat, and poultry. It is also delicious with eggs, soups, stews, rice, and pasta. It adds a unique taste twist to steamed vegetables, potatoes, and tomatoes. Freshly harvested tarragon leaves add a lovely surprise to green salads as long as they are used sparingly.

There are a couple of tricks to using tarragon in recipes. First, its leaves pack a powerful punch of flavor, so be careful not to use too much. Next, add fresh tarragon leaves to hot dishes just before they are finished cooking. Overcooking can cause leaves to lose their distinctive flavor.

An average family only needs enough space in the garden for one or two plants to satisfy their cooking and preserving needs. (And there should still be plenty of extra leaves to care for all those venomous snake bites!) Make room in your garden for French tarragon.

Resources

Albert, Steve. "How to Grow French Tarragon." *Harvest to Table* (blog), April 8, 2018. https://harvesttotable.com/how_to_grow_french_tarragon/.

Andrews, Glenn. *Growing & Using Tarragon.* North Adams, MA: Storey Publishing, 1999.

Grant, Amy. "French Tarragon Plant Care: Tips for Growing French Tarragon." Gardening Know How. Accessed April 4, 2018. https://www.gardeningknowhow.com/edible/herbs/tarragon/growing-french-tarragon.htm.

Hemphill, John, and Rosemary Hemphill. *What Herb is That?: How to Grow and Use the Culinary Herbs.* Mechanicsburg, PA: Stackpole Books, 1997.

Tucker, Arthur O., and Thomas DeBaggio. *The Encyclopedia of Herbs: A Comprehensive Reference to Herbs of Flavor and Fragrance.* Portland, OR: Timber Press, 2009.

Cayenne

⁂ by Kathy Martin ⁂

Ten years ago, I was given a small cayenne plant by a friend, and every year since then I've grown this variety by saving its seeds and planting them again the next spring. It's a great variety: bright red fruits that are long, thin, and very hot. Its thin skin dries beautifully, and I string the fruits into long ristras that hang in my kitchen until we use them up on pizzas and chili sauce during the winter.

Cayenne peppers are a cultivar of the plant species *Capsicum annuum*, which includes a wide variety of shapes and sizes of peppers, such as bell peppers, jalapeños, and New Mexico chiles. Cayenne peppers are long, tapering, generally skinny, mostly red-colored peppers, often with a curved

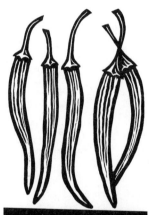

Cayenne	
Species	*Capsicum annuum*
Zone	1–10
Needs	☀☀☀ 💧💧
Soil pH	6.0–7.0
Size	1–3 ft. tall

tip. The fruits hang down from the bush as opposed to growing upward. Cayenne peppers can be moderately or fiery hot. They are relatives of wild peppers from South and Central America.

Are cayenne peppers an herb? A spice? A fruit? A vegetable? They are all four. In 2016, the International Herb Association selected peppers (*Capsicum* spp.) as the Herb of the Year. The fruits of cayenne pepper plants are often eaten ripe and fresh like a vegetable, but they are usually consumed dried and finely ground as a spice.

Growing Cayenne

Cayenne peppers are great fun to grow. Many years I have turned my dining room table into a planting bench by spreading out an old sheet. I usually plant several six-packs of cayenne seeds, several different varieties. I think homegrown and dried cayenne peppers are much more flavorful than store-bought, and every year I grow as many as I need until the next season.

Cayenne needs a long growing season, and since I live in New England, I start my seeds indoors. I plant in late March. Cayenne peppers like it warm for germination, above 78 degrees Fahrenheit (25.5°C), so the seeds I start go onto a heat mat until they sprout, which can take two weeks. I grow them under fluorescent tubes placed very close to the plants. In late April I transplant the seedlings into bigger pots. They go out to the garden only after the soil has gotten quite warm—late May for me.

Cayenne is generally a reliable pepper for ripening in the short northern growing season. Other pepper types can require even more heat and sun and often won't ripen to red for me. I can rely on a good harvest of ripe cayenne.

I grow my peppers in a raised bed and often use plastic mulch to warm the soil. I use drip irrigation and stake the plants, which generally grow about two to three feet tall. I always grow too many. In late summer I harvest baskets of cayenne.

A classic cayenne variety is called 'Large Red Thick'. It sets the standard for large-podded cayennes. Its pods measure six inches long by three-quarter inch wide. The variety my friend gave me many years ago has fruits that are smaller and thinner, maybe another heirloom called 'Cayenne Long Thin'. More recently I've grown other cayenne varieties, including 'Red Ember' (a moderately warm variety great for using fresh on pizza) and 'Red Rocket' (hot and quick drying). 'Charleston Hot' and 'Kilian' are fiery hot orange varieties of cayenne. 'Golden Cayenne' and 'Kristian' ripen to yellow. 'Cayenne Purple' is a beautiful heirloom variety.

Peppers are perennials in tropical climates, so you can bring your cayenne plants indoors in winter and grow them as houseplants. They will need more sunlight than a northern latitude provides, but a small plant will continue to grow and produce peppers if you if you give it a plant light.

Drying Cayenne

I love growing vegetables that I can preserve myself. Cayenne is perfect! I use it fresh, but those extra baskets of peppers I dry and save to use until my next harvest comes in.

Drying cayenne is easy. I pick the fruits when their shoulders are fully red and then spread them on plates in my kitchen. Thin-skinned peppers generally air dry nicely even in our relatively humid New England weather. It takes about a month for them to dry fully in my house.

I've also tied my cayenne into ristras that hang on the wall. Ristras are decorative and a good way to dry and store peppers. And I love that a ristra is something that grows—I can add to it as more peppers ripen. Cayenne peppers are a perfect pepper variety to use for a ristra.

If you want to make a ristra, first make sure you leave long stems when you pick the peppers. I then tie three whole, ripe, undried cayenne peppers together at the stem with string and make a loop with the end of the string. I make the loop about one inch long right where the string ties to the peppers. I then tie another bunch of peppers together the same way and loop one bunch over the loop on the other. I repeat the same process as I harvest more cayenne. Gradually, the ristra grows longer with the older dryer peppers at the bottom. I recommend that you only air dry a ristra if you know your humidity is low enough for peppers to dry. If it's too humid, the peppers will turn black and rot before they dry.

More recently, I've purchased a food dehydrator to dry my cayenne. This has been really useful for me, and I use it to dry lots of different vegetables and fruits. To dry cayenne, I spread whole cayenne peppers on the dehydrator trays and dry them at 125 degrees Fahrenheit (52°C) until they are dry to the touch. The length of time varies depending on the size of the pepper and the thickness of its skin, but is generally eight to twenty-four hours. When I walk into the room with the dehydrator running, I can smell the hot peppers! Alternatively, cayenne peppers can be dried in the oven at 150 degrees Fahrenheit (65.5°C) for six to eight hours. I store my dried cayenne crushed in canning jars or whole in baskets or ristras.

The dehydrator or oven can also be used to dry cayenne for a ristra. I find it best to dry the peppers first and then assemble. Instead of tying the stems together, I tie the string around the top of the dried pepper. I have some red cotton string that looks really nice for this.

Crushed cayenne pepper can be made from the dried peppers using a coffee or spice grinder or a mortar and pestle. Just be careful not to touch any surfaces that have cayenne power on them, and be careful not to breathe the air as you open up the grinder. More than once my eyes have ended up stinging from cayenne. Rather than grinding, I prefer to use my homegrown dried cayenne peppers whole, or I chop them one or two at a time with a knife as I use them.

Cayenne ristras make beautiful kitchen decorations and are a great way to dry and store cayenne peppers for use throughout the year. They are also said to ward off evil!

Cayenne Recipes

Cayenne is a requirement for Creole and Cajun cooking. I love to add it to Asian recipes and soups. It's also great on most cheesy dishes, like pizza, and in any type of chili sauce. I add a bit of cayenne when I'm cooking fish, beef, or chicken. Here are a couple of basic cayenne recipes I like.

Hot Cayenne Oil

> 1 cup of any oil (I like to use olive or sesame oil.)
>
> About a handful of dried cayenne peppers, crushed or whole

Heat oil in a small frying pan over low heat until hot. Add cayenne; don't remove the seeds as they will add a lot of spicy flavor. Cook about 1 minute and remove from heat. Let cool to room temperature. Strain through a fine mesh strainer if desired, and then transfer to a glass jar for storage.

Cayenne Pepper Sauce

This recipe is easy and even better than store-bought cayenne pepper sauce! It's very rich with lots of cayenne flavor. The heat will depend on the variety of cayenne you use.

> ⅓ pound fresh cayenne peppers, stems removed
>
> 3 large cloves garlic, peeled and hard tips cut off
>
> 1 teaspoon salt
>
> 1½ cups white vinegar (or just enough to cover the peppers)

Place the peppers, garlic, and salt in a medium pot with a lid. Add the vinegar and bring to a boil—use an exhaust fan as the vapor is spicy. Reduce heat, cover, and simmer for 20 minutes. Let cool.

Carefully pour the contents into a blender, reserving the pot. Puree until smooth (about 2 minutes). To remove the seeds, strain the sauce through a fine mesh strainer back into the pot. Bring sauce to a boil over high heat, then turn the heat off, and allow to cool. Pour into containers and refrigerate.

Keeps for at least 6 months in the refrigerator. Shake or stir before using. Makes about 1¾ cups.

Health Benefits of Cayenne

Cayenne peppers aren't only fiery and delicious, but they also have impressive health benefits. Cayenne is a very good source of carotenoids and vitamin A. **Carotenoids**, in particular lycopene, are the phytonutrients that give cayenne its bright red color. Studies have found that eating foods high in carotenoids is important for healthy vision, especially night vision, and protects against several cancers. Cayenne also contains vitamins C and K, the complete B complex vitamins, organic calcium, potassium, manganese, zinc, and dietary fiber.

Many recently studied and traditional health benefits of cayenne are produced by **capsaicin**, the phytochemical that gives cayenne its fiery heat. Cayenne or capsaicin is used as an herbal supplement available in the form of capsules or liquid extract. This supports a long list of healthful functions, including heart, cognition, the digestive system, and immune function, as well as pain relief.

Capsaicin's support of heart health and healthy blood circulation has been studied. Taken internally, capsaicin is more effective than aspirin in preventing pulmonary thromboembolism. Cognitive functioning studies in animals have also shown a significant benefit of capsaicin supplements. A traditional use of cayenne is to stimulate the digestive system. It is a powerful local stimulant of the digestive system that improves appetite, reduces atony of the intestines and stomach, and aids digestion.

When applied to the skin, capsaicin can act as an analgesic and relieve pain. It desensitizes local nerves and decreases pain due to conditions such as rheumatoid arthritis, osteoarthritis, psoriasis, and neuralgias caused by shingles or diabetes. Applying 0.25 to 0.75 percent capsaicin cream topically gives short-term pain relief.

Cayenne is also traditionally used to help fight infections, such as colds, sinus infections, and sore throats. Sprinkle a half teaspoon of finely chopped cayenne in a half cup of boiling water or hot milk, and take this slowly and carefully at the first sign of a cold. This extract can also be used as a gargle for laryngitis or a sore throat.

Saving Cayenne Seeds

Cayenne is great for seed saving. Sometimes I grow the peppers in a corner of the garden by themselves, but usually I plant them in a mixed bed with other peppers and let them cross as they will. Cayenne (like all peppers) self-pollinates, but when planted with other peppers, it will cross-pollinate if bees are around. My cayenne peppers have gradually become a bit shorter over the years, more like the Thai hot peppers I often grow next to them.

To save cayenne seeds, I usually just reserve a few of my best air-dried cayenne peppers in a labeled and sealed plastic bag in my seed box. In the spring just before planting, I crush the dried fruit, remove the seeds, and plant them. If you are not air drying your cayenne, slit open and remove the seeds from a fresh, fully ripened pepper and let these air dry on a paper towel for about two weeks before bagging and storing.

Of course, saving seeds is rewarding because they are free and you save all the resources that would have otherwise gone into the packaging, shipping, and selling of the seeds. But also, over the years, if you save the seeds from your best fruits, you gradually improve the variety so that it becomes adapted to your garden.

Resources

Vieira, A. R., L. Abar, S. Vingeliene, et al. "Fruits, Vegetables and Lung Cancer Risk: A Systematic Review and Meta-analysis." *Annals of Oncology* 27, no. 1 (January 2016): 81–96. doi:10.1093/annonc/mdv381.

Wang, J. P., M. F. Hsu, T. P. Hsu, and C. M. Teng. "Antihemostatic and Antithrombotic Effects of Capsaicin in Comparison with Aspirin and Indomethacin." *Thrombosis Research* 37, no. 6 (March 1985): 669–79. https://www.ncbi.nlm.nih.gov/pubmed/3992533.

Calendula

⫷ by Susan Pesznecker ⫸

Have you ever worked with calendula? It's an attractive and useful flower that's well worth adding to your gardening, culinary, and medicinal repertoires.

There are at least twenty marigold species in the *Calendula* genus. What we're discussing here is *Calendula officinalis*, known casually as pot marigold. The species name *officinalis* is given to plants that have both medicinal and general herbal uses. For example, other plants that bear this species name include common garden sage (*Salvia officinalis*) and lemon balm (*Melissa officinalis*). Some of calendula's other folkish names include garden or common marigold, ruddles, and English or Scottish marigold.

Calendula	
Species	*Calendula officinalis*
Zone	4–10
Needs	☼ ☼ ☼ ◗◗
Soil pH	7.0
Size	18–24 in.

Note that the "marigold" people typically grow in their yards—the one with flowers resembling small cheerleader pom-poms—are the common marigolds, genus *Tagetes*. The calendula we're discussing here has composite flowerheads made of separate florets, resembling large gold or orange daisies.

Written evidence documents calendula's earliest use in Egypt in the first few centuries of the common era. The plant was widely used medicinally throughout Europe as early as the twelfth century and is considered to be native to Europe. Penelope Ody reports that Macer's twelfth-century herbal instructed users to simply gaze upon calendula flowers to improve their eyesight, while William Turner advocated the petals' use as a dyeing agent, and Nicholas Culpeper advised it to treat smallpox and measles and strengthen the heart. Today, calendula has been naturalized widely throughout the temperate world and has become a much-beloved herb with a wide range of uses.

Cultivating Calendula

Calendula is native to many equatorial areas but grows readily in any mild or temperate climate. The seeds may be started indoors six to eight weeks before the final frost date or sown in a rich organic soil after frost danger has passed. In truth, the herb is easy to grow and will thrive just about anywhere that is warm and sunny.

Once the plants are established, don't overwater: they prefer a slightly dry soil. The plants grow to two or three feet, producing multiple daisy-like flowers that are two to three inches in diameter.

Calendula has a long flowering season. If deadheaded and fertilized regularly, the plants will bloom well into autumn.

They self-seed easily, so a patch of this year's plants may give rise to the next year's blossoms.

Harvesting

Calendula's flowering heads and flower petals are most commonly used parts. Harvest them when flowers are fully developed and at their peak, and harvest in the morning, after the sun has warmed the air but before the midday and afternoon heat drives essential oils from the petals. In temperate climates, the flowers can be harvested from midsummer and into autumn. The flowers follow the sun, opening wide on warm days and closing as darkness settles or when the air cools. On especially hot days, the petals may feel sticky as plant resins are drawn up and deposited on the petals.

The petals are best used fresh, but the heads and flowers can be dried slowly for future use. To dry, spread in a single layer on newspaper or a screen frame and allow to dry in a warm room out of direct light—this will take two to three days.

Please don't use a microwave for drying! Yes, microwaves dry herbs quickly, but the process also drives out most of the volatile oils and active constituents. The patience it takes to allow slow drying will yield a quality result. Use a mortar and pestle to grind the dried petals and heads into a powder.

An essential oil can be extracted from the petals, but the process is extremely expensive and takes a large number of flowers. Creating an infused oil (see the "Cosmetic Use" section of this article) makes a lot more sense, especially for everyday use.

For cooking with calendula, pick the leaves while they're still youthful and unblemished and use while fresh.

Medicinal Use

The plant's main medicinal use is as a skin rinse and antiseptic, treating wounds, scrapes, rashes, uncomplicated insect bites or stings, acne, minor (first degree) burns, diaper rash, athlete's foot, and red or inflamed eyes. For these purposes, create a water-based infusion of the petals, adding 1–2 tablespoons of fresh petals to 1 cup of just boiled water; allow to steep for 10–15 minutes and then strain, cool, and use as a rinse, compress, or footbath.

A cool calendula infusion makes a soothing mouth rinse or throat gargle, while a hot infusion may be drank as a tea to ease symptoms of bronchitis, quell coughing, and treat stomach or intestinal upset. Add additional herbs for a boost: a mixture of dried (cooked) elderberries, rose hips, ginger, and calendula makes a powerful tonic for colds and flu season.

Powdered calendula mixed with water or oil creates a paste that soothes rashes and insect bites or stings. My grandmother used to tell me that a poultice or paste of mashed fresh or dried calendula petals would remove warts. I can't confirm this, but perhaps it works—the grandmothers often have the best knowledge, after all.

Calendula is somewhat effective as a mosquito repellent. Its marigold cousins in the *Tagetes* genus are used as potent insecticides: be sure not to confuse the two!

Active Constituents and Their Effects

In herbal practices, a **constituent** refers to an element within the herb that has a specific physiological or medicinal effect. Some of calendula's most important constituents include the following:

Bitter Glycosides: Support improved digestion and nutrient absorption; historically regarded as an important tonic and immune stimulant

Carotenes and Flavonoids: Rich in antioxidants, with cellular health and antiinflammatory properties

Mucilages: Absorb water and help protect irritated or damaged tissues

Saponins: Exert mild estrogenic effects and mild hormonal actions; stimulate the uterus and regulate menses.

Triterpenes: Act as expectorants and encourage nutrient absorption

Volatile Oils and Resins: Antiseptic and antifungal actions

Vulnerary and Astringent: Support healing of skin and mucous membranes; antispasmodic

It's well known that deeply colored foods like blueberries, pomegranates, eggplants, and sweet potatoes tend to be rich in antioxidants. The same is true of calendula in terms of medicinal actions: the deeper orange the petals, the more powerful their constituents.

Allergy, Interactions, and Side Effects

People with ragweed pollen allergies or allergies to specific flowering plants may be allergic to calendula.

Calendula may cause additional drowsiness in people taking medications with sedative actions. Avoid using calendula in such situations without first checking with a physician.

Because of its estrogenic effects, calendula shouldn't be used by women who are pregnant or breastfeeding or who are under treatment for cancer of the breasts or reproductive organs.

Cosmetic Use

An infused oil of calendula makes a lovely lubricant for dry skin or for massage purposes. Warm 1 cup of neutral carrier oil (olive, sunflower, apricot, or coconut) over low heat. Add 2–3 tablespoons of fresh petals and steep for 30 minutes—this will create a deep golden-orange oil. Cool and use as a topical or bath oil.

To make the infused oil into a cream, liniment, or lip balm, add 1 ounce of grated beeswax or cocoa butter to the warm mixture. Adding a few drops of tincture of benzoin (available at the pharmacy) will act as a preservative. Otherwise, store these products in the refrigerator for longer keeping.

Stir infused oil into 1 cup of sugar or coarse salt in a bowl ½ teaspoon at a time to make sugar or salt scrubs or bath salts.

Calendula Crafts

Calendula petals are a lovely, colorful addition to potpourri mixtures and can be used in homemade soap, adding color, texture, or both. Stir the dried or powdered petals into melted wax for beautiful candles.

Dyeing with Calendula

The vivid petals can be used with a variety of mordants (ingredients added to dye solutions to help set or fix the color) to create a range of natural dyes in yellows, oranges, golds, and even soft browns. This method uses salt; three other commonly available mordants are vinegar, cream of tartar (found in the baking section of supermarkets), and alum (found in hardware store or pharmacy). To dye white wool fabric or yarn using herbalist Lesley Tierra's method, you'll need the following:

2–4 tablespoons calendula petals for every 1 cup water

Water

Fabric or small skein of yarn

1 teaspoon salt for every 4 cups dye liquid produced

In a large saucepan, make a large quantity of infusion and steep for at least 30 minutes. Strain.

Add the fabric or yarn to the pan; turn heat high enough to simmer without boiling. Simmer for 30–45 minutes, until the desired shade is obtained.

Remove the fabric or yarn. Stir in salt and dissolve. Add the yarn or fabric back to the pan and simmer for another 30 minutes until it's the color you want. Note that as the fabric or yarn dries, its color will lighten significantly—very much like paint on a wall. Therefore, when dyeing, get the material to a shade that's significantly darker than what you want for an end result.

Turn off the heat, take the saucepan off the heat, and let the material cool.

Once the solution is cool, remove the fabric or yarn and rinse under cool water until the water runs clear.

Squeeze gently in a clean towel and then hang to dry.

Calendula is a "calendar flower." The flowers start each day tightly closed, begin to open as sun strikes the petals, and open fully in mid-morning. The blossoms rotate through the day, following the sun's movement through the sky. In late afternoon, the petals slowly close, and the plant "sleeps" at night.

Culinary

Fresh calendula parts are on the menu for culinary use, and having a pot or plot in your kitchen garden will furnish you with a renewable supply of petals. When harvesting, leave as much stem as possible and then set the flowers in a vase of water until you use them. They'll stay plump and pretty.

The name *pot marigold* comes from traditional European stews that included calendula flowers. Stirring chopped petals into a soup or stew as it cooks will deepen the color. Add chopped petals to cooking rice or grains for a saffron-like hue. The petals have a slightly bitter taste, so add slowly and taste as you work.

Calendula petals can be used to color butter, cheese, ice cream, custard, and other dairy products as well as to make a delicious tea. The petals are also a colorful and tasty addition to green salads, and fresh calendula leaves can also be added to salads.

Toss a few petals to steep in your favorite oil and vinegar dressing. The flavor won't change, but the color will be stunning.

Next spring, toss a few calendula seeds into a garden plot, and you too can share in the bounty of uses that come from the beloved pot marigold.

Resources

Bremness, Lesley. *Herbs*. London: Dorling Kindersley, 1994.

Chevallier, Andrew. *Encyclopedia of Herbal Medicine*. 2nd ed. London: Dorling Kindersley Publishing, 2000.

Ody, Penelope. *The Complete Medicinal Herbal*. London: Dorling Kindersly, 1993.

Tierra, Lesley. *A Kid's Herb Book*. Bandon, OR: Robert D. Reed Publishers, 2000.

Sumac

≫ by Estha K. V. McNevin ≪

Much of my childhood was spent barefoot in the woodlands of Montana. Though we were not so privileged in other ways, the wilderness was a beloved resource of all manner of treasures, and none were more prized to me as a child than berries. And dear reader, I do mean every berry. While the teeny hairy berries of the sumac have nothing on a raspberry for eating, crushing these little gems and making wild pink lemonade was a tasty survival skill that we employed whenever roaming the "back forty," or the wild portion of my grandfather's ranch property. Not only did the berries delight, but the bright leaves and even the roots tasted sweet when chewed. We were

Sumac	
Species	*Rhus coriaria,* *Rhus glabra*
Zone	3–10
Needs	☼ 💧
Soil pH	6.0–8.0
Size	10–25 ft.

forever nestling under the umbrella-like branches and shoots of sumac in an attempt to move unseen through the brush, as we scuttled about reimagining our world as that of the forest moon of Endor, Sanctuary.

As an adult, I return time and again to the woods to wild harvest sumac for use in the herbal medicine chest as well as for use in my many exotic spice blends formulated to appease many a culinary curiosity. I seem only to learn new and innovative ways to use this plant, and I am forever finding hidden patches on the trails in and around my home city. Although I have yet to cultivate any of my own shrubs, I had the great luck to find them on the property I currently reside on.

Few bushes puzzle the imagination and evoke awe quite like the sumac. This anacardiaceous shrub is so evocative of the thick and verdant prehistoric forests of America. Sumac features widely in Native American myth and legend as being one of the original medicines of the early peoples of America. A large patch of the *Rhus* shrub can grow with primordial power as it works its wild way along the verge of a forest or creek with minimal effort in a matter of a few seasons. Above all else, sumac is cultivated commercially as a spice and makes for a rich display of seasonal color as an ornamental tree favored in the large lawn or walled garden.

The leaves put on a show throughout the year and range in color from the first fresh neon green leaves, so iconic of spring, to the autumnal splendor of fire-engine red, near-neon orange, and vibrant yellow as the leaves mark each season's transitions. Sumac is an ideal indicator of frost and environmental moisture and prevents erosion by helping rebuild the soil. Favored by landscape artists, this little unassuming shrub, with its fuzzy, tart berries, has a kind of prehistoric romance about it amongst herbalists and gardeners that captures the fancy and proves sumac has far more to offer than meets the eye.

Sumac in the Wild

Boasting over eighty genera and 893 different varieties, Anacardiaceae—the cashew or sumac family—contains a wide range of small trees and shrubs that grow as far north as midland Canada and as far south as Central America. As a general rule, cold-hearty varieties of sumac and those prone to dense root development like its cousins, mango and pistachio, tend to have even-pinate leaves while more closed-root sumacs are often trifoliate and rely heavily on reseeding due to annual dieback during harsh dry seasons. *Rhus metopium*, a poisonous native to Florida, and *Rhus malosma*, also known as laurel sumac, from the Carolinas and Mexico, are shrubs that are truly rejuvenated by monsoons and appear all but dead during the dry season.

Berries from sumac with red flowers are safe to eat.
White-flowered sumac is poisonous.

Only two genera, *Rhus* and *Toxicodendron*, are found across the frost belt of North America and Europe; most other varieties are equatorial. These two include over two hundred species, from evergreen and deciduous to tropical varieties. Short, crooked trunks with irregular branches give way to long, arching pinnate leaf fans. Over three hundred species of bird include sumac as a staple in their diet, and the trees will draw bees and butterflies to their red and white flowers with equal popularity.

Sumac is a self-pollinator, and seventy to one hundred fifty small red berries form in a bulbous cluster at the top of the bush. Each one contains a lentil-sized stone seed in the center, and millions of tiny little hairs on the skin of the berry give the glowing clusters a slight silver aura that causes them to glisten the sunlight.

Stagnant water is an environmental indicator of poisonous or toxic varieties of sumac, which will always have white flowers, such as those of shining, smooth, and staghorn sumac. These varieties seek out moisture and nitrogen-rich bogs and thrive in creek beds, swamp wetlands, and lowlands. Much of their toxins come from the higher levels of **urushiol**, a compound found in many anacardiaceous plants, such as sumac's uninhibited toxic cousins poison ivy, poison oak, cashew, and pistachio.

The leaves, bark, and fruits of these varieties are known for their thick waxy coating of urushiol-rich resins that produce an irritating and immediate reaction when directly exposed to the heat and oils of our own skin. Urushiol causes an allergic reaction in most people and will create pox or fissures on the skin that ooze pus in an effort to flush off the waxy toxin. Mud and clay-pack treatments are the only immediate way to pull urushiol resins out of the pores of the skin, and this is one reason calamine lotion and other treatments for Anacardiaceae allergy and rashes use silica and smooth minerals.

Each variety has its own range of leaf colors that turn from neon green in the spring to shades of red, orange, and yellow throughout the fall. When found in the wild, the trees are more usually connected in a dense cluster. Arching shoots are driven up from the soil in the first and second flush of growth during April and again in June. These shoots will grow to form whole new trees if not clipped back or harvested. Beloved by garden designers as an ornamental shrub, in the garden, sumac needs enough space to roam as well as enough pruning and direction not to climb from the garden bed into the more densely watered lawn.

Sumacs thrive in areas heavily populated by birds, as seeds sprout from the droppings. Unlike the northern hardy varieties like *Rhus glabra* or those that thrive from new spring shoot growth from the base of the shrub like *Rhus aromatica* and *Rhus typhina*, the tropical varieties produce fewer fruits as they age, making regular pruning essential for healthy fruit development of cultivated plants.

Cultivation

Many of the oldest plant families on earth have a wide range of growing zones, making it easy to find a local variety at any good organic garden nursery. When purchasing young shoots or potted shrubs, clear away the soil from the base and carefully inspect the pot for rot or disease. Mold, fungus, or any smell of rot will waste both time and money, as sumac will sometimes carry these things into the garden when transplanted and spread them about. This is because it is a thirsty little shrubs and is prone to need drenching in its early sages.

Many of the poisonous varieties of sumac live in the swampy waters of the lowlands and tidal marshlands like Florida, Georgia, and Louisiana. Sumac will grow just fine in damp and moldy conditions, but other plants and trees around it won't appreciate an infectious neighbor. Starting with a well-rooted yearling will yield the best results. Planting from shoots or seeds requires careful planning and a greenhouse to work in. This is because the stages of growth need to be carefully timed to create truly hardy shrubs; however, these methods are rewarding and can yield wonderful results if you are seeding a large area.

In early spring, sow seeds six inches apart in small pots of rich sprouting loam. Every eight weeks, repot into a larger size and feed with a few drops of fish emulsion. It's best to let them live in the greenhouse for a year once they reach eighteen-inch pots. While many northern varieties of sumac can handle harsh winter weather, the plants that produce larger berries, such as *Rhus glabra,* require a warm and cozy spot as well as mulching to insulate their fragile root bulbs from cracking in the frost. Though long term, this method will produce many strong shrubs that can then be planted to fill in areas by roadways or add color and transition to garden pathways and large retention zones. In the tropics they are planted six to eight feet from the foundation of a house to wick away moisture and help keep the porch shaded from harsh heat.

When ready, plant out in late spring, when all sign of frost is long past. Sumac loves morning sun and firm boundaries to explore and grow within. Dig four inches deeper than the pot is big and work a handful of bone meal into the bottom of the hole. When snug inside the soil, cover the base of the shrub with garden fabric and then layer over it with rocks and bark mulch. This system will inhibit shoots from spreading out into the lawn while also giving the plants a cozy layer of mulch to improve drainage and maintain soil temperatures during extreme weather.

Shoots will often appear in early spring and can be snipped and left in water for three weeks until they root out. These can then be placed in soil pots and staged out in the greenhouse in much the same way as the seed method. The important part of cultivating shoots is to feed them plenty of nutrients, especially B_{12}, as they will not have their own root system to start with and shoots need help to really get going. I like to use a rooting solution for all shrubs here on our farm because it also protects the wound from being infected by the garden shears or other shoots that it may be incubated with in the water bath. Once they are a year old, budding shoots can be planted out just as you would do with potted or seeded sumac. Though they will thrive in full sun, young shoots need lots of water and are a bit fussy about morning shade and frost zones, so take care to pick just the right spot when plotting your sumac patch.

Sumac is notoriously resistant to mineral deposits and flooding. The antifungal properties of the bark make the shrub hardy in flash flooding zones throughout the tropics. Like many other fruit-producing trees in the Anacardiaceae family, sumac relies on drought and drench cycles related to monsoonal or spring and autumn flooding. Marshland and creek beds provide rocky soil rich in clay pack and nitrogen.

Landscapers love to pair sumac with ash and oak trees to paint a palatte of color in the garden that draws the eyes from one tree to the next in a euphoric display of autumn glory. Wherever sumac blooms, a vibrant wall of color will grant a vertical perimeter, framing large garden features, re-taining walls, and fountains with a sense of sanctuary. Sumac will thrive in slightly acidic soil and loves other evergreens and many deciduous trees. Dogwood, lilac, wild rose, and mock citrus will also compete for space with sumac and can be used to train new sucker shoots to stay within a designated area. Larger trees will also help to rein sumac in and prevent light from reaching new shoots, somewhat deterring their sprawl. Without such tactics, sumac can become endemic and will take over an entire yard if watered and left to its own ramblings.

Like many shrubs, the spring suckers will follow the water line of the property, and after three or fours years, they will have dug a nearly permanent network of thick rhizome roots. These are not easily eradicated because when cut, hormones in the root trigger regeneration and they merely sprout a new sucker. In fact, to destroy a sumac shrub organically, gardeners build black boxes, starving the core of the shrub of food, light, and water for over a year, and simultaneously, they spore the tree with **lignicolous fungi**. The fungi will make quick work of a sumac patch, but if left unharvested and free to spore, they may infect other nearby trees within a five-mile radius due to wind, trail, or track. For environmental conservation and localized ecosystem integrity, fungi are often spored using inoculated plugs that are contained with a fungus patch or enclosed in a black box to employ a wind shield of some kind.

Uses around the World

Rhus is native to the Americas and known as lemonade berry. The common *Rhus coriaria*, *Rhus aromatica* (which is frangrent), *Rhus microphylla* (a dwarf variety), and *Rhus trilobata* have been cultivated around the world for medicinal value and are all related large berry varieties of sumac that are most favored in spices used in African, Spanish, and Middle Eastern cuisine. Sumac is a digestive aid, souring agent, dehydrator, citric preservative, flavor enhancer, and food-grade dye.

Large agricultural areas favor this perennial shrub as a fast-growing and effective hedge for woodlands, fields, sports yards, ponds, and roads because the sumac can be trimmed and trained to climb anywhere from ten to twenty-five feet. The shrub will create a wall of greenery blocking unwanted wind and noise while also visually transporting any back lot into a veritable rural oasis. Ornamental as well as medicinal, sumac is native to zones 3 through 9, and different parts of the plant are harvested at different times of the year because of how masterfully this shrub adapts to environmental conditions. Sumac loves dry, sandy soil and will conserve water during drought, even sharing its vital rhizome root moisture with other plants and trees nearby. Sumac taproots can help keep the whole area verdant.

Assiniboine natives along the Montana Highline use the leaves for craft dyeing and gather them at different stages of growth to derive different colors. These are artfully applied to leather and canvas using a natural acid wash. Once pressed or rolled up and aged, the leaves impart the color into the leather and are later rubbed with animal fat to cure and brighten the dyes, revealing vivid yellows, oranges, and reds as well as grays, browns, and blacks.

Cooking with Sumac

Sumac berries from the *Rhus coriaria* have been cultivated as an African spice since the second century BCE and are a vital component of *za'atar*. This enigmatic spice is used as a table salt blend and vegetable seasoning. Its flavor is ubiquitous to Moroccan savory stews and tagines as well as West African pan-fried curries. Za'atar with finely ground sumac is also mixed into yogurt for salads and marinades and is famous for its ability to preserve and tenderize smoked, kebabed, and pit-roasted meats.

This earthy and rustic berry is featured in many types of cuisine, from Mediterranean and Middle Eastern to Native American and ancient Mayan. Sumac was heavily cultivated and beloved as a spice throughout much of colonial America and is still a Montana summer treat when foraged in the wild and made into what my family calls "trail treasure lemonade."

Sumac lemonade can be made by crushing the berries in cheesecloth and steeping this in water like sun tea. The resulting juice extract can be sweetened and drunk to help beat the heat. As it works to regulate the body temperature by stimulating the lymphatic system, it is often used along with hibiscus in fruity sun teas. Slightly citric, tart, and mildly astringent, sumac berries are best known as a sweet and souring agent.

Montucky Pink Punch

 3 cups fresh sumac berries

 Cheesecloth

 2 cups boiled water

 1 cup honey or golden cane syrup

 1 cup lemon juice

 3 cups apple juice

Wrap the sumac berries in cheesecloth place them in the warm water. Let stand for 10 minutes. Then, crush the berries in the cloth with a potato masher until the pulp is separate from the seeds. Squeeze the cloth to expel the fruit juice of the berries. Discard the fruit material. Add the honey to the warm juice and stir until incorporated. Refrigerate this until cold or freeze in water bottles for later use.

Just before serving, combine lemon juice, apple juice, and chilled sumac juice together. Serve over ice and garnish with fresh mint to help beat the heat and savor the sweet and tart perfection of the sumac. Makes 8 cups—share and enjoy.

Sweet, Wild Medicine

Growing up wild has filled me with a deep love and respect for sumac because it is such a wonderful survival medicine to those roaming out in the isolated highlands. I grew up hearing all the different local uses, and many of them are still beloved today because of convenience and potency.

Sumac flowers themselves are iron rich and sweet with a slightly tannic and citric aftertaste. The Sioux and Flathead still use sumac juice and flower tea to treat women's issues. They can be harvested in early August and used in fresh salads or steeped in teas to promote menstrual regularity, relaxing the womb and thus eliminating cramps and revitalizing the blood.

Both the Sioux and Flathead decorated ritual tools and clothing with the sumac seed to evoke the power of the berry as a diuretic. Many still consume sumac to purify the kidneys and bladder, inducing the flow of healing. Kootenai natives used to crush the berries and use the paste for dyeing fabric and leather and for making mud poultices to apply to open wounds and rashes.

The antifungal, astringent, and antiseptic properties of the bark are shared by other Anacardiaceae, such as the Peruvian pepper tree (*Schinus molle*), mango (*Mangifera*), and pistachio (*Pistacia*), all of which produce rich **oleic** oils, which are extremely high in fatty acids. These penetrate the skin, repair damage, and kill fungi and bacteria as they moisturize, making them ideal for beauty products and healing ointments. The bark is an astringent, and when boiled in soup stock, it will also create a nourishing soup that fights tuberculosis, asthma, and deep coughing fits by removing bacteria and infected mucus from the sinuses, throat, esophagus, and lungs. This promotes sinus flushing in a similar way to black pepper. A famous Montana Flathead flu cure uses a host of wild foraged spices, such as bearberry, ginseng, and *Usnea* lichen, along with sumac, to create a lifesaver known as old man's beard or hag moss soup.

The leaves of the sumac are so renowned for their antiseptic qualities that many ceremonial tobacco blends favored by the Plains Native Americans contain sumac. The leaf smoke promotes respiratory health when inhaled before and after sweat lodge and acts as an expectorant to help eliminate bile and mucus from the lungs. The leaves also make a handy antiseptic and are a trail-ready poultice for acne, bug bites, poison oak, and poison ivy. When crushed and rubbed on the infected area, sumac leaves will greatly reduce the stinging itch of insect bites and nettles alike.

Springtime rhizomes are rich in antimicrobial and antifungal properties; sumac root helps fight tooth decay as well as heals mouth and skin ulcers. Harvesting and juicing the spring shoots produces a tannin-rich milk that can be used in herbal lotions and applied topically to treat athlete's foot and fungal infections. Both the Sioux and Kutenai have used the root for tooth and gum pain, and some modern medicine men and women use the juice of the root to treat STDs and fungal infections internally; however, a great deal of herbal and pharmacological expertise is necessary to extract and safely prescribe the juice for internal use. Externally applied, the juice is safe for common use and a small amount of the powdered root added into common lotion may help with everything from athlete's foot to candida. Many calendula-based lotions incorporate sumac root extract as a natural antibacterial agent and emulsion stabilizer.

Sumac Antimicrobial Spray

One of my personal favorite uses for sumac is as an antimicrobial spray. This is ideal to use in shoes, as an additive to bath and mop water, or in the garden to combat powder mildew and mold spores. Sumac spray can be used throughout the home as a natural cleaning agent. The sumac root juice will eradicate fungus so effectively that it is included in a lot of highland Native American hand and foot soaks to promote a balanced body biome, treating cracked, swollen, or infected skin and nail conditions.

> 2 cups crushed root or 1 cup of pure sumac root juice
>
> 8 cups of Everclear
>
> 1 cup of propanol alcohol

Combine to create your own antimold and antifungal spray.

Resilient Sumac

No matter how harshly you treat it, or how intensely you try to eradicate it, the wild sumac is a resilient shrub that can gift us with the ability to heal ourselves as well as our families with sheer grit and old-world know-how. Cultivating or ethically wild-harvesting medicines like sumac can really inspire our connection to the thriving earth. When rooted in these old ways, we are more able to endure hardship with a type of resilience that really is sprouting up all around us—if we know where to look!

Selected Resources

Bladholm, Linda. *The Indian Grocery Store Demystified*. Los Angeles, CA: Renaissance Books, 2000.

Burnie, Geoffrey. *The Practical Gardener's Encyclopedia*. San Francisco, CA: Fog City Press, 2000.

Devi, Yamuna. *The Art of Indian Vegetarian Cooking*. Old Westbury, NY: BALA Books, 1987.

Elpel, Thomas J. *Botany in A Day: The Patterns Method of Plant Identification*. 6th ed. Pony, MT: HOPS Press, 2013.

Griffin, Judith. *Mother Nature's Herbal: A Complete Guide For Experiencing the Beauty, Knowledge & Synergy of Everything That Grows*. St. Paul, MN: Llewellyn Publications, 1997.

Heart, Jeff, and Jacqueline Moore. *Montana Native Plants & Early Peoples*. Helena, MT: The Montana Historical Society & the Montana Bicentennial Administration, 1976.

Perrin, Sandra. *Organic Gardening in Cold Climates*. Missoula, MT: Mountain Press Publishing, 2002.

Gardening
Resources

Companion Planting Guide

Group together plants that complement each other by deterring certain pests, absorbing different amounts of nutrients from the soil, shading their neighbors, and enhancing friends' flavors. This table of herbs and common garden vegetables offers suggestions for plants to pair together and plants to keep separated.

Plant	Good Pairing	Poor Pairing
Anise	Coriander	Carrot, basil, rue
Asparagus	Tomato, parsley, basil, lovage, Asteraceae spp.	
Basil	Tomato, peppers, oregano, asparagus	Rue, sage, anise
Beans	Tomato, carrot, cucumber, cabbage, corn, cauliflower, potato	Gladiola, fennel, *Allium* spp.
Borage	Tomato, squash, strawberry	
Bee balm	Tomato, echinacea, yarrow, catnip	
Beet	Onions, cabbage, lettuce, mint, catnip, kohlrabi, lovage	Pole bean, field mustard
Bell pepper	Tomato, eggplant, coriander, basil	Kohlrabi
Broccoli	Aromatics, beans, celery, potato, onion, oregano, pennyroyal, dill, sage, beet	Tomato, pole bean, strawberry, peppers
Cabbage	Mint, sage, thyme, tomato, chamomile, hyssop, pennyroyal, dill, rosemary, sage	Strawberry, grape, tomato
Carrot	Peas, lettuce, chive, radish, leek, onion, sage, rosemary, tomato	Dill, anise, chamomile

Plant	Good Pairing	Poor Pairing
Catnip	Bee balm, cucumber, chamomile, mint	
Celery	Leek, tomato, bush bean, cabbage, cauliflower, carrot, garlic	Lovage
Chamomile	Peppermint, beans, peas, onion, cabbage, cucumber, catnip, dill, tomato, pumpkin, squash	
Chervil	Radish, lettuce, broccoli	
Chive	Carrot, *Brassica* spp., tomato, parsley	Bush bean, potato, peas, soybean
Coriander/cilantro	*Plant anywhere*	Fennel
Corn	Potato, beans, peas, melon, squash, pumpkin, sunflower, soybean, cucumber	Quack grass, wheat, straw, tomato
Cucumber	Beans, cabbage, radish, sunflower, lettuce, broccoli, squash, corn, peas, leek, nasturtium, onion	Aromatic herbs, sage, potato, rue
Dill	Cabbage, lettuce, onion, cucumber	Carrot, caraway, tomato
Echinacea	Bee balm	
Eggplant	Catnip, green beans, lettuce, kale, redroot pigweed	
Fennel	*Isolate; disliked by all garden plants*	
Garlic	Tomato, rose	Beans, peas
Hyssop	*Most plants*	Radish
Kohlrabi	Green bean, onion, beet, cucumber	Tomato, strawberry, pole bean
Lavender	*Plant anywhere*	
Leek	Onion, celery, carrot, celeriac	Bush bean, soy bean, pole bean, pea

Plant	Good Pairing	Poor Pairing
Lemon balm	*All vegetables*, particularly squash, pumpkin	
Lettuce	Strawberry, cucumber, carrot, radish, dill	Pole bean, tomato
Lovage	*Most plants*, especially cucumber, beans, beet, *Brassica* spp., onion, leek, potato, tomato	Celery
Marjoram	*Plant anywhere*	
Mint	Cabbage, tomato, nettle	Parsley, rue
Melon	Corn, peas, morning glory	Potato, gourd
Nasturtium	Cabbage, cucumber, potato, pumpkin, radish	
Onion	Beets, chamomile, carrot, lettuce, strawberry, tomato, kohlrabi, summer savory	Peas, beans, sage
Oregano	*Most plants*	
Parsley	Tomato, asparagus, carrot, onion, rose	Mint, *Allium* spp.
Parsnip	Peas	
Peas	Radish, carrot, corn, cucumbers, bean, tomato, spinach, turnip, aromatic herbs	*Allium* spp., gladiola
Potato	Beans, corn, peas, cabbage, eggplant, catnip, horseradish, watermelon, nasturtium, flax	Pumpkin, raspberry, sunflower, tomato, orach, black walnut, cucumber, squash
Pumpkin	Corn, lemon balm	Potato
Radish	Peas, lettuce, nasturtium, chervil, cucumber	Hyssop
Rose	Rue, tomato, garlic, parsley, tansy	*Any plant within 1 ft. radius*
Rosemary	Rue, sage	

Plant	Good Pairing	Poor Pairing
Sage	Rosemary	Rue, onion
Spinach	Strawberry, garlic	
Squash	Nasturtium, corn, mint, catnip, radish, borage, lemon balm	Potato
Strawberry	Borage, bush bean, spinach, rue, lettuce	*Brassica* spp., garlic, kohlrabi
Tarragon	*Plant anywhere*	
Tomato	Asparagus, parsley, chive, onion, carrot, marigold, nasturtium, bee balm, nettle, garlic, celery, borage	Black walnut, dill, fennel, potato, *Brassica* spp., corn
Thyme	*Plant anywhere*	
Turnip	Peas, beans, brussels sprout, leek	Potato, tomato
Yarrow	*Plant anywhere*, especially with medicinal herbs	

For more information on companion planting, you may wish to consult the following resources:

Mayer, Dale. *The Complete Guide to Companion Planting: Everything You Need to Know to Make Your Garden Successful.* Ocala, FL: Atlantic Publishing, 2010.

Philbrick, Helen. *Companion Plants and How to Use Them.* Edinburgh, UK: Floris Books, 2016.

Riotte, Louise. *Carrots Love Tomatoes: Secrets of Companion Planting for Successful Gardening.* Pownal, VT: Storey Books, 1988.

Cooking with Herbs and Spices

Elevate your cooking with herbs and spices. Remember, a little goes a long way!

Herb	Flavor Pairings	Health Benefits
Anise	Salads, slaws, roasted vegetables	Reduces nausea, gas, and bloating. May relieve infant colic. May help menstrual pain. Loosens sputum in respiratory illnesses.
Basil	Pesto and other pasta sauces, salads	Eases stomach cramps, nausea, indigestion, and colic. Mild sedative action.
Borage	Soups	Soothes respiratory congestion. Eases sore, inflamed skin. Mild diuretic properties.
Cayenne	Adds a spicy heat to soups, sauces, and main courses	Stimulates blood flow. Relieves joint and muscle pain. Treats gas and diarrhea.
Chamomile	Desserts, teas	Used for nausea, indigestion, gas pains, bloating, and colic. Relaxes tense muscles. Eases menstrual cramps. Promotes relaxation and sleep.
Chervil	Soups, salads, and sauces	Settles and supports digestion. Mild diuretic properties. Useful in treating minor skin irritations.
Chive	Salads, potato dishes, sauces	Rich in antioxidants. May benefit insomnia. Contributes to strong bones.
Coriander/cilantro	Soups, picante sauces, salsas	Treats mild digestive disorders. Counters nervous tensions. Sweetens breath.

Herb	Flavor Pairings	Health Benefits
Dill	Cold salads and fish dishes	Treats all types of digestive disorders, including colic. Sweetens breath. Mild diuretic.
Echinacea	Teas	Supports immune function. May treat or prevent infection.
Fennel	Salads, stir-fry, vegetable dishes	Settles stomach pain, relieves bloating, and stimulates appetite. May help treat kidney stones and bladder infections. Mild expectorant. Eye wash treats conjunctivitis.
Garlic	All types of meat and vegetable dishes as well as soup stocks and bone broths	Antiseptic: aids in wound healing. Treats and may prevent infections. Benefits the heart and circulatory system.
Ginger	Chicken, pork, stir-fry, gingerbread and ginger cookies	Treats all types of digestive disorders. Stimulates circulation. Soothes colds and flu.
Hyssop	Chicken, pasta sauces, light soups	Useful in treating respiratory problems and bronchitis. Expectorant. Soothes the digestive tract.
Jasmine	Chicken dishes, fruit desserts	Relieves tension and provides mild sedation. May be helpful in depression. Soothes dry or sensitive skin.
Lavender	Chicken, fruit dishes, ice cream	Soothes and calms the nerves. Relieves indigestion, gas, and colic. May relax airways in asthma.

Herb	Flavor Pairings	Health Benefits
Lemon balm	Soups, sauces, seafood dishes	Soothes and calms the nerves. Treats mild anxiety and depression. Helps heal wounds.
Lemongrass	Marinades, stir-fries, curries, spice rubs	Treats all types of digestive disorders. Reduces fever. May reduce pain.
Lemon verbena	Beverages, any recipe asking for lemon zest	Calms digestive problems and treats stomach pain. Gently sedative.
Lovage	Soups, lovage pesto, lentils	Acts as a digestive and respiratory tonic. Has diuretic and antimicrobial actions. Boosts circulation. Helps menstrual pain.
Marigold	Soups, salads, rice dishes	Effective treatment of minor wounds, insect bites, sunburn, acne, and other skin irritations. Benefits menstrual pain and excessive bleeding.
Marjoram	Vegetables, soups, tomato dishes, sausages	Calms the digestive system. Stimulates appetite.
Nasturtium	Nasturtium pesto, salad dressings, salads	Strong antibiotic properties. Treats wounds and respiratory infections.
Oregano	Chicken, tomato sauces and dishes	Strong antiseptic properties. Stimulates bile production. Eases flatulence.
Parsley	Soups, stocks, bone broths	Highly nutritious. Strong diuretic action and may help treat cystitis. Benefits gout, rheumatism, and arthritis.
Peppermint	Desserts, teas	Treats all types of digestive disorders. May help headaches.

Herb	Flavor Pairings	Health Benefits
Purslane	Salads	Treats digestive and bladder ailments. Mild antibiotic effects.
Rosemary	Roasted red meats, potato dishes, grilled foods	Stimulates circulation. May stimulate the adrenal glands. Elevates mood and may benefit depression.
Sage	Chicken, duck, and pork	Relieves pain in sore throats. May help treat menstrual and menopausal disorders.
Spinach	Sauteed, soups, salads, spinach pesto, stuffed in chicken, ravioli	Iron-rich; supports healthy blood and iron stores.
Summer savory	Mushrooms, vegetables, quiche	Treats digestive and respiratory issues.
Tarragon	Chicken, fish, vegetables, sauces—"classic French cooking"	Stimulates digestion. Promotes sleep—mildly sedative. Induces menstruation.
Thyme	Soups, stews, tomato-based sauces	May treat infections. Soothes sore throats and hay fever. Can help expel parasites. Relieves minor skin irritations.
Yarrow	Salad dressings, infused oils	Helps heal minor wounds. Eases menstrual pain and heavy flow. Tonic properties.
Winter-green	Ice cream, candies, desserts	Strong anti-inflammatory and antiseptic properties. Treats arthritis and rheumatism. Relieves flatulence.
Winter savory	Beans, meats, vegetables	Treats digestive and respiratory issues. Antibacterial properties.

Gardening Techniques

Gardeners are creative people who are always on the lookout for the most efficient, interesting, and beautiful ways to grow their favorite plants. Whether you need to save money, reduce your workload, or keep plants indoors, the following gardening techniques are just a sampling of the many ways to grow your very own bountiful garden.

Barrel

Lidless plastic food-grade barrels or drums are set on raised supports. Before the barrel is filled with soil, slits are cut into the sides of the barrel and shaped into pockets. A PVC pipe is perforated with holes and set into the center and out of the bottom of the barrel as a delivery tool for watering, draining, fertilizing, and feeding the optional worm farm.

Strengths

Initial cost is moderate. Retains moisture, warms quickly, drains well, takes up little space, maximizes growing area and repels burrowing rodents. Little weeding or back-bending required.

Weaknesses

Not always attractive, initially labor intensive, requires special tools to modify. Not generally suited for crops that are deep-rooted, large vining, or traditionally grown in rows, such as corn.

Hügelkultur

These permanent raised beds utilize decomposing logs and woody brush that have been stacked into a pyramidal form on top of the soil's surface or in shallow trenches and then packed and covered with eight to ten inches of soil, compost, and well-rotted manure. The rotting wood encourages soil biota while holding and releasing moisture to plants, much like a sponge. English pronunciation: "hoogle-culture."

Strengths

Vertical form warms quickly, drains well, reduces watering needs, increases overall planting surface, and reduces bending chores. In time the rotting wood breaks down into humus-rich soil.

Weaknesses

Labor-intensive construction and mulch tends to slide down sides. Requires two to three years of nitrogen supplementation, repeated soaking, and filling sunken voids with soil. Voids can also be attractive to rodents and snakes in the first few years.

Hydroponic

Hydroponics is based on a closed (greenhouse) system relying on carefully timed circulation of nutrient-enriched water flowing through a soilless growing medium in which plants grow. Aerial parts are supported above the water by rafts and, at times, vertical supports. With the addition of fish tanks to the system, hydroponics becomes aquaponics.

Strengths

Customizable to any size. Versatile, efficient, productive, and weedless. Produce stays clean.

Large systems are expensive and complicated to set up and maintain; require multiple inputs of heat, light, and nutrients; and are limited to certain crop types.

Lasagna

Based on sheet composting, lasagna gardens are built up in layers, starting with paper or cardboard that is placed on top of turf-covered or tilled ground to smother weeds and feed ground worm activity. This is then covered in repeating layers of peat moss, compost, leaves, wood chips, manure, and yard waste (green, brown, green), which eventually break down into rich, humusy soil.

Strengths

Excellent natural method to enrich poor soils, utilizes organic waste, supports soil biota, and improves drainage while reducing the need for fertilizers and excessive watering.

Weaknesses

Initially labor intensive and the proper breakdown of bed materials takes months, so is not suited to "quick" gardening. Requires ready and abundant sources of clean, unsprayed, organic materials.

Ruth Stout

This "no work" garden is based on deep, permanent layers of progressively rotting straw mulch, which simultaneously builds soil, feeds plants, blocks weeds, and reduces watering. Seeds and plants are placed into the lower decomposed layers. Fresh straw is added as plants grow and kept at a depth of eight or more inches.

Strengths

No tilling, few weeds, reduced watering and fertilizing. Warms quickly in the spring and prevents winter heaving. An excellent method for rocky, sandy, or clay soils.

Weaknesses

Requires an abundance of straw each season, which can be expensive and difficult to transport, move, and store. Deep mulch may encourage burrowing rodents and provide shelter for slugs, insect pests, and diseases.

Soil Bag

This simple method utilizes one or more twenty- to forty-pound bags of commercial potting soil or topsoil simply laid out flat on turf, mulch, or wood pallets. A rectangular hole is cut into the top and drainage holes are punched through the bottom. A light dusting of fertilizer is mixed in and plants and seeds are sown.

Strengths

Super easy, weed-free, no-till garden and a great way to start an in-ground garden. Fun for kids and those without a yard.

Weaknesses

Limited to shallow-rooted crops, needs consistent watering and fertilizing, and may flood in heavy rains. Cats may find this an attractive litter box.

Straw Bale

One or more square, string-bound straw bales are placed cut side up either directly on the ground or on top of a weed barrier and soaked with water for several days or even months and treated with nitrogen to help speed the decomposition of the straw. Alternatively, bales can be overwintered in place before using. Once ready, bales are parted down the center, filled with soil and compost, and planted with seeds or starts.

Strengths
Good on poor soils, even concrete. No tilling required, few weeds, handicap accessible, versatile, easy to configure, and renter-friendly. Spent bales make excellent mulch.

Weaknesses
Straw bales can be expensive, heavy, and difficult to transport. These gardens can initially be labor intensive, require frequent watering and fertilizing, and must be replaced every one or two seasons. Nitrogen from treated bales can leach into the local environment and affect the watershed.

Square Foot
This modern take on French Intensive gardening utilizes raised beds filled with a special soilless blend enclosed in a box frame that is further divided into twelve-by-twelve-inch squares, or one square foot. Each square is planted or seeded based on the correct spacing requirements of each plant. Large crops, like tomatoes, are planted one to a square, while small crops like radishes are planted sixteen to a square.

Strengths
Proper plant spacing utilizes space, increases yields, and reduces weeds. Adding trellises increases growing capacity. Raised beds drain well, warm quickly, hold mulch, look tidy, and are easy to mow around.

Weaknesses

Initial construction is expensive, labor intensive, and often impermanent. Requires frequent watering in dry spells and not all crops are suitable. Grids can be tedious to use and do not remove the gardener's need to learn proper plant spacing.

Vertical

Vertical gardens make use of nontraditional gardening space in two ways. The first is by training vining and climbing plants onto trellises, arbors, or fences and growing in raised beds, pots, urns, or tubs. The second is by firmly securing containers, troughs, rain gutters, or vertical garden felt pockets onto permanent frames supported by fences, walls, or other sturdy vertical structures. These gardens are typically irrigated by automatic drip or hydroponic systems. Soilless options are available.

Strengths

Attractive and weed-free indoor-outdoor garden perfect for small yards, renters, and disabled persons. Helps hide ugly structures and views and defines outdoor spaces.

Weaknesses

Construction of large systems and very sturdy structures can be initially expensive or labor intensive. Not conducive to all garden crops and requires frequent and consistent applications of moisture and fertilizer.

2020 Themed Garden Plans

Scarborough Fair Garden

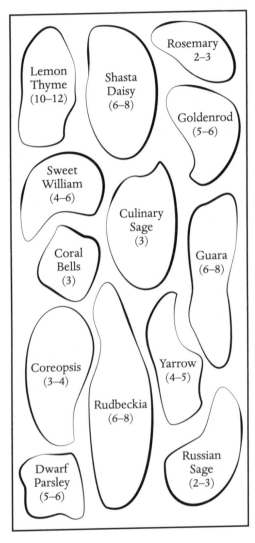

Rosemary
2–3

Lemon
Thyme
(10–12)

Shasta
Daisy
(6–8)

Goldenrod
(5–6)

Sweet
William
(4–6)

Culinary
Sage
(3)

Coral
Bells
(3)

Guara
(6–8)

Coreopsis
(3–4)

Yarrow
(4–5)

Rudbeckia
(6–8)

Dwarf
Parsley
(5–6)

Russian
Sage
(2–3)

Those of a certain age will remember Simon and Garfunkel's version of the English ballad "Scarborough Fair," a somber love song woven around the refrain: "parsley, sage, rosemary, and thyme." This sun-loving border garden celebrates that ballad. It is suitable to edge a sidewalk or to plant in a narrow border up against a wall. Either way, these perennials will guarantee enough flowers throughout the growing season to sell at the fair or to weave into your hair when you take in the festivities.

Apothecary Garden

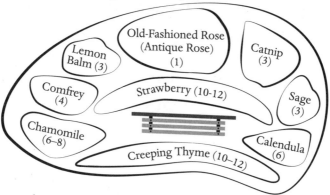

Once, no home would be without a medicinal garden to provide supplies to cure everything from colds to bug bites. Try French apothecary rose or any species with large rose hips like Rosa canina or Rosa rugosa 'Alba'.

Knot Garden

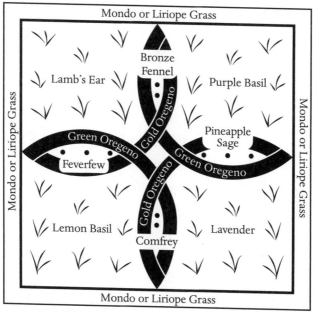

Modern concepts of knot gardens don't require the strict pruning and rigidity of old. The same effect is achieved with sun-loving oreganos that weave together. Finish with a border of liriope or mundo grass.

Planning Your 2020 Garden

Prepare your soil by tilling and fertilizing. Use the grid on the right, enlarging on a photocopier if needed, to sketch your growing space and identify sunny and shady areas.

Plot Shade and Sun

Watch your yard or growing space for a day, checking at regular intervals (such as once an hour), and note the areas that receive sun and shade. This will shift over the course of your growing season. Plant accordingly.

Diagram Your Space

Consider each plant's spacing needs before planting. Vining plants, such as cucumbers, will sprawl out and require trellising or a greater growing area than root crops like carrots. Be sure to avoid pairing plants that naturally compete or harm each other (see the Companion Planting Guide on page 272).

Also consider if your annual plants need to be rotated. Some herbs will reseed, some can be planted in the same place year after year, and some may need to be moved after depleting the soil of certain nutrients during the previous growing season.

Determine Your Last Spring Frost Date

Using data from the previous year, estimate the last spring frost date for your area and note what you'll need to plant before or after this date. Refer to seed packets, plant tags, and experts at your local garden center or University Extension for the ideal planting time for each plant. For information on planting by the moon, see *Llewellyn's 2020 Moon Sign Book*.

My 2020 last spring frost date: _____

Growing Space Grid

☐ = _____ feet

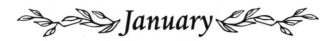# January

To Do	Plants	Dates

Notes:

_____

_____

_____

_____

_____

_____

_____

JANUARY

					1 ◑	3	4
5	6	7	8	9	○	11
12	13	14	15	16	◑	18
19	20	21	22	23	●	25
26	27	28	29	30	31

Layer Brown Paper under Mulch

After preparing the ground and installing plants in your garden, layer your beds with opened brown paper bags or flattened cardboard boxes before putting down mulch to keep weeds in check. Cut or tear the paper or cardboard so that it fits around the base of your plants.

February

To Do	Plants	Dates

Notes:

_____

_____

_____

_____

_____

_____

_____

Wine Bottle Frost Protector

Use a bottle cutter (available at craft stores or online) to cut glass wine bottles in half. Place the bottom of the bottle over small plants to protect them from frost.

FEBRUARY

◑

2	3	4	5	6	7	8
○	10	11	12	13	14	◐
16	17	18	19	20	21	22
●	24	25	26	27	28	29

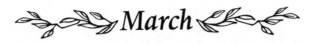

March

To Do	Plants	Dates

Notes:

_____

_____

_____

_____

_____

_____

_____

MARCH

1 ◐ 3 4 5 6 7

8 ○ 10 11 12 13 14

15 ◑ 17 18 19 20 21

22 23 ● 25 26 27 28

29 30 31

Water with Ice

Cut a recyclable plastic bottle in half and remove the cap. Nestle the neck end of the bottle in the ground at the base of a plant and fill it with ice cubes to slowly water a plant at its roots.

April

To Do	Plants	Dates

Notes:

_____

_____

_____

_____

_____

_____

_____

Easy Transplanting

Pot plants in paper bags or cardboard boxes before putting them in the ground, being sure to leave a bit of the bag showing once they go in. If you need to transplant, dig around the bag to preserve the plant's roots.

APRIL

			◗	2	3	4
5	6	○	8	9	10	11
12	13	◑	15	16	17	18
19	20	21	●	23	24	25
26	27	28	29	◗		

May

To Do	Plants	Dates

Notes:

_____

_____

_____

_____

_____

_____

_____

MAY

					1	2
3	4	5	6	○ 8	9	
10	11	12	13	◑ 15	16	
17	18	19	20	21 ●	23	
24	25	26	27	28 ◐	30	
31						

Recycled-Material Garden Kneepads

Cut open 4 plastic bags, layer them atop each other, then place between 2 pieces of baking parchment. Iron on medium heat to create a strong single sheet—make 2. Sandwich a piece of bubble wrap between the sheets and seal the ends with packing tape to make a waterproof kneepad.

June

To Do	Plants	Dates

Notes:

_____

_____

_____

_____

_____

_____

_____

Egg Carton Seed Starting

Use the grade-school trick of starting seeds in biodegradable egg cartons. When the plants are ready to go into the ground, they'll be easy to separate and transplant.

JUNE

	1	2	3	4	○	6
7	8	9	10	11	12	◑
14	15	16	17	18	19	20
●	22	23	24	25	26	27
◐	29	30				

July

To Do	Plants	Dates

Notes:

_____

_____

_____

_____

_____

_____

_____

JULY

			1	2	3	4
○	6	7	8	9	10	11
◐	13	14	15	16	17	18
19	●	21	22	23	24	25
26	◑	28	29	30	31	

Tin Can Waterer or Lantern

Carefully use an awl to punch holes into the sides and bottoms of tin cans, randomly or in patterns. Right-side up, the can can be filled with ice cubes and put at the base of a plant to slowly water it. Place the can upside down over a tea light to make a lantern.

August

To Do	Plants	Dates

Notes:

_____

_____

_____

_____

_____

_____

_____

A Tip from Colonial Williamsburg

Use short lengths of twine or string to bind tall leafy vegetables (like romaine and endive) once they have several layers of leaves. This will prevent the hearts from having a bitter taste!

AUGUST

						1
2 ○		4	5	6	7	8
9	10 ◗	12	13	14	15	
16	17 ●	19	20	21	22	
23	24 ◖	26	27	28	29	
30	31					

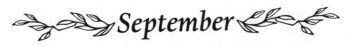

September

To Do	Plants	Dates

Notes:

_____

_____

_____

_____

_____

_____

_____

_____

SEPTEMBER

				1 ○	3	4	5
6	7	8	9	◑	11	12
13	14	15	16	●	18	19
20	21	22	◐	24	25	26
27	28	29	30

Berry Container Terrarium

Use clear, lidded plastic berry boxes as terrariums for seedlings and small plants (hint— you can also make these decorative with small stones and figurines!). The lid keeps in heat, while the holes in the bottom make for good drainage.

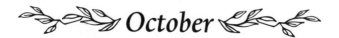

October

To Do	Plants	Dates

Notes:

_____

_____

_____

_____

_____

_____

_____

Recycled Cutlery Labels

Reuse plastic cutlery as plant labels. Clean the cutlery and write the names of plants and dates on the handles in paint marker; the spoon, fork, or knife end goes into the ground.

OCTOBER

					○ 2	3
4	5	6	7	8	◑	10
11	12	13	14	15	●	17
18	19	20	21	22	◐	24
25	26	27	28	29	30	○

 November

To Do	Plants	Dates

Notes:

_____

_____

_____

_____

_____

_____

_____

_____

NOVEMBER

1	2	3	4	5	6	7
◖ 9	10	11	12	13	14
● 16	17	18	19	20	◗
22	23	24	25	26	27	28
29	○

Fruit Peel Bird Feeders

Use thick-skinned fruits (navel oranges, grape-fruit, cantaloupe, etc.) as temporary bird feeders. Cut the fruit in half and scoop out the meat. Fill this "shell" with bird seed or seed-coated suet and nestle in tree branches or bushes to attract feathered friends!

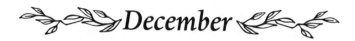

December

To Do	Plants	Dates

Notes:

_____

_____

_____

_____

_____

_____

_____

Chocolate Box Seed Storage

Reuse empty chocolate boxes to store seeds. Place a different type of seed in the each pod of the candy tray; use paint and markers to relabel the inside lid with seed names.

DECEMBER

		1	2	3	4	5
6	◑	8	9	10	11	12
13	●	15	16	17	18	19
20	◐	22	23	24	25	26
27	28	○	30	31		

Notes

Contributors

Anne Sala is a freelance journalist based in Minnesota. Last year, she and her family moved from a third-story apartment to a single-family home. Anne has never had to deal with animals eating her plants before and has since discovered the rabbits in her neighborhood are quite fond of the herbs she keeps in low-sided pots.

Autumn Damiana is an author, artist, crafter, amateur photographer, and regular contributor to Llewellyn's annuals. Along with writing and making art, Autumn has a degree in early childhood education. She lives with her husband and doggy familiar in the beautiful San Francisco Bay Area. Visit her online at www.autumndamiana.com.

Charlie Rainbow Wolf is happiest when she is creating something, especially if it can be made from items that others have cast aside. She is an advocate of organic gardening and cooking and lives in the Midwest with her husband and special-needs Great Danes. Visit www.charlierainbow.com.

Corina Sahlin homesteads on five acres at the edge of the wilderness near the Cascade Mountains, where she grows a lot of organic food. Together with her husband, Steve, she raises a variety of animals and a gaggle of three children, whom they homeschool. She teaches wilderness and homesteading skills to children and adults. Visit www.marblemounthomestead.com.

Dawn Ritchie is an organic gardener, cook, passionate beekeeper, and fledgling potter who writes about design, cuisine, gardening, travel, entertainment, and living well. She's a regular contributor to numerous publications in the US and Canada.

She's the author of *The Emotional House*, a home design/healing workbook.

Diana Rajchel lives in San Francisco, where she runs the Emperor Norton Pagan Social and handles the oft-squirrelly city spirit. She is the author of the *Mabon* and *Samhain* books in the Llewellyn Sabbat Essentials series and of the Diagram Prize–nominee *Divorcing a Real Witch*.

Diana Stoll shares her gardens with her grandchildren in the hopes they will each grow their own green thumbs. As a horticulturist and a garden writer, Diana writes a weekly garden column in the *Chicago Daily Herald* and shares her passion for all things gardening on her blog, *Garden with Diana*, at www.gardenwithdiana.com.

Elizabeth Barrette lives in central Illinois and enjoys magical crafts, historic religions, and gardening for wildlife. She has written columns on Pagan practice, speculative fiction, gender studies, and social and environmental issues. Her book *Composing Magic* explains how to combine writing and spirituality. Visit her blog at www.ysabetwordsmith.dreamwidth.org.

Emily Towne is a homesteader, gardener, and student of nature who enjoys digging in the dirt and curating an ever-growing seed bank on her multispecies Missouri homestead, Full Plate Farm, which she shares with her husband and son. She uses regenerative stewardship to grow and raise a variety of plants and animals.

Estha K. V. McNevin (Missoula, Montana) is a priestess and ceremonial oracle of Opus Aima Obscuræ, a nonprofit Pagan Temple Haus. She has served the Pagan community since 2003 as an Eastern Hellenistic officiate, lecturer, freelance au-

thor, artist, and poet. To learn more, please explore www.opus
aimaobscurae.org.

Holly Bellebuono (Massachusetts) is an international speaker,
author, and medical herbalist whose books and lectures feature
natural health, herbal medicine, and women's empowerment. She directs the Bellebuono School of Herbal Medicine.
Visit her online at www.HollyBellebuono.com.

James Kambos raises a large variety of herbs and flowers in
his Ohio garden. He's a writer and an artist. He has a degree
in history and geography.

JD Hortwort resides in North Carolina. She is an avid student
of herbology and gardening. She has written a weekly garden
column since 1991. She is a professional, award-winning author, journalist, and magazine editor. Recently retired from
journalism, she continues to write on topics as diverse as gardening and NASCAR.

Jill Henderson is a backwoods herbalist, author, artist, and
world traveler with a penchant for wild edible and medicinal
plants, culinary herbs, and nature ecology. She is a longtime
contributor to *Llewellyn's Herbal Almanac* and *Acres USA* magazine and is the author of *The Healing Power of Kitchen Herbs, A
Journey of Seasons*, and *The Garden Seed Saving Guide*. Visit Jill's
blog at www.ShowMeOz.wordpress.com.

Kathy Martin is a Master Gardener and longtime author of the
blog *Skippy's Vegetable Garden*, a journal of her vegetable gardens.
The blog has won awards, including *Horticulture Magazine*'s Best
Gardening Blog. Kathy has written four gardening apps and manages the Belmont Victory Gardens' 137 plots. She lives near Boston with her husband, son, and Portuguese water dogs.

Kathy Vilim is a Midwestern girl transplanted to Southern California who writes about the importance of creating outdoor living space using native plants and attracting pollinators. Kathy is a naturalist and photojournalist and finds herself in demand as a garden design consultant. Visit www.canative gardener.blogspot.com.

Linda Raedisch switched from coffee to tea about five years ago and has never looked back. When not making all-natural tea soaps or writing books and articles for Llewellyn, she enjoys exploring old houses, gardens, and Asian grocery stores. She lives in northern New Jersey, which has plenty of all three.

Mickie Mueller is the author/illustrator of *The Voice of the Trees*, the illustrator of *The Mystical Cats Tarot* and *The Magical Dogs Tarot*, author of *The Witch's Mirror*, and *Llewellyn's Little Book of Halloween*. Her art has been seen as set dressing on SyFy's *The Magicians* and Bravo's *Girlfriends' Guide to Divorce*. Visit her online at MickieMuellerStudio.etsy.com.

Mireille Blacke, MA, LADC, RD, CD-N, is a registered dietitian, bariatric program coordinator at Saint Francis Hospital, and professor at the University of Saint Joseph in Hartford, Connecticut. Mireille worked in rock radio for two decades before shifting her career to psychology, nutrition, and addiction counseling.

Monica Crosson is the author of *The Magickal Family* and *Summer Sage*. She is a Master Gardener who lives in the beautiful Pacific Northwest, happily digging in the dirt and tending her raspberries with her family and their small menagerie of farm animals. Monica is a regular contributor to Llewellyn's annuals as well as *Enchanted Living Magazine* and *Witchology Magazine*.

Natalie Zaman is the author of *Color and Conjure* and *Magical Destinations of the Northeast*. A regular contributor to various Llewellyn annual publications, she also writes the recurring feature Wandering Witch for *Witches & Pagans* magazine. When not on the road, she's busy tending her magical back garden. Visit Natalie online at www.nataliezaman.blogspot.com.

Susan Pesznecker is a mother, writer, nurse, college English teacher, and Baden-Powell Service Association scout living in the Pacific Northwest with her poodles. Her previous books include *Crafting Magick with Pen and Ink, The Magickal Retreat,* and *Yule.* Follow her at www.facebook.com/SusanMoonwriter Pesznecker.

Suzanne Ress runs a small farm in the Alpine foothills of Italy, where she lives with her husband. She has been a practicing Pagan for as long as she can remember and was recently featured in the exhibit "Worldwide Witches" at the Hexenmuseum of Switzerland. She is the author of *The Trial of Goody Gilbert*.

Thea Fiore-Bloom, PhD, is an arts and culture journalist with a doctorate in mythology. Artists and writers of all levels looking for audacious inspiration, information, and encouragement are warmly welcomed at her new blog, www.thecharmedstudio.com.

Gardening Resources

Cooking with Herbs and Spices compiled by **Susan Pesznecker**
Gardening Techniques written by **Jill Henderson**
2020 Themed Garden Plans designed by **JD Hortwort**
2020 Gardening Log tips written by **Natalie Zaman**

GET MORE AT LLEWELLYN.COM

Visit us online to browse hundreds of our books and decks, plus sign up to receive our e-newsletters and exclusive online offers.

- **Free tarot readings • Spell-a-Day • Moon phases**
- **Recipes, spells, and tips • Blogs • Encyclopedia**
- **Author interviews, articles, and upcoming events**

GET SOCIAL WITH LLEWELLYN

Find us on  🐦 @LlewellynBooks

www.Facebook.com/LlewellynBooks

GET BOOKS AT LLEWELLYN

LLEWELLYN ORDERING INFORMATION

Order online: Visit our website at www.llewellyn.com to select your books and place an order on our secure server.

Order by phone:
- Call toll free within the US at 1-877-NEW-WRLD (1-877-639-9753)
- We accept VISA, MasterCard, American Express, and Discover.
- Canadian customers must use credit cards.

Order by mail:
Send the full price of your order (MN residents add 6.875% sales tax) in US funds plus postage and handling to: Llewellyn Worldwide, 2143 Wooddale Drive, Woodbury, MN 55125-2989

POSTAGE AND HANDLING

STANDARD (US):
(Please allow 12 business days)
$30.00 and under, add $6.00.
$30.01 and over, FREE SHIPPING.

INTERNATIONAL ORDERS,
INCLUDING CANADA:
$16.00 for one book, plus $3.00 for each additional book.

Visit us online for more shipping options.
Prices subject to change.

FREE CATALOG!

To order, call
1-877-
NEW-WRLD
ext. 8236
or visit our
website

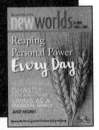